The Quest for the Hittites

Uncovering a Forgotten Civilization

Fausto Labruto

McFarland & Company, Inc., Publishers
Jefferson, North Carolina

LIBRARY OF CONGRESS CATALOGUING-IN-PUBLICATION DATA

Names: Labruto, Fausto, 1976– author.
Title: The quest for the Hittites : uncovering a forgotten civilization / Fausto Labruto.
Other titles: Uncovering a forgotten civilization
Description: Jefferson, North Carolina : McFarland & Company, Inc., Publishers, 2023 | Includes bibliographical references and index.
Identifiers: LCCN 2023031552 | ISBN 9781476692395 (print) | ISBN 9781476650166 (ebook) ∞
Subjects: LCSH: Hittites—Historiography. | Hittites—History.
Classification: LCC DS66 .L33 2023 | DDC 939/.30722—dc23/eng/20230717
LC record available at https://lccn.loc.gov/2023031552

BRITISH LIBRARY CATALOGUING DATA ARE AVAILABLE

ISBN (print) 978-1-4766-9239-5
ISBN (ebook) 978-1-4766-5016-6

© 2023 Fausto Labruto. All rights reserved

No part of this book may be reproduced or transmitted in any form or by any means, electronic or mechanical, including photocopying or recording, or by any information storage and retrieval system, without permission in writing from the publisher.

Front cover: Bas relief of Hittite storm-god, circa 1000–900 BCE (British Museum)

Printed in the United States of America

McFarland & Company, Inc., Publishers
Box 611, Jefferson, North Carolina 28640
www.mcfarlandpub.com

To Julie the dreamer

Table of Contents

Preface — 1
Introduction — 3

1. The Beginning — 7
2. Hittites and Where to Find Them — 16
3. Anatolia — 28
4. Writing Letters — 44
5. Hattusa — 54
6. Eat Bread, Drink Wine — 73
7. The Hittites Start to Tell Their Story — 85
8. Troy — 97
9. Between the Two Wars — 107
10. From Plague to Family Dramas — 120
11. Luwian — 137
12. The Late Bronze Age Collapse — 151

Epilogue — 164
Chapter Notes — 167
Bibliography — 177
Index — 185

A note on the spelling of Hittite names:
The conventional transliteration of the Hittite language uses the letters ḫ and š, pronounced as a voiceless velar fricative < x > and a voiceless postal-veolar fricative <ʃ>, respectively. However, there is no certainty about the historicity of these pronunciations. For the benefit of readers unfamiliar with phonetic conventions, in this book, the letter *h* is used in place of the letter ḫ, and the letter *s* in place of the letter š. For example, the name of the city Ḫattuša is rendered in its anglicized form, "Hattusa."

A note on the spelling of Turkish names:
Care has been taken to respect the current spelling of Turkish names of people and places, except for direct quotations from others' work and their bibliographic references, in which alternative spellings can be seen.

Preface

There are many books about the Hittite civilization.

Most books approach the Hittites from a single angle, some concentrating more on their political or military history or archaeology, others discussing the intricacies of their language. Rather than adding another title to the list, I wanted to write a book on *how* we have learned about the Hittites.

The Hittites eluded historians and archaeologists for thirty centuries. The story of how the riddle of the Hittites was finally solved is surprising and compelling. It is the story of inspiring researchers who, armed with passion, talent, and cunning intuition, started from a few scattered clues and, over a hundred years of study, were able to retrace the steps of a forgotten civilization.

With this book, I wanted to convey the feeling of mystery and adventure which surrounded the early days of this re-discovery, which started at the end of the nineteenth century. It is a story that unfolds between the halls of academia in the Old Continent and the excavation sites in the Near East.

This story develops at a time when Europe and the Near East were undergoing historical events of great importance: the end of the Victorian Age, the Great War, the fall of the Ottoman Empire, and the ascent and fall of the Third Reich. Rather than leaving these events as a simple backdrop, I took care to make the historical context come alive, and I tried to convey how it shaped the work and the lives of the researchers.

And it is primarily they, the explorers, archaeologists, and linguists who contributed to solving the mystery of the Hittites, who are the protagonists of the book. Their life journeys are unique, as unique as their mission of studying a lost civilization.

Although the style of this book is informal and the contents are aimed at the non-specialistic general public, the contents are thoroughly researched with scientific rigor, as witnessed by nearly two hundred bibliographic references.

Preface

This book is divided into 12 chapters. Each chapter brings the reader to a different location, where a great discovery took place or a great character worked. Each chapter adds a piece to the puzzle, leading to an understanding of the Hittite civilization, as seen through the eyes of the researchers who studied it.

Through a series of subplots, flashbacks, and flashforwards, the reader will be walked through the first discoveries of ancient Hittite artifacts and how the archaeologists studied them or will be shown the hints hidden in the ancient texts and how the linguists used them to decipher the Hittite language.

In the end, the reader will feel *they* unraveled this three-thousand-year-old secret.

Introduction

In the heart of London, at the corner of Waterloo Place and Pall Mall, stands an elegant neo-classic building that is an icon of Victorian history. It was built in 1830 to house one of England's most prestigious gentlemen's clubs: the Athenaeum. The Club was founded by members "of distinguished eminence in science, literature or the arts" and became immediately one of the most popular places for London intellectuals to get together. Academicians, writers, and scientists would regularly attend the Athenaeum, dining with Charles Dickens or chatting with Charles Darwin under the light of one of the earliest gas-fittings in London.[1]

On August 4, 1879, Archibald Sayce (1845–1933), priest of the Church of England and professor of philology at Oxford University, arrived at the Athenaeum. When he entered the building through the double row of Doric columns of its patio, Sayce was excited and hurried. Although his mentor at the Club, the poet Matthew Arnold (1822–1888), had admonished him: "You are the youngest member of the Club, you must not shock its susceptibilities by running up its stairs!" on that night, Sayce could not slow down his pace. It was an extraordinary moment: he was to deliver a lecture to a select group of members. He was to present a bold, revolutionary theory on an ancient, little-known people he had studied for some years: the Hittites.

The Club was named after the Greek goddess Athena, and its façade was adorned with an exorbitantly expensive frieze copied from the marbles of the Parthenon. Perhaps it is for these reasons that, by 1870, the Athenaeum had become a favorite haunt for distinguished British historians and archaeologists. When he was accepted as a member, Sayce was very proud and called this honor "the greatest ever conferred upon me." The dinners hosted by the Oriental archaeology group, in particular, were his favorite events at the Club. Held every Sunday night at seven, the dinners had a strict menu of fish curry, which concoction was supervised by famous art historian James Ferguson (1808–1886). Other regular attendees were Arthur Grote (1814–1886), a colonial administrator and expert on Indian history; William Sandys Wright Vaux (1818–1885), London's most respected antiquary and numismatist; Thomas Chenery (1826–1884), the editor of *The Times*; Sir Henry Rawlinson (1810–1895), the father of Assyriology; Austen Henry Layard (1817–1894), the excavator of the Mesopotamian city of Nineveh; Henry Blosse Linch (1807–1873), the explorer; and William Willoughby Cole (1807–1886), 3rd Earl of Enniskillen and paleontologist. Sayce felt at home in the company of these gentlemen. In his autobiography, he declared "here I found the society I most enjoyed" and would stay up until late, involved in academic discussions into the night before retiring to one of the guest bedrooms in the attic of the Club.[2]

That night, in front of his fellows interested in Oriental archaeology, Sayce delivered a historical lecture. He proposed a new theory on the Hittites. An audacious and revolutionary idea that would change the way historians looked at this poorly known civilization. That night, with Sayce's lecture, Hittitology was born.

Early 1800s historians did not think much of the Hittites. They regarded the Hittites as just one of several ancient tribes who inhabited the hills of Palestine within the territory known as Canaan at the time of the biblical Exodus when the Israelites reached the Promised Land and subjugated them. In its original version, the Old Testament did not even contain the word Hittite. The expression mostly used, especially in the book of Genesis, is the Hebrew בני-חת (*bny-ḥt*) which can be translated as "children of Heth," Heth being the great-grandchild of Noah, the survivor of the deluge. This is all the Bible said about them, and this is all historians knew about the Hittites.

It may sound strange

Professor Archibald Sayce (1845–1933), of Oxford University in England, considered the father of Hittitology. In 1879, his "unifying theory" put the Hittites on the map of the Ancient Near East for the first time. Bain News Service, publisher, public domain, via Wikimedia Commons.

that 1800s historians would base their understanding of ancient civilizations on the stories told in the Bible. However, at that time, the tradition passed on by the Bible was so ingrained in European culture that it prevailed over scientific research.

Using the Bible as a history book had its drawbacks. The Old Testament was not written by historians, so it provides only hazy information about the people who inhabited the Ancient Near East. One of these populations was the Hittites.

Outside of the Bible, there was simply no mention of the Hittites in any other available source. Not in the writings of Ancient Greek historians and ethnographers, not in the main literary works of antiquity, nor in any other known sources. To the eyes of early 1800s historians, the Hittites were just a scarcely significant Canaanite tribe, side characters of the Old Testament.

But the new discipline of archaeology was starting to develop, and the earliest archaeological expeditions in Egypt and Mesopotamia were soon to obtain discoveries and knowledge which would bring a new understanding of the Ancient Near East.

1

The Beginning

The story of the re-discovery of the civilization of the Hittites, virtually forgotten for thirty centuries, begins in Egypt.

Egypt had been an unceasing passion for Europeans for centuries. One of the reasons for this fascination was that Egyptian hieroglyphics were undeciphered until modern times, which gave an aura of mystery to anything coming from Egypt. Decipherment of Egyptian hieroglyphs happened thanks to the discovery of the famous Rosetta Stone, an incidental finding of French surveyors during Napoleon Bonaparte's military campaign in Egypt. The Rosetta Stone, a heavy, thick stone slab, was instrumental in deciphering Egyptian hieroglyphs because it carried an inscription in two languages, a so-called bilingual. A bilingual is a key to decrypting an unknown language because the philologist can leverage the knowledge of one language to study the other. The two languages on the Rosetta stone were Ancient Greek and Egyptian; however, the Egyptian text was written in two writing systems: hieroglyphs and demotic.

When the stone came to Europe, the foremost linguists of the age started to compete at cracking the code. None of them could have a better head start on the matter than a young French language genius named Jean François Champollion (1790–1832). Champollion was of humble origins, a true child of the *Révolution*. His father was a drunkard, his mother uncaring; since a young age, he relied heavily on the support of his older brother, who had prudently left home in rural Occitaine and had settled in Grenoble, where Champollion joined him. In Grenoble, Champollion was just eleven when he visited the house of the local Prefect, the mathematician Joseph Fourier (1768–1830). Fourier—who, by the way, was the scientist who introduced the theory of the Greenhouse Effect—had been to Egypt as a member of the Napoleonic expedition in 1798 and had taken home a collection of Egyptian art. Little Champollion was charmed by the collection and made inquisitive queries about what he saw. When someone told him that the Egyptian hieroglyphs were an undeciphered form of writing, Champollion declared that he, one day, would be the one to decipher them.

Whether this story is true or not, Champollion was lecturing at the Grenoble Academy on Coptic language and its relationship with hieroglyphs at the astonishing age of just sixteen. From that moment, studying Ancient Egypt and deciphering hieroglyphs became his life mission. The mission, however, was not a short journey. Champollion's obsession with breaking the code almost broke him. His early academic career was an epic seesaw of jealousies, political upheavals, and rivalries, which almost consumed him until 1822. Champollion had started his decipherment by concentrating on the proper names of rulers like Ptolemy and Cleopatra, which were readily recognizable because they were inscribed within a sign called a "cartouche." Then he leveraged his knowledge of Coptic to identify some verbs like the verb "to be born" in the hieroglyphic spelling, given that the same verb was also present in some names of pharaohs.

That year, Champollion finally deciphered the hieroglyphic text of the Rosetta Stone.[1] There are legendary tales about this event. According to the lore, Champollion frantically arrived at his brother's home, walked through the door, and triumphally shouted "I got it!" then, overwhelmed by emotion, promptly fainted, dropping to the ground in the dramatic style of the age.

Almost overnight, the fainting-prone Champollion became a towering personality in European archaeological circles. The deciphering of hieroglyphs created a wave of discoveries. The study of ancient Egypt, until then little more than a leisurely activity for bored European intellectuals, became the focus of Ancient World archaeology: Egyptology was born. Egyptologists started translating the countless inscriptions discovered in Egypt, little by little unlocking the most intimate secrets of its history. Europe was hit by true Egyptomania, influencing all fields of art and fashion. The upshot of this wave of popularity was that both publicly funded and privately funded archaeological expeditions to Egypt proliferated.

Shortly after his 1822 decipherment, Champollion traveled to Egypt on one such expedition and investigated most archaeological sites along the Nile. He was particularly fascinated by Karnak, a magnificent temple complex near Luxor, modern-day Thebes, the capital of Upper Egypt, and made sure the memory of his visit would be preserved by carving his signature on one of the monumental stone pillars of the Main Temple. At Karnak, Champollion became intrigued by a hieroglyphic inscription that, he thought, may have significant historical value. The inscription was visible, in similar text, at two sites: one on a wall of the Main Temple, the other at the *Ramesseum*, the complex of funerary monuments, and the tomb of the Pharaoh Ramesses II. Ramesses II was one of the most powerful Pharaohs in the history of Egypt. In his reign, which lasted over forty years, from 1279 to 1213 BCE, at the beginning of what is known as the Egyptian "New Kingdom," Ramesses II campaigned, defeated, conquered, and subjugated more than any other Pharaoh, and he had the habit of leaving monumental inscriptions to commemorate his campaigns everywhere he went.

Champollion copied the inscriptions and brought the copies back to France for study. It was not until 1844, after his death, that his translation was published. Once they were out, the contents of the two inscriptions, one in thirty lines and one in a more concise version of ten lines, made news worldwide. The inscriptions were not a simple commemoration of a battle or a conquest: Champollion had discovered the first peace treaty in history. It was a peace treaty between Pharaoh Ramesses II and a king called Kheta-sira, the king of a land Champollion read as *Scheto*. What land was this Scheto, which fought against Egypt? Because of the sound of the name, Champollion believed it to be the land of the Scythians, an ancient population of the Eurasian steppes.[2] However, his reading was uncharacteristically wrong. It wasn't until fourteen years later that German Egyptologist Karl Heinrich Brugsch (1827–1894) corrected the reading as *Kheta*.*[3]

Karl Brugsch was self-taught in Egyptian since the age of sixteen and was the foremost authority in demotic of his time. Still, the translation did leave him puzzled: no one had ever heard of a kingdom called Kheta, especially not a kingdom so strong to wage war against the Egyptian Empire at the height of its power and force it to a peace treaty. Where did this mysterious land lay? Brugsch reasoned that if the treaty discussed an agreement on sharing a territory in Syria, Kheta must have been located somewhere in the Levant, the region of the Ancient Near East, which comprises the modern-day countries of Syria, Jordan, Lebanon, Palestine, and Israel. Knowledge of Egyptian chronology helped him to place the treaty in the thirteenth century BCE. Brugsch knew only of one people who inhabited that area at that time and had a similar-sounding name: the "Children of Heth" cited in the Old Testament, the Hittites. Brugsch went on to become one of the most celebrated Egyptologists in history. He was highly respected by the Egyptians, who gave him the title of "pasha" (the highest nobiliary rank assigned to a foreigner), and he carried his dedication to Egyptology *literally* to the grave (since his tombstone was the re-used

---

* In his work, Brugsch wrote *Chetâ*, however, this is based on a transliteration system which Brugsch himself abandoned a few years later. According to the current transliteration convention, the name should be rendered as *Ḫt*. However, for ease of understanding, here it is transliterated in the anglicized form *Kheta*.

cover of an Egyptian sarcophagus). But Brugsch deserves a special place in the history of Hittitology as well because he identified the previously unknown and powerful kingdom of "Kheta" as the Hittites.

The treaty studied by Champollion and Brugsch is a very advanced piece of diplomacy. It addresses the question of a Syrian territory, about which both parties agreed to "act in harmony." Egyptians and Hittites also agreed on not waging war on each other for other matters and promised each other an "eternal alliance." According to this alliance, if third parties had attacked either of them, each would have acted in defense of the other. Moreover, the Pharaoh agreed to support (presumably militarily) the succession to the throne of the Hittites. Finally, the treaty stipulated rules for the extradition of political refugees to their respective countries.

Even seen with today's eyes, this peace treaty written over three thousand years ago appears surprisingly modern and sophisticated. The only difference between the Egyptian-Hittite peace treaty and a modern-day diplomatic agreement is that it is concluded with an oath to the gods. The oath stipulated that if the treaty were ever violated, the oath-breaker would be "cursed by the gods, who shall destroy his house, land, and servants." Conversely, if the oath-takers maintained their vows, they would be rewarded by the gods, who "will cause them to be healthy and to live." In the treaty, Egyptians and Hittites appeared to believe in different gods as the oath is dedicated to no less than "a thousand gods," "both male and female," of the lands of Egypt and Kheta. Finally, the agreement was witnessed by "the mountains and rivers of the lands of Egypt, the sky, the earth, the great sea, the winds, the clouds."

Historians were captivated by the discovery, which added an entirely new dimension to their knowledge of the Ancient Near East. Until a moment earlier, the Hittites were hardly known and had a very tiny place in the history books; now, scholars recognized them as one of the strongest political powers of the Late Bronze Age, the period which, in the Near East, lasted from 1550 to 1200 BCE, approximately.

At the same time as some archaeologists were learning about the Hittites in Egyptian sources, others had started to organize expeditions in Mesopotamia, the part of the Near East which lies between the rivers Tigris and Euphrates, roughly corresponding to modern-day Iraq. In Mesopotamia, they discovered a plethora of Assyro-Babylonian monuments and inscriptions. Assyriologists, however, were encountering the same challenges Egyptologists faced decades earlier; no one could read the sources in Akkadian (the language of Assyria) because they were written in the hitherto undeciphered cuneiform writing system. Hundreds of ancient texts were lying around museums and universities, but nobody could make sense of them. A decipherer, a "Champollion of cuneiform," was needed.

The process of cracking the cuneiform code unfolded similarly to deciphering Egyptian hieroglyphs. The main difference was that, while the Egyptian hieroglyphs were used to write the Egyptian language only, cuneiform was the writing system used by several different languages of antiquity. Just like the Latin alphabet is used for writing languages as diverse as English and Turkish, throughout history, cuneiform has been used to write over a dozen, often radically different languages. Rather than being a drawback, this played to the advantage of linguists because they could use their knowledge of one language to decipher the script and then use the known script to study the other languages.

Among the several languages written in cuneiform, scholars figured that the best starting point for decipherment could be Old Persian, a language spoken in Iran between 600 and 300 BCE. The main advantage of Old Persian was its lexical similarity with modern Persian, which may have made decipherment easier. In the first half of the nineteenth century, linguists from the most prestigious universities across Europe attempted to read Old Persian cuneiform using this method. However, when success came, it did not come from the halls of a university but from a far less likely place.

Georg Friedrich Grotefend (1775–1853) was a German scholar whose knowledge of Latin and Italian philology would have easily secured his tenure at any university but who chose to remain all his life in his most prized position, headmaster of the gymnasium in Frankfurt and then in Hannover, where he worked until his retirement. The students at the schools he led admired this jovial intellectual who wrote academic papers and schoolbooks alike. Grotefend had a brilliant mind and a passion for puzzles. One night he was having drinks with his friends when the conversation fell on the cuneiform texts found by archaeologists in Mesopotamia. Grotefend came up with a bizarre idea: he would be the decipherer of the cuneiform script, he declared and placed a bet with his friends. The bet was not just a joke, Grotefend was serious, and the day after, he started to study Old Persian texts.

Soon he devised a strategy: he would work on proper names in inscriptions, in particular names of kings. He reasoned that names would be easier to identify amid the text because they were conventionally followed by honorifics, which are largely formulaic. Soon, he identified famous kings' names in Old Persian inscriptions. As early as 1802, he enthusiastically communicated his findings to the Royal Academy of Göttingen; however, the other scholars dismissed his theories with contempt.[4] The fact that Grotefend did not come from the academic world probably penalized him. By 1805 the account of his hypotheses appeared only as a trifling appendix to an even more trifling history book published by a friend of his in Germany.⁵ Grotefend's work would have been forgotten if it wasn't that one of his few readers was the most influential linguist of the time: Champollion.

Champollion was highly impressed by Grotefend's deductions and, in 1823, just after his historic breakthrough on the Rosetta Stone, wanted to put them to test. He asked his friend and orientalist Antoine-Jean Saint-Martine (1791–1832) to accompany him to visit a collection of antiquities at the *Cabinet des Medailles*, a museum in central Paris, to see a fabulous alabaster vase of Persian origin from the fifth century BCE, known as the "Caylus Vase." Champollion was intrigued by the vase because it carried a bilingual inscription in Egyptian hieroglyphs and Old Persian cuneiform. No one better than Champollion could appreciate the value of bilinguals in decoding a writing system. So, Champollion and Saint-Martine united forces and applied Grotefend's principles to read the names on the vase.⁶ It was a success, and they could read several names on the vase. This time, the discovery did not carry the signature of the headmaster of a German school but the names of two stars of linguistics, so the academic world immediately picked it up and applied it. Working mainly on proper names, linguists from all over Europe could now decipher the cuneiform script and read texts in Old Persian.

By now, everyone in the world of linguistics knew what the next step should be: they needed to find a multilingual cuneiform text to work their way from Old Persian to Akkadian. This time, however, fate wanted that the suitable multilingual text was not carved on a vase placidly lying on the dusty shelves of a Paris museum, nor on a heavy rock slab at the side of a road in Egypt, but on a 15-meter tall and 25-meter long inscription which stood, almost defiant-looking, a hundred meters above ground, carved on the limestone side of a mountain in a deserted region of Iran, one of the most inaccessible places of the Near East.

The cuneiform inscription, written in three languages, Old Persian, Elamite (one of the oldest languages spoken in the area and unrelated to Persian), and Akkadian (in its Babylonian dialect), is known as the Behistun Inscription. Persian scribes carved it ca. 500 BCE to celebrate the life and achievements of King Darius the Great. The monument had been admired by generations of Persians traveling between the cities of Ecbatana and Babylon. However, once these cities were abandoned and the road became less traveled, European travelers who happened on it glaringly misinterpreted it and assumed it to be Christian in origin, with pilgrims even interpreting Darius' troops depicted beside the inscription as the twelve apostles. The inscription is perched on the top of a dizzying precipice, and European scholars had only gotten access to a portion of it, the one in Old Persian, which was visible from the furthest away. A copy of the remaining text was badly needed, but this was no easy feat: obtaining it would have required stubbornness and courage. Luckily, a stubbornly courageous man was stationed nearby as an officer of the British East India Company. His name was Henry Rawlinson (1810–1895).

Rawlinson was just seventeen when he became proficient in Persian, but rather than channeling his gift for oriental languages into an academic career as Champollion had done, he realized his skill could bring him to visit the places he dreamed of visiting, so he began a military career which saw him traveling between London and Baghdad, Persia, and Afghanistan. He retired from his military career at age 45 to become active in politics: he was elected to Parliament, knighted by Queen Victoria, and nominated Fellow of the Royal Society. Thanks to his intimate knowledge of the Near East, he covered diplomatic posts while retaining his position of Trustee of the British Museum until his death.

At the beginning of this brilliant career, Rawlinson was stationed in a solitary outpost in the Iranian desert. He was captivated by Old Persian inscriptions in cuneiform and had studied the Behistun inscription, which was located nearby and of which he realized the value. He repeatedly climbed the cliff, built a makeshift bridge between rock ledges to access the section of the inscription furthest away from him, and even suspended an unwitting local boy with a harness and ropes to get him close enough to the inscription and make a cast of it, which he then generously made available to European scholars for attempting the translation.[7] Once he and other scholars started working on deciphering the Akkadian portion of the inscription, essential advancements were made. By 1851, Rawlinson could read not only the text on the inscription but other fragments of Akkadian as well.

Once Akkadian started to be translated, thanks to Rawlinson's pioneering work, historians could finally understand the texts found at many Mesopotamian archaeological sites. A decade earlier, British archaeologist, Austen Henry Layard had discovered and excavated Nineveh, one of the major Assyrian cities on the outskirts of modern-day Mosul, Iraq, and found the library of King Ashurbanipal, a royal archive containing tens of thousands of documents. Now, at long last, scholars could read these documents. Akkadian became a widely studied language. Riding on the wave of the novel understanding of Akkadian, another primary language of ancient Mesopotamia, Sumerian, could be translated as well. This was possible because, although Sumerian had died out as a spoken language centuries before Akkadian, it was still in use by Assyrians as a written language in religious texts. Moreover, some Akkadian texts contained dictionaries and word lists of Sumerian, thought for the benefit of the scribes but extremely useful to comparative linguists.

The floodgates were open. The main languages of Mesopotamia were finally understood, and it would have been just a short time before translators would come across the name of the Hittites again.

By 1857, university scholars all around Europe were making bold claims about translations of Akkadian texts. Still, the Royal Asiatic Society, the leading British body for archaeological research in the Near East, was somewhat skeptical about the accuracy of these translations. A senior member of the Society, the eclectic Henry Fox Talbot (1800–1877), decided to settle the matter once and for all and proposed a test.

Fox Talbot was a scientist and inventor who dedicated his life to developing photography techniques but cultivated Assyriology as a side passion. He sent the Society his translation of a recently discovered Akkadian text and asked that three eminent Assyriologists—Sir Henry Rawlinson, Irishman Edward Hincks (1792–1866), and French-German Julius Oppert (1825–1905)—submit their translations for comparison. The texts chosen for the competition were the so-called prisms of King Tiglath-Pileser I.

Tiglath-Pileser I was a king of Assyria during the Middle Period who obtained many military successes during his thirty-eight-year kingdom between 1114 and 1076 BCE. He was a ruthless warrior-king who referred to himself as "King of the Universe" and left several inscriptions describing his military, hunting,

The terracotta prism of Assyrian king Tiglath-Pileser I, from Assur, Iraq, circa 1110 BCE. The prism was translated by Sir Henry Rawlinson and others in 1857. It records the king's military campaigns, including the conquest of Karkemish "in the Land of Hatti," providing for the first time a geographic detail on the Hittite territory. Osama Shukir Muhammed Amin FRCP(Glasg), CC BY-SA 4.0, via Wikimedia Commons

and building achievements which became very useful to historians. The record of his first five years of reign was inscribed on four clay prisms embedded in the walls at the corners of the temple of Anu and Adad at Assur, the capital of Assyria. The prisms had been found in Iraq and were sent to the British Museum, where no one had yet been able to translate them.

The test went well—Fox Talbot and all the other scholars translated with only minor differences—but the prisms delivered an unexpected twist to the plot. The fifth year of Tiglath-Pileser's reign was a record year in which he crammed six whole military campaigns. According to the prisms, one of the campaigns was against the land of "Hatti" and its capital Karkemish.[8]

It was the first time Assyriologists had come across the name Hatti, but the connection was made immediately. The name, the time, the geography, all pointed in one direction: the land of Hatti was the "Kheta" of the Egyptian peace treaty: the land of the Hittites. This was another critical turning point for historians: until a few years earlier, no one suspected the Hittites of the Bible would be more than a small Canaanite tribe. The eighth edition of the *Encyclopaedia Britannica*, under the entry "Hittites," contained a mere seventy-eight words. By 1858, this was about to change. Hittites became recognized as one of the leading military powers of the Late Bronze Age, fighting for dominion over the Ancient Near East.

But now that the Hittites had been suddenly thrown under the limelight of ancient history, questions became more numerous than certainties. If the Hittite Kingdom had been so powerful, where were the remnants of this civilization? Why didn't anyone ever come across traces of the Hittites, like ruins of their cities or inscriptions in their language?

The search for the Hittites started.

2

Hittites and Where to Find Them

The age of studying the Ancient Near East in the dusty old books of university libraries was over. Champollion, who traveled the length of the Nile and brought back to France casts of hieroglyphs, and Rawlinson, who climbed up cliffs to copy cuneiform inscriptions, inspired a new generation of European scholars to leave their universities and reach the sites where the Ancient World was waiting to be discovered. From the deserts of Egypt to the planes of Persia, the Near East became the new frontier of archaeology. A frontier, though, the exploration of which required a good spirit of adventure. Traveling in the Near East often meant traversing inhospitable territories on horseback in harsh climates, at risk of thirst, hunger, or disease. It was, above all, an exercise in fitting in; being conspicuous and being prayed on by bandits seemed to go naturally together.

Explorers of the Near East learned to pick up local languages and adapt to local customs as a matter of self-preservation. No explorer showed better skills at assimilating than the French-Swiss Johann Ludwig Burckhardt (1784–1817). He was born the son of a wealthy silk merchant, and after completing his university studies in Germany, he moved to England to pursue a career in civil service. He did not find employment in the civil service but was offered the opportunity to join the British African Association in an expedition from Cairo to Timbuktu to study the course of the river Niger. This experience changed his life. Crossing the Sahara, he encountered foreign cultures for the first time. He soon discovered versatility for languages, especially Arabic, and showed an almost chameleonic ability to fit in among foreigners. From that moment, he dedicated his tragically short life to exploring the Orient. He moved to Aleppo, the most ancient town in Syria, then part of the Ottoman Empire, to immerse himself in Arabic culture and customs; he changed his name to Sheikh Ibrahim Ibn Abdallah and started dressing like a Syrian. Soon, he spoke

2. Hittites and Where to Find Them

Arabic like a local and, dressed in a white turban and tunic, could easily pass for a native.

Burckhardt traveled incessantly, crisscrossing the whole Near East from Syria to Sudan, from Arabia to Egypt. He was the discoverer of the ruins of Petra, in modern-day Jordan, one of the most iconic archaeological sites in the world, and the first European in three hundred years to complete the hajj, the pilgrimage to Mecca which is a yearly custom for Muslims but strictly prohibited to Westerners. But he also lived through moments of utter despair: multiple times robbed, kidnapped, marooned in the desert by betraying guides, or imprisoned in Nubia under the suspicion of being a spy.

During his travels in Syria in 1812, visiting the city of Hamah on the banks of the Orontes River, Burckhardt saw a mysterious artifact that stood out from the architecture of the town. He noted in his journal: "Embedded in the corner of a house in the bazaar is a stone, with several small figures and signs, which appear to be a kind of hieroglyphical writing, though it does not resemble that of Egypt."[1] Burckhardt realized that this was an odd find: at that time, the only known hieroglyphs in the Near East were the Egyptian ones, but he didn't think more of it, and his observation lay forgotten in his travel journal.

Five years later, while in Cairo, he became severely ill with dysentery. No cure seemed to help; his condition deteriorated quickly, and he died alone in Cairo at just forty-three. Almost two years later, his belongings, including a precious collection of more than eight hundred ancient Oriental manuscripts, were sent back to England, where they can still be admired at the Cambridge University Museum. His precious travel notes were organized and published posthumously in 1822. Still, the publication did not receive much attention.

His mysterious finding in Hamah went ignored for almost fifty years until the stone was noticed again by two other sets of eyes, the ones of the American consul in Beirut, J. Augustus Johnson (fl. 1870–1890), and American missionary Henry Harris Jessup (1832–1890). The two of them were traveling together through Syria, half leisure, half exploration, when they called at Hamah and spied the ornate stone. They were intrigued by its unusual appearance and asked the locals about it. The locals pointed them to another three similar slabs located at different points of the town, all embedded in the walls of buildings. The ancient stones, with their incomprehensible drawings, had attracted an aura of superstition on themselves: Muslims in town would touch the stones believing they could be cured of all sorts of ailments.[2]

When Johnson and Jessup's published the report of their explorations in Europe, scholars became interested in the mysterious hieroglyphs.

Among them was the brilliant, bizarre, and controversial British orientalist Sir Richard Burton (1821–1890). Burton was a celebrity to the Victorian public for having competed against explorer John Hanning Speke (1827–1844) in the race to discover the source of the Nile. His explorations stretched from the Atlantic coast of Africa to India. He had an uncanny versatility for learning languages: no matter where he traveled, he was able to strike a conversation with locals (he is said to have mastered as many as 29 languages) and was the first translator of masterpieces of literature from diverse languages like the Portuguese *Lusiades* and the Arabic *One Thousand and One Nights*. He had a haughty, perpetually stern gaze and an almost animalistic nature.

As a soldier, he was known for his brutal ferociousness in single combat. He was a swordsman and a hunter. Other scholars considered him scandalous for publishing ethnological studies and discussing sexual practices from all latitudes. Throughout his life, he toggled smoothly between academia, the military world, exploration, scientific expeditions, and politics. He adopted several alternative personas, which became his true alter egos, complete with aliases and religious conversions. One time he dressed like a Persian dervish and traveled in disguise to Mecca, the first European after Burckhardt; another time, he reached the scarcely less alarming Ethiopian city of Harar, also forbidden to all Westerners.

Throughout his explorations, when Burton sniffed an interesting archaeological finding, he could quickly put his academic hat on and produce sensible, accurate, and novel scientific research. When he read about the hieroglyphs of the Hamah stones, they immediately intrigued him. He unleashed his contacts in Syria and obtained some casts of parts of the slabs; he studied them, wrote a detailed article, including their first published illustrations, and speculated about their origin.[3] However, his attempts to bring back the stones to Europe for closer investigation failed, mainly because the town of Hamah was a remote stronghold of religious fundamentalism, whose inhabitants distrusted foreigners (especially foreigners who tried to chisel out stones from the walls of their bazaar). There was no success at securing the stones until 1872 when a man called William Wright (1837–1899) had a chance at them.

William Wright was a god-fearing Irish missionary who dwelled in Syria from 1865 to 1876 (*stirring* years according to his autobiography) on behalf of the British and Foreign Bible Society, a non-denominational Christian Bible society whose purpose was to make the Bible available throughout the world.* In 1872 he was based in the capital Damascus when

---

* William Wright, the erudite missionary, is not to be confused with William Wright (1830–1889) English orientalist and professor of Arabic at Cambridge University.

he was invited to visit Hamah by the then governor of Syria, Subhi Pasha. Besides being a respected Ottoman dignitary, Subhi Pasha was an intellectual, a polyglot, a poet, and a numismatist who loved to show his country to European orientalists.

Wright, who knew about the stones, decided to turn his visit to Hamah into a mission for the rescue of the contended slabs. To do so, he decided to resort to the least elaborate plot: he bought them. Unfortunately, however, whomever he bought them from did not guarantee that the transaction would be smooth. When they heard that a Westerner was going to take away their "sacred" stones, the local population was angered. Wright feared the locals could attempt to destroy the stones rather than release them.

His fear was well-grounded: just three years earlier, in Jordan, archaeologists who tried to purchase the famous Moabite Stone, a 2800-year-old slab with inscriptions in the Moabite language, an object of unique archaeological value, had the slab broken before their eyes by a mob of angry Bedouins who would rather see it in pieces than handed over to the Europeans.[4]

Wright had to obtain guarded surveillance throughout the operation of retrieval of the stones, all the while fearing for his life probably as much as for the integrity of the artifacts. The work to remove the stones from their position went on throughout the night–"an anxious and sleepless night," he noted in his journal—while the displease of the locals was brewing. It certainly didn't help that the clear sky that night was illuminated by a meteor shower: a group of resentful locals interpreted it as the proverbial "sign from the sky" and by morning was surrounding the palace of the Pasha, demanding the restitution of the stones.

Subhi Pasha had to resort to all his influence to prevent a riot and, at the same time, organize as quick as possible a transfer of the *corpus delicti*. This was no effortless job (the reports describe fifty men and four oxen dragging the stones over a mile in one day). Finally, Wright's fear that the stones would be broken became a reality because two of the stones were so cumbersome that they had to be split in two for ease of transportation. Eventually, the four stones made it safely to the museum of Constantinople (the capital of the Ottoman Empire, today Istanbul), where they can still be admired.

At Constantinople, Wright made better gypsum copies of the stones and submitted them to the British scientific community. Just months later, in the summer of 1873, the Palestine Exploration Fund of London (an independent membership society funded in 1865 "for the purpose of investigating the Archaeology, Geography, manners, customs and culture, Geology and Natural History of the Holy Land") hired the elegant Dudley

Gallery at the Egyptian Hall in Piccadilly, for an exhibition of watercolor sketches and photographs of Palestine and a collection of various objects that came from the Holy Land. The casts of the Hamah Stones were placed at center stage as the *pièce de résistance* of the exhibition. The photograph of the stones was included in the selection of 100 images of the exhibition, which the visitors could buy for £4 (£5 for non-subscribers!).[5]

There was something mysterious about the stones, which intrigued scholars and museum visitors alike: linguists attempted to make sense by advancing diverse theories about their origin. According to one, they were written in a variant of the Cypriotic alphabet; for another, they were not writings but just ornaments; and there were several other hypotheses. An unexpected observation came from over the Atlantic when William Hayes Ward (1835–1916), New York journalist and orientalist—later president of the American Oriental Society—realized that the hieroglyphs were written in boustrophedon. "Boustrophedon" is a Greek word for "as the ox plows," an exceedingly unusual writing system in which text is written one line from left to right, the following line from right to left, and then again from left to right in an alternate manner. Ultimately, no one could place the boustrophedon hieroglyphs of the Hamah stones: they did not resemble anything previously seen in the region and did not bear any similarity with any known Syrian language.

The humble Wright, the man who recovered the stones, had his theory. Wright was a clergyman who knew the Bible almost by heart, so he started from what he knew best: the Old Testament. In the Old Testament, Hamah (or Hamath) is cited numerous times as a region just at the northern border of Israel, a place which, in other passages, is described as being populated by Hittites. Therefore, Wright came up with an article suggesting that the hieroglyphs could be Hittite. The theory was conjectural, and Wright's article was deeply imbued with a religious spirit, resembling more a sermon than a research paper, so it was accepted for publication only in a journal for theologians and biblical archaeologists.[6]

His Hittite theory did not quite make it to the right circles and gained limited popularity, so most scholars, unconvinced, kept on referring to the language of the stones with the neologism "Hamathite," or coming from Hamah. But the Hamah hieroglyphs were not meant to be forgotten forever, and the next person to stumble across them, albeit at a different location, would be able to finally connect them with the Hittites. His name was George Smith (1840–1876), and he was a legend of British archaeology.

Since childhood, Smith, who was of simple origins, had a deep, almost romantic fascination for ancient writings. He was just fourteen when he was earning a living engraving banknotes at a famous press in central London; in his lunch breaks, he would sneak out of the building and visit the halls of the British Museum to admire the cuneiform writings unearthed in Mesopotamia. Soon he was noticed by the museum curators, who were impressed by his self-obtained knowledge. Sir Henry Rawlinson, fresh back to London after his pioneering research on cuneiform, took young Smith under his wing and gave him a job as his assistant in translations. Working among piles of cuneiform tablets for years, Smith soon became proficient in Mesopotamian languages, and at the age of thirty-two obtained something very few archaeologists can claim to have obtained: an appearance on the first pages of the newspapers.

Smith was translating from Sumerian the famous eleventh tablet of the Epic of Gilgamesh, the oldest literary work in the world, when he came across the passage in which it is described how the gods sent a flood to destroy the world and Utnapishtim, who was forewarned, built an ark to escape it. It was the first—and understandably revolutionary—evidence of a flood myth that predated Noah's biblical account. When Smith held a lecture about his discovery on December 3, 1872, in front of the members of the Society of Biblical Archaeology, and the Archbishop of Canterbury and Prime Minister William Gladstone (1809–1898),* he instantly became world-famous. In the wake of his notoriety, Smith traveled to Mesopotamia on two separate archaeological campaigns.

In 1876, however, his third campaign to the Near East had a different destination: Syria. Smith planned a low-key expedition; his main aim was to survey archaeological ruins along the Euphrates River, a reconnaissance job to prepare for future excavations. He arrived in Constantinople at the start of March and was welcomed by a Bulgarian man named Peter Mateev (fl. 1870). The British Museum had recruited Mateev to accompany Smith in his exploration: he had excellent local knowledge and spoke good English, but Smith wasn't convinced. They were about to embark on a long journey through inhospitable territories and he did not want to take any risks. He figured Mateev would be more respected by the locals if he were a British citizen like him, so he visited the British consulate in Constantinople and persuaded them to produce a British passport for Mateev under the alias of Peter Matthewson.

Smith and Mateev/Matthewson started their long horseback journey, and after many hard days on the saddle, they called at Aleppo, where they met up with the British consul, James Henry Skene (1812–1886). Skene gave them a map of the area and marked a spot along the banks of the river Euphrates, a place called Tell el Jerablus. "Make sure you inspect this site"— he exhorted them—"I have seen scattered ruins there." The duo resumed its horseback journey along the Euphrates, which they followed upstream. When they came to Tell el Jerablus, the first sight was unimpressive. The low, deserted mound covered in low shrubs on the bank of the river did not promise much.

They divided and started inspecting the mound in search of ancient ruins when Matthewson, almost immediately, spotted a huge basalt stele covered in unusual inscriptions lying about on the ground and called Smith, who was on the other side of the mound. When Smith arrived and set his eyes on the stele, in pure Champollion style, he fainted and dropped to the ground. Mathewson revived him with some providential cognac as Smith, frazzled, explained why he was so shocked.[7]

From his knowledge of the Tiglath-Pileser prisms, Smith knew that when the Assyrians conquered the land they called Hatti, they took its city Karkemish. No one exactly knew where Karkemish lay; however, the Old Testament described it as being on the banks of the river Euphrates in north Syria, just where they were standing now. When he saw the inscription on the slab, Smith immediately realized it was written in the same unique hieroglyphs of the Hamah stones, which he knew as Hittite. Hittite hieroglyphs on the banks of the Euphrates River: Smith realized that he must have come across the biblical city of Karkemish. He was exultant. He convinced Matthewson to rush back to Aleppo, where he took paper and pen and immediately wrote to the Director of the British Museum in London:

> My dear Sir, … I have used my time here in making examinations of the country, and I have discovered the site of Carchemish, the great Hittite capital. I found many sculptures and an inscription of the Hittite period on a monolith, which I tried in vain to move. I wanted to send it to the Museum; it would form a unique monument there. The characters are in Hittite hieroglyphics (so-called Hamath character), and it is the longest inscription yet found—the site of Carchemish would be a magnificent one to excavate, could we not get a *firman** to excavate 'in the district of Aleppo' and spend £500, which would be enough to give you splendid results in an entirely new field. The place is very easy of access, and one could excavate and remove to England with less trouble than any other site I know of.[8]

When the news reached the British Museum, Smith's mentor, Sir Rawlinson, was thrilled; just days later, on 19 May 1876, at the 53rd Anniversary Meeting of the Royal Asiatic Society in London, he was eager to give a preliminary account of Smith's discoveries. He proudly announced that the inscriptions found by Smith at Karkemish were Hittite and that thanks to Smith's findings, the Hittites could be demonstrated to be the chief people occupying the region between Egypt and Assyria.[9]

---

* A *firman* was a royal mandate or decree signed by a sovereign in an Islamic state. In this case an authorization to dig signed by the Sultan.

"Smith has done it once again," his friends at the British museum must have thought and prepared themselves to welcome him back to London as a winner. Unfortunately, Smith would never make it back to London. A few weeks later, he contracted dysentery and died in Aleppo, just thirty-six, but a giant of Near East archaeology. Immediately after Smith's death, the new British Consul in Aleppo, Patrick Henderson, obtained the firman on behalf of the British Museum, and excavation at Karkemish started.[10] The destiny of the Karkemish site would be mixed. After a pompous start, the excavation was rapidly abandoned for lack of funds; a new excavation project would start decades later, in 1910, guided by archaeologist David George Hogarth (1862–1927) and a young, brilliant Oxford graduate called Thomas Edward Lawrence (1888–1935). Later in this story, we will meet Lawrence again, in a very different role.

In England, the news of Smith's death shocked the archaeological community. He was a talented researcher, but most of all, he was a good man loved by his fellows. Sir Rawlinson was inconsolable. Smith's necrology appeared on the pages of the prestigious scientific journal *Nature*,[11] an honor reserved for a few selected scholars. It was written by Archibald Sayce, who had known him, worked with him, and co-authored papers with him,[12] the same Archibald Sayce soon to become the father of Hittitology.

That Sayce was a genius was apparent from an early age. Born near Bristol in 1845, he read Latin and Ancient Greek at the age of ten and was able to translate Sanskrit, Hebrew, and Ancient Egyptian by eighteen. Despite his various interests, Sayce had one overarching purpose in his life: magnifying the Lord. After becoming a curate of the Church of England, his life was a journey along two parallel paths, which he managed to bridge into one coherent existence. One path was religion, which he experienced with absorbing devotion, the other was archaeology, to which he dedicated himself with incredible energy for a man of a sickly constitution. In the second half of the nineteenth century, the British intelligentsia was divided. On one side were intellectuals who, influenced by the advancements of science—in particular by the theories of Charles Darwin, which discredited the biblical stories of creation—promoted a more liberal approach to religion or even flatly denied it. On the other side were intellectuals who reacted to this cultural revolution with staunch Anglican orthodoxy.

In between these two factions, Sayce's life story is an attempt to demonstrate that science and religion not only could but *should* be practiced together, and his way of showing this was by proving the truthfulness of the Bible through rigorous archaeological research. In practice, this meant that, throughout his life, Sayce was criticized by religious people for being too scientific, by scientists for being too religious, and by both for being non-traditional in his traditionalism. However, he was also a determined man of the vintage that only Victorian England has seen, and he kept his course with an almost hieratic sense of duty, in the end winning the highest level of respect both as a theologian and as a historian. His biggest achievement was to connect the dots. He noticed similarities in archaeological finds from distant locations and was the first to intuit what these archaeological finds had in common: they were all unrecognized traces of the Hittite people.[13]

Sayce agreed with the Wright hypothesis, according to which the hieroglyphs of the Hamah stones were the first identified trace of Hittite culture. His friend Smith's discovery of the same hieroglyphs in the Hittite city of Karkemish confirmed the hypothesis. So, where did the elusive Hittites live, he wondered? What was the extent of their territory?

The answer came to him accidentally and could not have been more surprising. It was 1879 when he came across a travel report by the clergyman and explorer Edwin John Davis (fl. 1860). Davis described how in his travels he had seen a large rock relief with hieroglyphs identical to the ones of the Hamah stones near a village called İvriz. The description was convincing, the carvings were so similar they may have been made by the same hand, but there was something very odd about this claim: İvriz was in Anatolia, the region of the Near East which corresponds quite precisely to modern-day Asian Turkey, almost one thousand kilometers away from Karkemish.

Davis was the epitome of the nineteenth-century explorer, his travel memoirs merrily skipped from a description of the Cilician post system to a review of the types of pears produced in Cappadocia. According to his journal, he was traveling through the region of Lycaonia, in the heart of Anatolia, when he stopped to rest at İvriz. The locals told him about an ancient stone relief situated in a valley nearby, sculpted on the side of a cliff by the bank of a small creek.[14] Davis was no archaeologist but, moved mainly by curiosity, made his way to the valley where he found a beautiful 4 × 2-meter rock relief.

The sculpture was partially worn by the elements, but it was easy to recognize a royal figure depicted in the act of worshipping a much larger figure (likely a god) who carried wheat and grapes (symbols of fertility). To complete the scene, an aqueduct fed water to a mill, which suggested the deity was being thanked for bringing the water which made agriculture possible. Adorning the relief were hieroglyphs. Davis concluded that the hieroglyphs of the İvriz rock relief were identical to the ones seen on the Hamah stones.

It turned out that Davis was not the first to publish a description of the rock relief: in the 1600s, a Turkish author called "Kâtip Çelebi", also known as Hajji Khalifa (1609–1657), an extraordinarily prolific and versatile character who wrote fluently in Arabic, Turkish and Persian, had written about it. Hajji Khalifa specialized in reference works and authored, among others, an entire encyclopedia and a reference list of books, including 15,000 titles, so European historians may be excused for overlooking the report of this rock relief amidst his colossal production.

Later, the Swedish-born French diplomat and traveler Jean Otter (1707–1748) also mentioned the relief in his travel diaries (without having ever seen it), and the German traveler Major Fischer (fl. 1840–1860) published a sketch of it in a geography book published in Germany in 1858. However, none of these reports gave a detailed description of the hieroglyphs.

Sayce was puzzled. How could the traces of the Hittites, already very scarce in Syria, be found a thousand kilometers away in Anatolia? Just a few years earlier, he, like everyone, knew the Hittites as a scarcely significant Canaanite tribe. Now he was looking at people who left traces all over the Near East.

Sayce started researching all the literature he could find about ancient monuments of Anatolia and realized that several earlier explorers had described similar monuments scattered all over the region: a rock relief in Karabel, west Anatolia, or the ornaments of some ruins near the village of Boğazköy, in Central Anatolia.

The Karabel rock relief was visited in 1834 by a French architect turned archaeologist, Charles Texier (1802–1871). Texier was traveling through west Anatolia when he came across this monumental rock carving on the side of a cliff. He was trained as a historian and was familiar with the writings of the father of historiography, Herodotus, so he identified the relief as the one described in chapter 106 of the second book of *Historiae*. This chapter is dedicated to the Egyptians' customs and their rulers' deeds. In it, Herodotus discusses Pharaoh Sesostris of the 12th Egyptian dynasty (nineteenth century BCE), known for his extensive conquests. Herodotus wrote about the Karabel rock relief and incorrectly concluded that it was dedicated to Sesostris:

> The pillars which Sesostris erected in the conquered countries have for the most part disappeared; but in that part of Syria called Palestine, I myself saw them still standing.... In Ionia also, there are two representations of this prince engraved upon rocks, one on the road from Ephesus to Phocaea, the other between Sardis and Smyrna. In each case, the figure is that of a man, four cubits and a span high, with a spear in his right hand and a bow in his left, the rest of his costume being likewise half Egyptian, half Ethiopian. There is an inscription across the breast from shoulder to shoulder, in Egyptian hieroglyphics, which says "With my own shoulders I conquered this land."[15]

In reality, the sculpted figure is much taller than what Herodotus wrote. Herodotus also got left and right mixed up because the spear is in the left hand and the bow is in the right, and the clothes of the figures in the relief are neither Egyptian nor Ethiopian in fashion.

Texier published the accounts of his travels only in 1861. When Sayce saw the accurate drawings of the Karabel relief in Texier's book, he was struck by the similarities to the İvriz relief: the figures were dressed in the same style, wearing a cone-shaped hat, short-skirted tunics, and shoes with upturned tips, but, most importantly, he concluded that Herodotus was wrong. Those on the Karabel relief were not Egyptian hieroglyphs: they were the same hieroglyphs of the İvriz relief, of the Hamah stones, of the Karkemish slab: the language of the Hittites.

The Boğazköy site too was visited by Texier. Boğazköy, which in Turkish means "Gorge Village," is located in the heart of Anatolia, about 200 kilometers from modern-day Ankara. The ruins lay on a hill not far from the village. Texier described how the ruins were surrounded by an impressive wall at least three kilometers long. He was still following Herodotus' accounts, so he believed that the ruins at the Boğazköy site represented the ancient city of Pteria.[16] Just across the valley from the ruins of the town, at a place called Yazilikaya, Texier visited another site, a small esplanade surrounded by large, carved boulders. The site appeared to him like a rudimentary temple, a sanctuary, and, under the impression of looking at Greek art, he interpreted the carvings on the rock walls of the sanctuary as the depiction of figures of Greek mythology.

Sayce studied Texier's travel report in detail but found even more information in the account of another traveler, French archaeologist Georges Perrot (1832–1914), who had visited the site during his eight months of travels through Cappadocia, in central Anatolia, in 1861. Sayce was enthusiastic about Perrot's work. Until then, he read scant travel journals with clumsy drawings, which left him always wondering how much he could rely on them. Perrot's account of Cappadocia was on a whole different level, consisting of dozens upon dozens of elegant ink and watercolor sketches drawn with the hand of an experienced professional surveyor and even some excellent black-and-white photographs of the sculptures.[17]

Sayce studied the images down to the last detail. The more he looked at the rock art, the more he could find similarities: the fashion of the clothing on the stone figures, the carving method, the hieroglyphs, everything told him that the two sculptures, which were situated almost 800 kilometers away in different parts of Anatolia, were the work of the same people.

Sayce started to pull all the elements together. Hamah stones, İvriz relief, Karabel relief, Yazilikaya sanctuary: there were too many

One of the Hama stones. The stones, found in the city of Hama in Syria, carry hieroglyphic inscriptions in what was then understood as the Hittite language. The hieroglyphs observed on the stones led Archibald Sayce to study hieroglyphs from Anatolia, and observe similarities. Rabe!, CC BY-SA 4.0, via Wikimedia Commons

similarities, and they pointed all in one direction: these were all remnants of the same culture, the Hittite culture, and they were spread hundreds of kilometers apart throughout Syria and Anatolia. It was time to bring these observations together into a daring "unifying theory." It was time to go to the Athenaeum and let everyone know about his discovery.

3

Anatolia

That night of August 4, 1879, at the Athenaeum, Sayce held the lecture which marked the beginning of Hittitology. In front of his illustrious orientalist friends, the crème of London archaeology, he proposed that all the monuments with hieroglyphic inscriptions recently found in Syria *as well as* in Anatolia should be attributed to the Hittites. The theory was revolutionary because it meant that, at its apogee, the Hittite Empire included the whole of Anatolia and Syria, making it one of the largest in the Ancient Near East, far larger than anyone had imagined it to be until then. The historians in the audience were thrilled: in just a few years, the Hittites had been promoted from a small Canaanite tribe sparsely mentioned on the pages of the Bible to a major Near East empire, not unlike Assyria or Egypt.

Just one week after that historical evening, Sayce departed from England for a campaign in Anatolia. He wanted to see with his own eyes the Hittite ruins. Most researchers would have planned a generously funded excavation campaign, but not Sayce. Sayce had a personal, almost intimate relationship with ancient history. He wasn't a discoverer of cities like Burckhardt, a namer of lakes like Burton, a climber of cliffs like Rawlinson, or a surveyor of sites like Perrot; he wanted to admire and study. At that time, the Near East was full of archaeologists who worked out the most efficient ways of unearthing the biggest number of artifacts and carrying them back to Europe, but not Sayce. He would stand in the rain for hours carefully studying the weather-worn Hittite reliefs, taking only a few gypsum casts and his travel book notes as a memory of the visit.

British archaeologists on a mission to the Near East would customarily begin their journey at Constantinople and pay a courtesy visit to the British Ambassador. Sayce was no exception, and as he arrived, he too called at the Embassy, but his was not an ordinary institutional visit. The Ambassador was none other than his old friend, the orientalist Austen Layard.

After his exploit excavating at Nineveh, Layard returned to London celebrated as a rising star of archaeology, and started a successful career in politics (as well as being Trustee of the British Museum and owner of a Venetian glassware gallery). He became a member of the Parliament and was sent to cover prestigious diplomatic posts like the one in Constantinople.

Layard's surge to the jet-set of British diplomacy had been an improbable one. In 1839 he was a self-willed young man who dreamed of moving to the Orient to break away from his desk job at his uncle's solicitor firm in the City. He headed out on an adventurous overland journey to Ceylon, where his father had previously lived and had some contacts which could get him a job. He wasn't even halfway through his seven thousand miles trip, just past the Jordan river, when he ran out of money and was presently captured by Bedouins who held him enslaved for six months. When he miraculously escaped and reached the British Consulate in Damascus, tattered, he was given some money. Still, instead of spending it on getting the prospect of a job in Ceylon* or going back to his desk at the family firm, undaunted, he resumed his travels on foot through Anatolia.

Layard lived among the locals, picking up languages as if they were stones, until he called at Constantinople. There he won the trust of the British Ambassador Sir Stratford Canning (1776–1880), who sent him on short missions throughout the Ottoman Empire in all sorts of capacities on account of his local knowledge (and readiness). While on a mission at Mosul, in modern-day Iraq, Layard stumbled upon the ruins of the ancient Mesopotamian city of Nineveh, sniffed the opportunity, obtained funding for the excavation, and, he who had not previously worked in archaeology, suddenly found himself at the top of notoriety after unearthing the Assurbanipal library, the most important trove of cuneiform tablets ever discovered.

Forty years after calling at Constantinople ragged and destitute, Layard was now back, this time luxuriously accommodated in the British summer embassy in Therapia, a suburb on the European side of the Bosphorus. Despite being very respected by local authorities, perhaps also on account of his knowledge of the language—"omnipotent" wrote Sayce about him—Layard was not particularly liked by London bureaucrats: he wasn't of noble birth, and he wasn't highly educated, he had gained his skills "on the field," and this was not popular with Westminster, especially with Prime Minister Gladstone.

There was a famous caricature of Layard, published in *Punch*, which showed him as the proverbial bull raging through a china shop, the bull being though a sacred Mesopotamian winged bull and the china being the delicate diplomatic relationships between the United Kingdom and the Ottoman Empire. Layard's summer residence was housed in a majestic,

---

* Years later Layard's younger brother Edgar attempted the move to Ceylon as well. He succeeded, and became a respected zoologist with a mollusc, a squirrel and a warbler named after him, a fact which never ceased to amuse Layard.

white, three stories building with turrets at each corner, situated just meters from the shore. On the day Sayce arrived, Layard threw a delightful dinner party in his honor, with "singing all evening," according to the pages of Lady Layard's diary.

In the following days, Layard used all his influence to introduce Sayce to the right circles and obtained for him an audience with the Sultan, a meeting which, in Sayce's own words, considerably "smoothened" his travels through Anatolia. Layard even accompanied Sayce for a part of his explorations.[1]

The first port of call in Sayce's visit through west Anatolia was the site of the Karabel Relief, at a mountain pass no more than twenty kilometers from the town of Smyrna (today İzmir). When Sayce visited the site, the scenic countryside, and picturesque vegetation on a pleasant September morning starkly contrasted with the dangerousness of the place. The Sultan had deemed thirty soldiers not too many to safeguard Sayce from the attack of the local populations. Throughout the three hours which took Sayce to make casts of the rock relief, all of the soldiers stood with their rifles aimed at an equal number of armed brigands watching from the hills in a nerve-wracking stand-off. Besides the alarming company, Sayce was dismayed to see that Yuruk nomads had previously pitched a tent near the cliff and used the niche of the sculpture as a fireplace. However, he was satisfied with confirming his earlier observations on the relief and of his new, better casts of the hieroglyphs.

From Karabel, Sayce, still surrounded by the soldiers of the Sultan, made his way to the site of another west Anatolian rock sculpture he had studied. Not far from the town of Magnesia, at a mountain called Mount Sipylos, a sculpture had been carved on a limestone cliff wall. The monument represented a woman sitting on a throne with long hair and a headdress. The sculpture had a peculiarity: when it rained, because of how the water trickled over the head of the statue, it appeared as if the woman was crying.

Sixteen hundred years earlier, the Greek traveler and writer Pausania had visited the site and reported that this was a monument to the mythical Niobe, carved by her brother Broteas. In Greek mythology, Niobe is known as "crying Niobe." She was the daughter of King Tantalus and was punished by the gods for her arrogance, especially for being too proud of having numerous children. According to the legend, the gods killed her children, turning her into a weeping rock statue.

To Pausania, it made sense that a rock statue of a woman who appeared to weep would represent Niobe. However, when Sayce studied it, he realized that the monument was much older than what Pausania assumed it to be and that its style was consistent with other Late Bronze

Age Anatolian art he had studied. It was yet another unrecognized piece of the Hittite puzzle that Sayce picked up along his journey. Comparing the monument to accounts of later mythology, Sayce deduced that the sculpture represented the main female deity of Anatolian tradition, known sometimes as Atergatis or Derketo, sometimes as Kybelê.

The fact that Greek historians like Herodotus and Pausania (ironically both of them natives of Anatolia) never mentioned the Hittites and misinterpreted the origin of Hittite monuments taught Sayce that already by the fourth century BCE, the historical memory of the Hittites was permanently lost. Already at the time of Ancient Greeks, the Hittite Empire was, as he would call it, a "forgotten kingdom."

Sayce returned to England enthusiastic about the findings, which confirmed his theory. Back at his post at Oxford University, he made the Hittites the focus of his research. On July 6, 1880, in London, he held a memorable lecture before the members of the Society of Biblical Archaeology. The crowd of listeners was mesmerized: he told about Hittite history, showed pictures of Hittite artifacts, and drew maps of their territory. His passionate introduction to this previously virtually unknown civilization fascinated even the general public and was published in one of the most popular literary reviews of the time, the very fashionable "Fraser's Magazine."[2]

Sayce's sources on Hittite history were still minimal, but the more the Egyptologists translated the heaps of hieroglyphic texts from Egypt, the more the Hittites were mentioned. More than twenty years had gone since the first, puzzling mention of the "Land of Hatti" in the Egyptian–Hittite peace treaty, and archaeologists had now found and translated a dozen other inscriptions which revealed the background of the treaty. What led to the famous truce was a story of war and heroism, one of the highest moments of Egyptian history, grandiosely celebrated in war bulletins and epic poems, the most known of them by the poet Pentaur, written in the thirteenth century BCE.[3]

Through lines upon lines of elegant hieroglyphs, Pentaur reveals a gripping rivalry between the Egyptian and Hittite kingdoms at the beginning of the thirteenth century BCE, when both wanted to establish supremacy over Syria. Pharaoh Ramesses II, thirsty for imperial expansion, started campaigning in the Levant very early during his reign, which lasted over three decades. In the spring of 1275 BCE, when tensions between Hittites and Egyptians reached a boiling point, Ramesses II and the Hittite king converged onto the city of Kadesh, one of the main Hittite strongholds in the Levant, for a face-off, a "pitched battle" to decide the destiny of the territory they both coveted.

It was May when the Egyptian army crossed the river Orontes near the modern-day Syrian Lebanese border. The army consisted of four divisions of 4000 soldiers each, proudly named after the main gods of the Egyptian pantheon and was led directly by their god on earth, Pharaoh Ramesses the Great. The troops were very close to the walls of Kadesh when they captured two Hittite deserters. Questioned, the two men declared the Hittite army was still at Aleppo, over 200 kilometers north. The Egyptians relaxed, believing the enemy was several days away. But the Hittites had a cunning plan: the two deserters were covert agents instructed to deceive the Egyptians. The truth was that the Hittite army was already at Kadesh, having set up camp north of the city where they could not be seen getting ready to lay an ambush, and the Hittite King was already safe within the city walls.

In a twist of luck, however, the Egyptians captured two Hittite scouts snooping around the camp. The two scouts were put under torture and confessed the actual position of the Hittites but, bitterly, added that they would soon be vindicated because the troops of their King were "more numerous than the sands on the shore." And numerous they were; in fact, the Hittite army was nearly twice as big as the Egyptian one and was strengthened by thousands of foreign mercenaries, which the Egyptians, proud citizens of the oldest nation in history, found contemptible. What happened next is shrouded in mystery because the account of the war leaves the way for romance and epic.

According to Pentaur, the Egyptians were victims of an ambush by the Hittites. The clash which followed is still, over three thousand years later, the largest battle chariot engagement on record. Hittites charged with heavy three-man chariots and smashed the Egyptian vanguard, which used lighter, two-man chariots. The Egyptians were overwhelmed, the rear-guard retired, and the bodies of thousands of soldiers were left behind to be plundered by the Hittites. When he heard about the ambush, Ramesses II was furious. He invoked the wrath of the gods and led the charge of a fierce counterattack. He outmaneuvered the Hittites (the epic account states that he *literally* single-handedly destroyed the enemy) and reverted the defeat leaving scores of Hittite soldiers agonizing on the battlefield.

The losses on both sides were enormous, so both parties retreated for the day. Back at the camp, the situation did not look good for the Pharaoh. He had undoubtedly demonstrated outstanding leadership in chasing back the Hittites to their side of the battlefield (although some speculate that he succeeded in doing that thanks to the timely arrival of reinforcements from the Egyptian colony of Amurru).[4] Still, his army had suffered a loss of about a quarter of its capacity. The stakes were high, and a second clash would have put him in the difficult position of losing everything or even being captured. It was a stalemate. Ramesses, disheartened, decided to retreat to Egypt, while the Hittites withdrew north of Kadesh. In the aftermath of the battle, both sides cooled off their hostile intents, and, where the weapons could not settle the matter, diplomacy did. Within fifteen years, King Muwatalli II's second successor, King Hattusili III, signed the peace treaty. The two nations would forever keep the peace and entertain a cordial relationship.

Sayce was fascinated by the accounts of the Battle of Kadesh and all other mentions of the Hittites found in the Assyrian archives. He kept collating as much information as possible to conduct elaborated research to reconstruct the history of the Hittites and the geography of their empire. The sources available to him provided evidence that the Hittites had expanded militarily into west Anatolia and Syria and had forged alliances with northern Anatolian tribes; therefore, he reasoned, their place of origin had to be in Central Anatolia. He studied the geography of Anatolia and reconstructed in painstaking detail the main ancient roads, mapping those old enough to date back to the Hittite age. Like a detective who puts red dots on a map where each crime has been committed and reconstructs the whereabouts of the culprit, Sayce mapped all the sites at which Hittite ruins had been found. His main intuition was that the largest supposed Hittite settlements were close to copper deposits. Because he also knew from Perrot's surveys in Boğazköy that the Hittites were able to produce bronze artifacts, he correctly suggested that the Hittites had advanced skills in metallurgy, which, he maintained, would have contributed to their military power. His work progressed slowly but steadily, adding a little morsel of information at a time. "Little by little…"—he wrote— "the obscurity is being cleared away from the earlier history of Asia Minor."[5]

The few recognizably Hittite monuments of Anatolia became key in Sayce's interpretation. Besides the ones he visited himself, he included in his studies the ruins of Boğazköy and the neighboring site Hüyük, which were well-documented in the beautiful photographs and drawings of Georges Perrot. The images of Boğazköy showed a wall surrounding the site. The wall had a large gate, and enormous carved sphinxes stood on each side of the gate. Within the site walls, Perrot documented the ruins of a large palace. On the palace walls, well-preserved bas-reliefs showed hunting scenes, as well as lions in the act of devouring a ram. Sayce concluded that the sphinx gate was inspired by Egyptian art, albeit with local adaptations.

Then he studied an ornament carved on a wall of the palace: the figure of a double-headed eagle. This must have been an important symbol in Hittite culture, as Sayce noticed it was also visible at Yazilikaya sanctuary. He correctly deduced that the symbol had been adopted many centuries later by Turkish princes, who likely saw it on the Hittite ruins. The crusaders who visited Anatolia in the Middle Ages brought the symbol of the double-headed eagle back to Europe, where it became the emblem of the German emperors, who, in turn, passed it on to Austrian and Russian royal families.[6]

From the monuments, Sayce was able to catch the first dim glimpses of the Hittite customs: their unique clothing with unusual cone-shaped headpieces not seen in other ancient Near East cultures, or the mittens they appeared to wear, which told of a people used to cold climates like the ones of mountainous Anatolia, or the shoes with their unique upturning toes, probably made for walking in fresh snow. Indeed, the image of the Hittites painted by Sayce was largely based on conjectures and deductions, but later archaeology would prove him right on most accounts.

Still, the most intriguing theories advanced by Sayce were about Hittite religion and mythology. He studied the accounts of Anatolian religious customs from later traditions, for example, those reported by the Greek author Lucian of Samosata (125–180) at Mabog (Modern-day Mabij, later known to Greeks and Romans as Hierapolis, not to be confused with the Hierapolis in Anatolia) in northern Syria in the second century CE. He compared them to those reported in documents found at Karkemish and noticed similarities with the scenes depicted in Hittite sacred sites, so he drew extensive comparisons. He could establish that the heritage of the Hittite traditions was still identifiable in the Near East hundreds of years later.

Besides identifying traces of Hittite cultural heritage in populations that inhabited Anatolia and the Levant centuries later, Sayce put forward exciting theories on the influence of Hittite culture on contemporary civilizations outside Anatolia and the Levant as well.[7] For example, he went as far as hypothesizing that the Greek myth of the Amazons may have originated among the Hittites. In Greek mythology, the Amazons were a nation of female warriors whose native home was Cappadocia; according to Greek folklore, many of the cities of west Anatolia had been founded by Amazons, and the Amazons sided with the Trojans in the *Iliad*.

Sayce maintained that the myth of the Amazons was derived from the tradition of priestesses of the main Anatolian female deity, the same sculpted at Mount Silypos, whose cult the Hittites had acquired when they conquered Karkemish. Today (2023), over a century after Sayce's work, the debate over which influence, if any, the Hittites had on prehistoric Greek culture is one of the hottest in archaeology. As we will see in the following chapters, it became a central field of study for some Hittitologists.

But besides speculating on the history and customs of the Hittites, Sayce had another question to answer. In Sayce's time, the concept of race was crucial. Thanks to the advancements in genetics, today we know that classifying human populations into physically discrete races is impossible. The genetic variation, even among individuals who appear very different, is too small to make any sensible discernment. However, in the 1800s, the so-called "scientific racism," the belief that people could be divided into anthropological typologies by all sorts of methods ranging from measuring the darkness of their skin to the size of the skull or their hairstyle or the shape of their nose, was prevalent among scholars.

The sad upshot of this belief was that the classification could be used to support concepts of racial superiority or inferiority. It is unfortunate that language was among the parameters used by 1800s anthropologists to divide people into races because, while divisions based on skull shape and skin color are pointless, dividing languages into different families is scientifically relevant and helps to understand language evolution.

In Sayce's time, peoples of the Near East were usually described as belonging to one of three races: Semites (like Assyrians or Egyptians), Aryans (like Medes or Persians), and Mongols (like Turks). Scholars decided as early as the 1860s that the Hittites were not Semites. Their view was based on their names: when translations of the accounts of the Battle of Kadesh or the Egyptian–Hittite Peace Treaty started to appear, French scholar François Joseph Chabas (1817–1882) was the first to realize that the names of the Hittite kings were not Semitic. Looking at the drawings representing the Hittites on Egyptian monuments, Sayce believed the Hittites had "yellow skins and mongoloid features," and Samuel Birch (1813–1885) of the British Museum, contemporary of Sayce, noted that Hittites had ponytails, which according to him were characteristic of Mongols.[8] Therefore, following the day's understanding, Sayce hypothesized that the Hittites were of the "Mongol race" in his lectures and articles.

Notwithstanding his unsound racial stereotyping, Sayce's enthusiasm for the Hittites was contagious, and in the 1880s, his research gained tremendous traction. Articles were published, and lectures were held on the topic. The Hittite entry of the *Encyclopaedia Britannica*, which a few years earlier was only two and a half lines long, now occupied two full pages. In 1884 Wright, the missionary who had rescued the Hamah stones published the first monograph on the Hittites, titled "The Empire of the Hittites," of which Sayce co-authored a chapter.[9]

However, the older generation of archaeologists was still lukewarm about the Hittites. They argued that too little was known about the Hittites and that most literature was based on conjectures. In 1893, American-German historian Wilhelm Max Müller (1862–1919), in his book *Asia and Europe in the Ancient Egyptian Monuments*, described the Hittites as "the current fashion-people of amateur historians." He wrote: "When they were discovered a few years ago, and the connection between the Hittites-Hatti and the monuments with the Hamah hieroglyphs were found, this finding was seized with greed, and now ... they have become the stopgaps of ancient oriental history, usable for everything inexplicable. They are allowed to live now in this part and now in that part of Syria, mostly in Palestine or near Kadesh, in the first case as Hamitic Canaanites, in the second, of course, as indefinable Semites."[10]

Clearly, Müller failed to appreciate that research on the Hittites was a work in progress; however, he highlighted a serious underlying issue: more sources were needed. However valuable Egyptian and Assyrian sources could be, and however satisfying the study of the Hittite monuments, the most valuable sources that were still nowhere to be seen were those written by the Hittites themselves. So far, Sayce and the other Hittitologists could only count on a handful of poorly preserved hieroglyphic inscriptions scattered between Anatolia and Syria, which linguists were far from deciphering.

Once again, the holy grail of decipherment was needed: a bilingual inscription. Sayce knew this and was searching for more examples of Hittite hieroglyphs when he came across an article by German orientalist Andreas David Mordtmann (1811–1879), ambassador of the Hanseatic League in Constantinople. In his article, Mordtmann described how he had been approached by a shadowy Russian numismatic collector in Constantinople, a certain Aleksandar Jovanov (fl. 1850), who showed him a curious small ancient artifact: a metal boss. In antiquity, embossing was often used for seals, which are stamps used to sign correspondence. However, this particular boss was more likely an ornament, for example, the kind used on the handle of a dagger. The article did not show a picture, but it described how the boss represented a warrior dressed in a fringed tunic, wearing boots with upturned ends, and carrying a dagger and a spear. The figure was surrounded by a cuneiform text, however, around the figure, there were tiny signs "similar to hieroglyphs."

When Sayce read the article, he immediately suspected the boss to be a Hittite handicraft and that the tiny signs could have been Hittite hieroglyphs. Could this be the bilingual text he had been looking for, Anatolia's "Rosetta Stone"? Sayce was determined to find an image of the boss. Mordtmann had just passed away, so there was no chance to ask him for further clarifications. Sayce had to go through all earlier publications by Mordtmann; one, in particular, was hard to locate because Mordtmann had referenced it under the wrong year and place of publication. Sayce, however, managed to track it down and was rewarded: a drawing of the Hittite boss was attached, and the signs looked consistent with Hittite hieroglyphs.

3. Anatolia

But drawings are prone to mistakes. Sayce had to be sure that the copy was correct. He wrote to everyone he knew to gather more information on the Hittite boss. Through his contacts in London, he discovered that Jovanov had offered the seal to the British Museum. Still, nobody at the Museum had ever seen anything like that before and suspecting it was a forgery, they rejected it. Finally, Sayce received a letter from his friend, French orientalist François Lenormant (1837–1883), who had seen the seal when he was still in Constantinople and had taken a cast of it, which he forwarded to Sayce. When the parcel arrived, Sayce unpacked it and saw the cast; he was ecstatic: the hieroglyphs were undoubtedly of the Hittite type. Meanwhile, Jovanov too had died, and Sayce was dismayed because he could not locate the boss: it had quickly changed hands, and no one knew its whereabouts (it was later found that the boss was shipped from Athens to America to be purchased by a Mr. Henry Walters, who donated it to the Baltimore Museum, where it can be admired today).

The first thing to do was to translate the cuneiform text on the boss. The cuneiform characters were known to him, although the words they spelled were not exactly consistent with Akkadian. Nevertheless, Sayce obtained the sentence: "Tarqu-dimme, King of the country of Erme." He assumed the name Tarqu-dimme to correspond to the Greek name Tarkondemos which he knew from ancient Greek history as a king of Cilicia in southern Anatolia, and the name Erme to correspond to the name the Greeks had given to a group of Anatolian mountains, the Arima mountains. But with so little text, making any sense of the hieroglyphs was challenging. Sixty years earlier, Champollion had the whole text of the Rosetta Stone to study; Sayce had scarcely a sentence, rather just the epithet of a king, so he could only make some educated guesses. A hieroglyph looked like a mountain with three peaks. Surely that could be the sign for "country"?[11] Especially if the country in question is a mountainous one, like Anatolia. However, Sayce's attempts at decoding the hieroglyphs went no further. The appointment with the cracking of the Hittite code had to be postponed one more time.

While interest in the Hittite Empire was growing among archaeologists, more curious researchers were converging into Anatolia in search of a significant find which could make them famous. In 1882, after the French and British had visited the archaeological site of Boğazköy, it was the turn of the Germans. The initial German contacts with Boğazköy were not the most successful. However, Germans would have time to make up for that later. The first German archaeologist to visit Boğazköy was a cantankerous but determined engineer named Carl Humann (1839–1896). Like most archaeologists of the age, Humann came to this discipline almost fortuitously and with self-taught skills. In his homeland, he was an engineer and surveyor who battled tuberculosis, but when he moved to the warmer climate of Constantinople for the benefit of his lungs, traveling and surveying Palestine and Anatolia on behalf of the Ottoman Government, his interest in antique ruins bloomed, and he soon expanded his horizons into archaeological excavations.

Throughout his career, he never hid his contempt for a scholarly approach to archaeological remains and loathed the study of literature, linguistics, and the like. He was tall and strong, with a military haircut and imposing mustache. His ways were hasty and coarse, but he had a talent for commanding teams of workers into the most advanced excavation techniques, a skill which led him to become famous in the European archaeology circles thanks to a singular, grandiose achievement: supervising the disinterment and transportation to Berlin of the great altar of Pergamon, a 35 × 33 meter structure, masterpiece of Hellenistic sculpture and architecture, complete with columns, a staircase, and two dozen giant statues, a treasure of archaeology which lay almost entirely buried in the ground—but in a good state of preservation—near Pergamon in western Turkey.

Humann came across the ruins of the Pergamon acropolis while surveying the area and immediately detected the potential of the find. Armed with his legendary resolution, he went to great lengths, liaising with the Berlin Sculpture Museum and the echelons of the Ottoman Empire to obtain authorization for digging out the altar and transporting it to Germany. Due to the structure's magnitude, this was a daunting effort that took over ten years, but Humann eventually made it. The altar was transported to Berlin, where an entirely new museum was constructed around it: the Pergamon Museum, to date one of the finest archaeological museums in the world.

In 1882 Humann, the engineer turned archaeologist, accompanied by countryman and archaeologist Otto Puchstein (1856–1911), visited central Anatolia. The two of them could not have been more different. Puchstein was short and plump, soft-eyed, and mild-mannered, a pure intellectual. The contrast with Humann was almost comic. Yet they got along famously and participated in several successful expeditions together. They would set out on horseback and visit remote parts of Anatolia. None of them was fluent in Turkish, but they somehow found their way to Mar'asch (modern-day Kahramanmaraş), a small, quaint town in the interior of southern Turkey, located between high hills, lakes, and rivers. The town had been a Byzantine military post for centuries and featured a busy fortified citadel.

Humann and Puchstein were studying the grounds when they made an outstanding discovery. The finding was the classic crowd-pleaser, one of those artifacts which tick all the boxes to become the *pièce de résistance* of a museum: a meter-long black basalt statue of a lion dating back to the Late Bronze Age. Elegant, majestic, with an open mouth and a row of fangs showing, it is a masterpiece of Anatolian art. But besides pleasing the eye of archaeologists, it pleased epigraphists because the lion's mane was inscribed with perfectly preserved hieroglyphs.

The Mar'asch lion was immediately transported to the Istanbul Museum, where the German explorers made sure that casts of its inscription would be sent to Berlin for study. Humann and Puchstein continued their Anatolian exploration and finally reached Boğazköy, where they surveyed the same Hittite ruins that Texier and Perrot had seen before them and even took casts of the rock carvings on the walls of the Yazilikaya religious monument nearby. None of them realized they were looking at ruins of the Hittite Empire; they still mistakenly believed that the walls and ruins represented the remains of the city of Pteria,[12] a view they probably took from Texier.*[13]

At the same time as the Germans were surveying Anatolia, back at Oxford, Sayce had a different understanding of the Boğazköy site. He had narrowed it down as the most likely capital of the Hittite Empire. Not only was it the largest Hittite site in Anatolia, but it was also the site of the largest sanctuary (Yazilikaya). Moreover, the site was located in the geographic area he believed was the epicenter of the Hittite civilization; the key to understanding this mysterious ancient people had to be Boğazköy. Sayce could not wait to travel again to Anatolia on an expedition to see with his own eyes. On June 23, 1883, corresponding with his German fellow historian and friend Eduard Meyer (1855–1930), he wrote, "…if only excavations could be made on certain sites, I feel sure that a new and important chapter in the history of civilization would be disclosed."[14]

The British Museum was hard to persuade, so Sayce tried to talk his German friend, the famous archaeologist Henrich Schliemann (1822–1890), into this idea. The two had developed a friendship over dinner at a club during one of Schliemann's visits to London. That Sayce may have had a friendship or even basal respect for Heinrich Schliemann is nothing less than surprising because the two men were the exact opposite in everything. Sayce was a pious philologist whose life was equally divided

---

* Pteria was a major Assyrian town in Anatolia. Archaeologists had tried to locate it for a long time but were misled by Herodotus' unclear description. In view of recent research, the real Pteria is currently believed to lay about fifty kilometres away, at a site called Kerkenes Daği.

between library and church, between sermons and history books. Schliemann was a divorced ex-businessman who hated his father and had a fetish for women called like his mother. Whimsically, one day, armed with no more than basic, amateurish knowledge of ancient history,[15] he decided that he would become the man who found Troy, the lost city in which Homer's *Iliad* takes place.

Almost incredibly, in 1870 Schliemann did, in fact, find the buried ruins of a Bronze Age city, which is likely to be Troy, attracting to himself at the same time praise for what he did and loathing for *how* he did it. Schliemann was accused of making personal profits with the artifacts he discovered, associating with shady figures, ignoring the rights of local populations, acting in disregard of international laws on excavation, being unscientific, causing massive damage to historical remains by using rough digging techniques, lying about his discoveries for personal interest and manipulating his associates.[16] Due to the roughness of his methods, his *modus operandi* at some sites has been compared to "an act of vandalism unworthy of any people imbued with a sense of the continuity of history."[17]

Schliemann was not available to excavate at Boğazköy: he was busy in Orchomenus, an archaeological site in Boeotia, a region of Greece where he believed to have identified the tomb of the legendary Minyas, so he declined.

While Sayce was desperate for not being able to dig in Anatolia, in France, Georges Perrot had come to the same conclusion that the key to the Hittites was to be found in Boğazköy. Therefore, Perrot pushed French benefactors to pay for an expedition and lobbied for one of his pupils, anthropologist Ernest Chantre (1843–1924), vice director of the museum of Lyon, to lead it. Some—like Sayce—came to archaeology from the historical study of the Bible, others—like Rawlinson—through their interest in ancient languages, and others—like Layard—stumbled upon it while following their sense of adventure. Chantre came to archaeology through his passion for anthropology, the science that studies human beings' natural history. He learned the basics of human development under the father of French neuroanatomy Paul Broca (1824–1880), and the pre-historian Gabriel de Mortillet (1821–1898). He became one of the most brilliant young scientists in France. A level-headed, conscientious researcher, he had started to make a name for himself in Near East anthropology by studying the populations of Armenia and even had an African water bird named after him. Chantre arrived in Constantinople in May 1893, accompanied by his wife and other scholars.

The French party started moving east towards the heart of Anatolia.

The first six months of the expedition went smoothly: by early 1894, the team had visited many Hittite sites (including Boğazköy, twice), carrying out small excavations here and there and collecting an impressive amount of small Hittite artifacts like figurines, vases, and metalwork. Everything was going well until they found themselves in the throes of a cholera epidemic. Ailing with what Chantre called the "dreadful scourge," the following months were challenging; between limited drinkable water and uncomfortable accommodations, they repeatedly contemplated cutting the expedition short; however, the final mortification came in June.

The party was stationed in Hüyük when they realized that the local administrative authority, the *Mutassarif*, had prohibited all locals from selling them food or other goods. With their stocks dwindling, the archaeologists had no choice but to interrupt their journey, packing up and heading home. The cause for this *de facto* expulsion from the country was never clarified. Chantre speculated that his good relationship with the local Armenians was seen negatively by the Ottoman authorities; Chantre had studied Armenian culture during his years as an anthropologist and was fluent in Armenian. Probably the Ottoman authorities suspected him of fomenting a revolution among this minority.[18]

The expedition ended abruptly, but Chantre was not exactly empty-handed. Besides the many artifacts, he had secured some incised clay tablets. The discovery of 3,000-year-old written materials was made by chance by Madame Chantre at Boğazköy when she observed the tiny fragment of a clay tablet inscribed with cuneiform characters lying on the ground. Digging in the same area, the party found more fragments. It was quite a considerable bounty of tablet fragments. However, as Chantre and his partners were about to embark on a ship to France at the Turkish port town of Mersin, Ottoman authorities at the douane confiscated most of them. Of the few fragments they managed to secure, most were small and with just a few cuneiform signs inscribed; only one was larger and better preserved.

Chantre was not an expert in ancient languages, so when he came back to France, he had to involve other scholars to try to translate them. One of the expedition's participants, Alfred Boissier (1867–1945), made initial attempts. Boissier was a French-Swiss philologist, the son of the Dean of Geneve University; Chantre's expedition to Cappadocia had been his maid mission. Because of his juniority, he worked under Joachim Menant (1820–1899), a Magistrate from Rouen who had turned to oriental studies and had become an expert on cuneiform. On August 23, 1895, in front of a large public at the *Académie des Inscriptions et Belles Lettres* of Paris, Menant presented Boissier's results. The translation he showed[19] generated

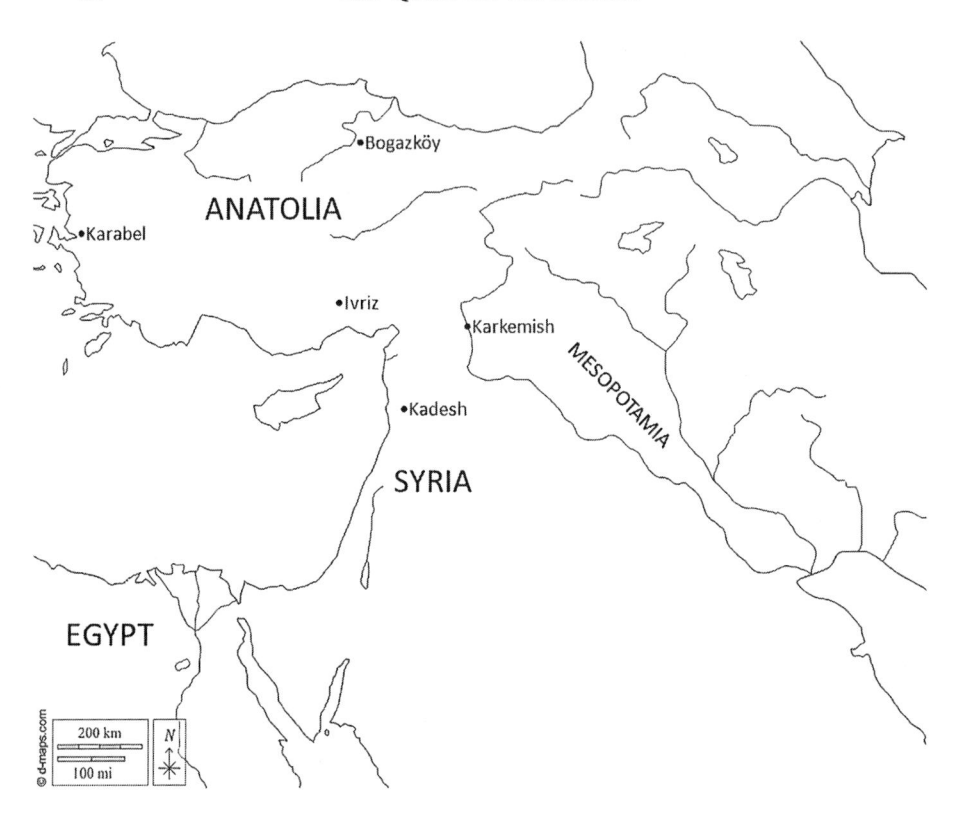

The Ancient Near East. By 1879, evidence of Hittite presence was demonstrated in both Syria and Anatolia, redefining the previous understanding of the extent of their territory. By the author, www.d-maps.com

a bit of confusion. In the smaller fragments, Boissier and Menant recognized some Akkadian names of celestial bodies like *Dilbat* (the planet Venus) and deduced they were astrological records.

The others, they supposed, were fragments of letters. However, the largest fragment contained a list of cities. Boissier and Menant knew these were names of cities because a cuneiform symbol preceded each name. This kind of symbol is called "determinant," and this particular determinant indicated that whatever followed was the name of a city. Among the names of the cities, some, like Assur, were identifiable, while others were unknown.

The problem was that the French scholars were approaching the texts assuming they were written in a variant of Akkadian. They did not know they were holding in their hands the first cuneiform Hittite text ever unearthed in Anatolia. One of the city names they transliterated was *Hattusipaizzi*. Chantre remarked that the name sounded Semitic to him, owing to its end in -*iz*. But the transliteration was wrong. Unbeknownst to him, what was written was actually *Hattusi paizzi*, which is Hittite for "He comes to Hattusa," and Hattusa was the name of the glorious capital of the Hittite Empire. Once again, the appointment with the Hittite language had to be postponed. The truth about the Hittite language was just about to emerge. The key, however, did not come from Anatolia, it came from a different country, actually from a different continent altogether.

4

Writing Letters

It was the summer of 1887, and a peasant woman was digging to scavenge old bricks from some ancient ruins in a town called Tell el Amarna in Middle Egypt. What she found changed our understanding of ancient history. Buried under the ground were some ancient clay tablets with inscriptions on them. At that time, Egypt was perpetually scouted by shady European art merchants sniffing for artifacts they could buy cheaply and sell high on the markets of Paris or London. The peasant woman thought of making a small profit and sold the tablets to one of them. The deal didn't go unnoticed, so other locals went to the same spot, found more tablets, and put them on the market.

At the same time, British William Flinders Petrie (1853–1942) was visiting Tell el Amarna of his own accord, having spent the last few years as an independent excavator at Egyptian archaeological sites. His passion for archaeology was almost innate. He was just eight years old when he put forward his theories on carrying out a scientifically sound, systematic excavation of archaeological sites, which until then were a rather haphazard affair. When he was twenty-seven years old and got the opportunity of joining archaeological missions in Egypt as a surveyor, from the moment he set foot at a site, he revolutionized the excavation technique of the age. Digging in Egypt became his life mission and only focus, to the point that, to be closer to the site, he famously moved into a pharaonic tomb, using it as his home for three years.

The picture of Flinders Petrie with long hair, long beard, barefoot and dirty, resting by the door of his makeshift dwelling, has become a classic in the history of archaeology. But while the appearances made him look more like a grave robber than an archaeologist, Flinders Petrie was a genius. A genius in the classic sense of the word: his baffling ability for mental calculation of impossibly large numbers was the subject of research in scientific journals.* By the age of thirty-nine, he was assigned the first chair of Egyptology at the Royal College of London, which he accepted, but on the condition of staying in Egypt. From there, working knee-deep in the dirt daily, he trained an entire generation of archaeologists. Although his favorite sites lay in Lower Egypt, he could not resist the attraction of the distant site of Tell el Amarna in Middle Egypt because of its unique past. Tell el Amarna was the site of Akhetaten, a city funded by Pharaoh Akhenaten (who ruled 1353–1336 BCE) for worshiping the god Aten and abandoned shortly after the end of his reign.

When Flinders Petrie heard about the tablets found among the ruins of Akhetaten, he located the exact spot and turned it into a large-scale excavation. When he reached an underground chamber, his surprise was immense. There lay a room full of inscribed tablets: what was left of the state archives of the 18th dynasty Pharaohs Amenhotep III, Akhenaten, and Smenkhkare (or Tutankhamun, this is unsure), who reigned over Egypt in the fourteenth century BCE. Three hundred eighty-two neatly stacked clay tablets with letters or copies of letters sent to the pharaohs or by the pharaohs, the diplomatic correspondence between rulers of kingdoms of the Late Bronze Age, the first known example of an international diplomatic system. It is impossible to overstate the value of this archive: the Amarna Letters represent a true window into the past.

Most of the letters were between the pharaoh and his vassal states. At that time, Egypt was at the height of its expansion. Some of the rulers of satellite kingdoms in the southernmost region of the Levant, like Amurru, Byblos, Damascus, and Kadesh, would use flattery and cajolery to request favors from the pharaohs. Others would pledge eternal allegiance, like King Adda-danu of the vassal city-state of Gezer, who declared: "A brick may move from under its partner; still I will not move from under the feet of the Pharaoh, my lord."[1]

The letters which most captivated historians were the correspondence between the heads of state of the powers of the age: Egypt, Babylonia, Assyria, and, above all, Mitanni, a powerful state populated by the Hurrian people, in a territory between northern Syria and Anatolia, between 1500 and 1200 BCE. Written in Akkadian, the *lingua franca* of the Late Bronze Age Near East, they give a unique insight into the etiquette and the strategies of the diplomacy of 3000 years ago. In a largely cordial tone, the

---

* The research was conducted by eclectic British scientist Francis Galton (1822–1911), a cousin of Charles Darwin and friends with Flinders Petrie and collaborated with him on projects of other nature as well. Galton is known for his ideas on scientific racism and held the first chair of eugenics at the University College of London.

great kings address each other as "brothers," negotiate marriages between royal families, discuss alliances and conflicts, honor each other with presents, and even spread the occasional gossip.

Two letters came to the Pharaoh from the Hittites.* One more complete, the other partially preserved, they were written by the "King of the land of Hatti," Suppiluliuma. Unfortunately, they were not the kind of letters that allowed the archaeologists to learn much more about the Hittites. They were short and fragmentary; they did not show where or when they were written, nor did they refer to any event or person which could be unequivocally placed in time; even the name of the pharaoh they were sent to was unreadable. Yet, they confirmed how powerful the Hittite Kingdom was, as its king Suppiluliuma referred to an old friendship with the Pharaoh of Egypt and made demands and promises about the exchange of gifts:

> Now, my brother, you have acceded to the throne of your father, and similarly as your father and I have sent each other gifts of friendship, I wish good friendship to exist between you and me. I have expressed a wish to your father. We certainly shall make it come true between us. Do not refuse, my brother, what I wished to receive from your father. It concerns two statues of gold, one standing, the other sitting, two silver statues of women, a chunk of lapis lazuli, and some other things. They are not gifts in the true sense of the word but rather, as in most similar cases, objects of a commercial transaction. If my brother should decide to send these, may my brother send them? If my brother should decide not to send them, as soon as my chariots are ready to carry the cloth, I shall send it to my brother. Whatever you, my brother, may want, write to me, and I shall send it to my brother.[2]

While most of the letters were gathered into one collection, some were circulating in the black market of Egyptian art. One, code-name EA (for El Amarna) 31, came to Berlin Museum in 1888 through a collector. When the three-thousand-year-old clay tablet EA31 arrived at the Museum, the curators knew exactly what to do. They called at the University and asked to speak to a man named Hugo Winckler (1863–1913), who was just twenty-four years old and fresh off his doctorate in philology; a serious, impatient young scholar who had a unique talent: he could read Akkadian like we read a newspaper.

Winckler looked at the tablet and came back to the Museum curators with a simple but perplexing conclusion: the letter was written in cuneiform, but the language was not Akkadian. It was a never-seen-before

---

* There were actually four letters addressed by the Hittites to the Pharaoh, however two of them were so fragmentary and so poorly preserved, that they were misinterpreted for years and only correctly identified in recent times.

4. Writing Letters 47

language. Interspersed in the text, he could recognize some Akkadian and Sumerian signs (more correctly described as "logograms"). It was not strange that an Akkadian expert like Winckler would also be knowledgeable of Sumerian. The two languages are completely different: Akkadian is a Semitic language while Sumerian is a so-called language isolate, i.e., unrelated to any other known language (the linguist who proved this was Frenchman François Lenormant—the same who helped Sayce by providing him with a copy of the Tarkondemos' seal), however, when the Akkadian language started to be committed to writing, scribes adapted the Sumerian cuneiform to their language and, in doing so, they retained several Sumerian logograms, which linguists call "Sumerograms."

That Sumerograms would appear in an Akkadian text was not surprising for Winckler. But that both Sumerian logograms and Akkadian logograms would appear in a text written in a new, unknown language as in EA31 was a new and revolutionary finding. At the same time, news came from Cairo that another Amarna letter, code name EA32, was also written in the same unknown language interspersed with Sumerograms and Akkadograms. Winckler received a copy of it and confirmed.

Winckler had in front of him a linguistic puzzle to decipher. He did not have the luxury of a bilingual text, which had helped Champollion and Rawlinson in their endeavors. Still, he had another advantage: diplomatic letters of the Late Bronze Age were largely formulaic and tended to follow a fixed structure. The stereotypical formula at the opening of a diplomatic letter usually followed this pattern: "Thus says so-and-so, ruler of such-and-such place: say* to so-and-so, ruler of such-and-such place."

The words for "king" and "land" were Sumerograms, so there were no difficulties there, and the names could be simply read as they were spelled out using the Akkadian cuneiform syllabary. So Winckler was able to translate the opening of the letter as: "Thus says Nimuwareya, great king, king of Egypt (speaks) as follows: say to Tarhundaradu, king of the land of Arzawa...."[3]

"Nimuwareya" he recognized as the cuneiform spelling of the name of pharaoh Amenhotep III (who ruled from 1386 to 1349 BCE). Nimuwareya is not the rendering of his given name Amenhotep, but rather of his regnal name Nebmaatra (or "Ra is the Lord of Order"). Non-Egyptians were confused by the fact that Pharaohs had multiple names; in foreign sources, some Pharaohs ended up being called by their given name, others by their regnal name. EA31 was a letter written by the Pharaoh to the king of Arzawa. The other letter turned out later to be the reply from the king of Arzawa.[4]

---

* "Say" is aimed at the clay tablet. It was meant as if the tablet could read out the words written on itself.

No one had any idea of where the Kingdom of Arzawa was.

Historians could not place the name anywhere in the Ancient Near East, and neither Egyptologists nor Assyriologists had ever encountered it. But Winckler had his theory. He remembered that names starting with *Tar* were typical of a region in southern Anatolia, sometimes referred to as the "Lower Lands" of Anatolia, roughly corresponding to the area later called "Cilicia" by the Romans, so he proposed that Arzawa would be located there. This theory made perfect sense: if Arzawa had been in Mesopotamia or Syria, the scribes would have probably written in Akkadian. Also, if Arzawa was in distant Anatolia, it would explain why there was no mention of it in the literature of other Mesopotamian kingdoms.

Winckler translated most of the brief letter, leaving some blanks for the words he could not derive from Sumerograms or Akkadograms and making educated guesses about the structure of the language. But the real surprise came from the famous line twenty-seven of the tablet. In this line, there was the unmistakable Sumerogram for "land," followed by the name "Hattusa." "Land of Hattusa": the country of the Hittites. Winckler could not translate the context, but he could conclude that the letter in the unknown language undoubtedly referred to the Hittites.

On December 13, 1888, Winckler communicated his revolutionary findings to the German Royal Academy.[5] In his historical lecture that night, he proposed that the one he held in his hands was the first ever found letter in the Hittite language. This was perfectly logical, even from the point of view of diplomacy. The scribes of the Pharaoh, who used Akkadian to correspond to all their neighbors, would not make an exception and write in a different language for the benefit of a small and insignificant kingdom in Anatolia. Much more likely, they would have used the language of the mighty Hittite Empire to address a king who lived within the geographic area of influence of the Hittites.

When he learned about the findings of Winckler in EA31, Archibald Sayce was beside himself in excitement. He was just returning from Cairo, where he obtained as many accurate copies of the Amarna Letters as he could, including a copy of EA32. EA31 was missing from his collection, so he asked Winckler for a copy, which Winckler sent without hesitation. A few months later, Sayce published his conclusions on EA31, the "Arzawa letter" studied by Winckler. Sayce largely agreed with Winckler's translation.[6] On June 4, 1889, at the Society of Biblical Archaeology of London, he held a lecture in which he supported Winckler's theory: the language of the Arzawa letters was Hittite.

But this statement clashed with his previous research. Wasn't the Hittite language written in hieroglyphs? The undeciphered hieroglyphs of the Karabel relief, of İvriz, mount Silypos, Yazilikaya, of the Karkemish stele discovered by Smith, or of the lion statue found by Humann, weren't they Hittite?

Sayce reasoned that the hieroglyphs must have represented the earliest form of writing of the Hittite language, while the cuneiform, borrowed from Assyrians, was a later writing system for the same language. This was, after all, the same process the Egyptian language went through, transitioning from a mostly logographic (hieroglyphic) to a mostly alphabetic script (demotic).

These were groundbreaking theories. Until a few years earlier, no scholar imagined that such a thing as a Hittite language had even existed. Now the first text in Hittite had emerged, and the challenge was on: who would be able to translate it? The race to understand the Hittite language, however, was not a crowded one.

In September 1892, the ninth International Congress of Orientalists was held in London. In keeping with the mindset of the day, which put exceeding stress on racial labels, the congress was divided into two main sessions: research on Indian–Aryan populations and Semitic populations. Within the Semitic session, for the first time, a special Assyrian–Babylonian subsection was detached, and Sayce chaired the session. In his opening speech, he claimed for Assyriology the dignity it deserved within oriental studies: "To be a student of the Assyrian inscriptions was for many years regarded in several quarters as equivalent to being a charlatan. The small band of workers has now become a goodly multitude, and Assyriology, especially in America, is one of the fashionable studies of the day. Chairs have been founded for the promotion of it in France and Germany, in Italy and America, and finally in our own country in the ancient University of Oxford."[7]

Assyriology was gaining ground, but Hittitology was still considered the "ugly duckling." The scarcity of information about the Hittites was still felt as a major disappointment. With such a limited knowledge of their history, it was hard to elicit interest in the Hittites. In 1898 in his novel *Fiancée d'Avril*, author Guy Chantepleure (pseudonym of Jeanne-Caroline Violet [1870–1951], wife of the French consul in Athens) describes a Hittitologist named Michel Tremor as a sort of dreamy, bohemian student of abstract matters with no construct. "The Hittites. That's it. Well, are you working on your history of the Hittites, now that, to obtain the material, you have made a journey to Egypt, one to Greece, and two to Syria?"—she wrote—and her character's reply is emblematic: "Oh!—cried Michel—my history of the Hittites wouldn't flood me with bank notes."[8]

With just about a dozen Hittite hieroglyph inscriptions that nobody had been able to translate and with two of the Amarna Letters, which may (or may not) have been in Hittite, research was stagnating. But this was soon to change when a new theory made its way to academia: the hypothesis that Hittite could be an Indo-European language.

To be fair, both Sayce and Winckler had timidly hypothesized that the language of the Arzawa letters, which they believed to be Hittite, had characteristics suggestive of Indo-European languages. However, the first monograph to make this bold claim came at the beginning of the new century from a Norwegian philologist: Jørgen Alexander Knudtzon (1854–1917).

Like many scholars of his time, Knudtzon started as a theologian; however, his interest in the Old Testament brought him to become an expert in Semitic languages. In the early 1800s, this would have meant primarily Hebrew; however, by the second half of the century, knowledge of Akkadian was increasing, and Knudtzon expanded his studies into Assyriology. The Amarna Letters became his main field of study. He was particularly fascinated by the Arzawa letters, which he studied in Winckler's translation. In this translation of EA31, Winckler had taken advantage of the formulaic structure of diplomatic letters of the Ancient Near East: After the salutation, they most often included a report on the prosperous state of the land of the writer, including a list of items which were plentiful, followed by the wish that the recipient's land may enjoy the same richness.

Thus, although missing some words which were in Hittite and which he could not translate, Winckler had worked out that the opening paragraph went something like: "good—houses—wives—children—noblemen—soldiers—horses—lands—good." The following section had the same structure, with the same items written in the same order, but where the words in the opening line had an ending in -*mi*, the words of the following section had an ending in -*ti*. Winckler correctly concluded these suffixes had to indicate the possessive adjective "my" in the opening paragraph and the possessive adjective "your" in the next section, as in "my houses, my wives, my children are good" followed then by "your houses, your wives, your children, may they be good as well."

It was at this point that Knudtzon had an epiphany. In this Anatolian language—which Winckler and Sayce believed to be Hittite but which Knudtzon still referred to as "Arzawan"—the -*mi* and -*ti* endings did not sound at all like Semitic languages but sounded eerily familiar. Where else had he seen these word endings? The answer was shockingly simple: he had seen them in contemporary Indo-European languages, the languages of the continent of Europe, including his mother tongue Norwegian. In Indo-European languages, an *m* sound is characteristic of first-person possessive adjectives (English my, Spanish *mi*, Croatian *moj*, etc.), and a *t* sound is typical of second-person possessive adjectives (English thy, Spanish *tu*, Croatian *tvoj*, etc.). Knudtzon realized that in the Arzawa letters, the possessive adjectives placed at the end* were identical to that of other Indo-European languages, like Persian.†

Moreover, Knudtzon noticed that among the unrecognizable words of the second paragraph was the word *eštu*. He thought this could be a verbal form that expressed a wish, as in "may you be good as well," and he pointed out the similarity between *eštu*, Ancient Greek εστω, and Latin *esto*, which both mean "let it be" or "may it be."[9]

Furthermore, Knudtzon noticed that some words which he presumed to be in the accusative case (that means objects of action, like something which was sent to the Pharaoh) ended in *-an*, an ending which is not unlike the ending of Latin or Greek words in the same accusative case.

Most of Knudtzon's observations built on Winckler's analysis of the text; it goes to Knudtzon's credit, though, to have tied all this research together in a large monograph under the bold title: "The two Arzawa letters, the oldest known in an Indo-European language," which he published in 1902.[10] In his paper, in German, Knudtzon, rather than "Indo-European," used the term "Indo-Germanic." This was customary in German literature. The term "Indo-Germanic" was introduced by the French-Danish scholar Conrad Malte-Brun (1755–1827) in 1810. However, three years later, linguist Thomas Young (1773–1829) proposed the more balanced "Indo-European." Young's version prevailed in European scholarly circles; however, "Indo-Germanic" remained popular in German literature. This title was bold not only because of the novelty of the theory but also because of the racial connotation. At the time, languages were studied in the framework of racial categories.

Ancient populations were divided into races, like Semitic as opposed to Indo-European. It would be another thirty years until Nazi propaganda would turn these distinctions into a basis for genocide. Still, the toxic belief that human beings should be divided into races and that one race should be considered superior to another was already prevalent at the beginning of the twentieth century. Eugenics and scientific racism were considered legitimate in European academia. Therefore, determining to which family the Hittite language belonged was an extremely sensitive matter: before Knudtzon, no one had evidence that an Indo-European

---

* The -mi and -ti endings which helped Knudtzon were actually due to a flaw in composition. The Arzawa letters were written by non-native Hittite speakers. A native Hittite speaker would have more likely used a genitive marker rather than attaching a possessive pronoun.

† Persian too is an Indo-European language, despite being written in the same script as Arabic, which, in contrast, is a Semitic language. For example, "brother" in Persian is "baradar"; "my brother" is *baradar-am* while "your brother" is *baradar-at*, with the possessive adjective after the name, just like in the Arzawa letters.

language was spoken in Anatolia before Alexander the Great's conquest in the fourth century BCE.

If Knudtzon's theory was correct, the two letters would represent the most ancient recorded example of an Indo-European language. They would mean that an Indo-European language was spoken in Anatolia, an area that is geographically external to Europe. The discovery could have a substantial political impact: should Anatolia then be considered part of Europe? And what about the Turkish people who inhabited Anatolia? Should they be now considered Indo-Europeans as well, or rather usurpers of a territory which by right should be European? The questions were not voiced, but they were in the mind of all the scholars who believed in the wicked equation that language equals race and that belonging to a certain race equals having a specific position in the rank of civilizations.

Knudtzon wasn't interested in these aspects. He was a philologist interested in languages, his work on the letters was deep and accurate, and he was oblivious to the racial implications. His work focused on the translation of the letters and their philology, but it also included speculations on where the land of Arzawa would be. Once again, Knudtzon built mainly on Winckler's work and agreed that Cilicia would be a likely location for the Kingdom of Arzawa. The hypothesis would later turn out to be incorrect; as we will see later, Arzawa lay in western Anatolia. Knudtzon even went as far as hypothesizing a cultural connection between the land of Hatti, which he knew from separate sources, and Arzawa. He rightfully concluded that the two lands would have been neighboring and that their languages may be related.

When his 140 page monograph was sent to the press, supported by the commentaries of two other well-known Norwegian Indo-Europeanists (Sophus Bugge [1833–1907] and Alf Torp [1853–1916] of the University of Oslo), Knudtzon was hopeful of receiving international recognition.

Unfortunately, Knudtzon's brilliant intuitions were not well received, probably also because of the existing racial prejudices. Few scholars endorsed his conclusion, including Danish philologist Holger Pedersen (1867–1935).[11] The rest of the Indo-Europeanists of the age were decidedly more diffident. To famous German linguist Paul Horn (1863–1908), Knudtzon's theory was tantamount to heresy. Writing on the pages of the leading journal of Indo-European studies of the age, he wasted no time in demolishing Knudtzon's work and addressed him with the words "Be gone, Satan!" as if he was reacting to a blasphemy, calling his attempt a failure.[12] In the same month, another German linguist, Paul Kretschmer (1866–1956), wrote a scathing review of Knudtzon's book.[13] Yet another German scholar, Leopold Messerschmidt (1870–1911), affirmed that Knutdzon had "failed in his conclusion" and defined his etymological method as "wild,"[14]

4. Writing Letters

followed by American linguist Maurice Bloomfield (1855–1928) who rejected Knudtzon's work entirely, accusing him of sensationalism.[15]

The reviews were so harsh they were demoralizing. Knudtzon became one of the foremost scholars of the Amarna Letters, but his theory on the Indo-European origin of the Arzawa letters was criticized so harshly that even he, writing years later, manifested his doubts about it.[16] The detractors maintained that Knudtzon had based himself on a tiny sample and a few observations, which could have been just the result of coincidences. Messerschmidt objected that the *m* sound of possessives was not exclusive to Indo-European languages, being present even in Turkish. At the same time, Horn and Kretschmer were not convinced by the unicity of *eštu* or the accusative ending in *-an* either.

Whether the objections were purely based on scientific observations or colored with prejudice—the prejudice of seeing an Anatolian civilization among the Indo-European "cast"—will never be known. Still, one thing was evident: more sources were needed. But where to find them?

Once again, Winckler had the answer. With Sayce, he observed that some words of the Arzawa letter were identical to the words on the tablet fragments which Chantre and his Madame had accidentally found at Boğazköy during their expedition in Cappadocia seven years earlier. Winckler and Sayce had no doubts: the answer to the riddle of the Hittites was to be sought in Boğazköy.

Professor Jørgen Knudtzon (1854–1917) of the Royal Frederick University in Christiania, Norway. In 1902, Knudtzon published a monograph which hypothesized that the language of the letters was of Indo-European origin.

5

Hattusa

To dig in Boğazköy, foreigners had to negotiate and obtain a firman from the Ottoman authorities. In previous times, this had been easy because regulations were loose. However, the Ottoman *intelligentsia* had finally realized the importance of governing archaeology in their territory and stopping the bleeding of ancient artifacts only to enrich the most prestigious European museums. A new generation of Ottoman leaders who interested themselves in archaeology emerged. Among them was the towering figure of a refined Turkish intellectual, artist, and scholar: Osman Hamdi Bey (1842–1910).

Hamdi belonged to an affluent family of the Osmanian elite: his father had been Gran Vizir and Ambassador to France, where Hamdi spent his youth and studied. From a young age, he was interested in painting and even exhibited three of his works at the 1867 Universal Exposition in Paris. Later, Hamdi became the father of Turkish archaeology and led the first scientifically planned archaeological campaigns with Turkish-only teams. At thirty-nine, he became the Director of the newly founded Imperial Museum in Constantinople, which he directed until his death. Many of the masterpieces admired at the Museum today have been unearthed under his supervision.

As Director, Hamdi understood that if, on the one hand, he had to limit foreign expeditions on Ottoman territory to stop the smuggling of works of art, on the other hand, he needed to attract foreign expertise and investments to carry out more extensive archaeological campaigns. Therefore, although in 1883 and 1884, he wrote laws limiting the export of archaeological finds, he later lobbied with foreign missions to share the costs of archaeological expeditions under the agreement of dividing the finds. But which foreign nation should be allowed to dig on Turkish soil?

In the last two decades of the 1800s, the Near East was the object of desire of the three European archaeological powers of the age: Germany, Great Britain, and France. Through diplomacy, the three nations had put

5. Hattusa

into being what was, in essence, a subdivision in spheres of interest: south Palestine, Sinai, and Upper Egypt became the prerogative of the British, Lebanon, the stronghold of French archaeologists, and Anatolia was the "archaeological backyard" of Germany,[1] however, all three were very interested in digging at Boğazköy.

During his successful expedition at Boğazköy, Frenchman Ernest Chantre immediately realized the importance of the site. As soon as he came back to France, on May 8, 1884, feeling the pressure of competition from German archaeologists, he wrote to the Minister of Public Instruction: "I will insist, Minister, on the considerable interest which such an exploration must present for the knowledge of the Hittite people. Most of what we know about these people is due to French scholars, and it would be very regrettable today if the study of the most important monuments of this civilization that we have discovered would remain the exclusive prerogative of German research."[2]

Chantre thought the timing was good, as France was steadily attempting to intensify its presence in the Ottoman Empire by developing cultural activities. What France lacked, though, was a permanent archaeological mission on Ottoman territory. Archaeological expeditions in Anatolia had to be organized by the nearest French archaeological mission, the French School of Athens, founded in 1846. In the late 1800s, public funding for archaeological missions in France was scarce.[3] Even Chantre's expedition to Anatolia in 1893 had not received any public funding, private sources entirely funded it, and Chantre himself had to put his hand in his pocket on numerous occasions.

A strong voice invocating the opening of a permanent French archaeological mission at Constantinople was the one of diplomat Paul Cambon (1843–1924), who, during his post as Ambassador at the *Sublime Porte,* had looked with envy at the advancements of German archaeology in Anatolia. But the money just wasn't there, and the Department of Public Education did not want to upset the French School of Athens, which was not keen on sharing its funding with Constantinople, so Cambon's lobbying failed. It wasn't until 1930 that, at long last, the French Government opened a permanent archaeological mission in Constantinople, which by then had changed its name to Istanbul.

If the French failed to set a timely "foot in the door" of Anatolian archaeology, the British couldn't do better. The most invested scholar was obviously the father of Hittitology, Archibald Sayce. Ever since he visited Anatolia, he had dreamed of opening a British archaeology school in Smyrna (modern-day Izmir). In his autobiography, he wrote: "I was very keen that excavations be undertaken in Boghaz Keui, the Hittite capital. The ruins were vast, and the French excavator, Chantre, had discovered fragments of cuneiform tablets there, so much so that I was convinced that an archive had existed on the site."[4] Sayce never succeeded at opening the British school at Smyrna. Like the French, the British had to lean on the permanent mission in Athens (this one not even funded by public money) for any activity in Anatolia. Sayce did obtain that Oxford University would grant a scholarship for Anatolian studies; however, this experience was short-lived and did not eventuate into any full-fledged expedition.

On the other hand, Germans had a head start over France and Great Britain. During the 1880s, the archaeological duo Humann and Puchstein, the same who had discovered the Marʿash Lion, was scouting the rest of Anatolia on several separate and quite successful missions. Their most notable finding was the monumental tomb of King Antiochus, at Nemrut Dağ, in south-east Turkey, which later became a UNESCO world heritage site. The interest of the two German archaeologists converged on Boğazköy because of a singular, fortuitous event.

In August 1894 a German army lieutenant called Schäffer carried out a survey of Cappadocia for military purposes. While walking among the ruins at Boğazköy, his eyes fell on an inscribed clay tablet lying on the ground. This happened just shortly after Chantre had found several tablet fragments, however, Chantre's finds were not yet published and therefore not known in the European archaeology circles. Schäffer published a brief report of his survey, which concludes with a seemingly innocuous sentence, referring to the fragment of the tablet with cuneiform writing: "I hope this finding will lead to further excavations at Boğazköy."[5]

His words were prophetic: Boğazköy would become the epicenter of Hittitology for the coming hundred years. When Puchstein heard of the tablet found at Boğazköy, he immediately realized the importance of the find. The opportunity of unearthing an extensive collection of tablets was too rich to be missed, and he started pulling all strings to obtain a permit to dig there.

In the same year, Hamdi Bey, who was in charge of all archaeological initiatives within the Ottoman Empire, attempted to mediate. He proposed an excavation with the Germans, but under the condition that they would carry out the expedition on behalf of the Imperial Museum at Constantinople. With a Turkish-German joint venture, they would not have needed a firman. However, Hamdi Bey did not guarantee that the Germans could bring any artifact back to Berlin, so Friedrich Sarre (1865–1945), a voluntary assistant at the Berlin Museum who had offered to finance the expedition personally, rejected the proposal.[6]

Meanwhile, the German government listened to Puchstein's ideas and decided to act pragmatically. In pure German style, it launched a full-force campaign for the cultural invasion of Anatolia. To begin with,

5. Hattusa

it established a German consulate in Baghdad. Soon after, in 1896, it funded the *Vorderasiatische Gesellschaft* (the Near Eastern Society, a scientific archeological society), whose presidency was given to Hugo Winckler. One year later, it founded the *Königliche Kommission zur Erforschung der Euphrat- und Tigrisländer*, the Royal Commission for the Study of the Euphrates and Tigris Territories. Another year later, the *Deutsche Orient-Gesellschaft*, the German Orient Society. All these institutions lobbied incessantly with the Ottoman intellectuals to try to obtain digging rights.[7] Germany forcing its way into the European archaeological scene was also coupled with the proliferation of archaeological literature in German: the year 1898 saw the publication of the new *Orientalische Literatur Zeitung*, which specialized in oriental studies, and became hugely popular in the academic circles of all Europe.[8]

But the real battle, the Germans were fighting at a much higher level: their emperor, Kaiser Wilhelm II (1859–1941), an extremely strong-headed and proud ruler, saw the Ottoman Empire within his sphere of interest, a territory to control both commercially and culturally, so he established ties with its ruler, Sultan Abdulhamid II (1842–1918), and generously supported the development and modernization of the Ottoman Empire attempted by the Sultan.

It wasn't just the archaeologists or the Kaiser who were so incensed about digging in Anatolia. All German intellectuals were frustrated because they felt that Germany was well behind in the race to enrich their museums. Germans would travel to Paris or London and admire the Louvre or the British Museum. Still, until the late nineteenth century, no museum in Germany had a notable art collection from the ancient Orient; national pride was at stake.[9]

On March 15, 1898, at the *Reichstag*, member Rudolf Virchow (1821–1902), who had an interest in archaeology,* interpreting the feeling of most German intellectuals, addressed the Minister of Education Julius Robert Bosse (1832–1901) lamenting the risk that British and French could win the race for Oriental archaeology:

> … how can we not be disappointed when the French and the English brought back so many treasures that the Germans had to be satisfied with casts. Much the same is happening in the regions of the Middle East, which have long been very neglected, and where the English and French have been left almost alone to search. The French, in particular, collected extraordinary treasures in Asia Minor, and the English explored Assyria. We received very little, for a long time, we have been content to make large plaster casts, which were solemnly

---

* Aside from being one of the foremost figures in the history of medicine: before becoming a politician, he was regarded as the Father of Pathology.

placed in museums. This is of considerable interest, but it cannot be denied that the originals are more interesting than the plaster casts.[10]

Touched on his pride, the Kaiser, who also was an amateur archaeologist, decided to take the matter into his own hands: in October of the same year, he traveled to the Levant to visit the most important archaeological sites, started showering the German Orient Society with generous donations and, since 1901, endorsed it with his protectorate. His plan was simple: Germans were the officers sent by his administration to Istanbul to help reorganize the state finances, Germans were the engineers sent to plan and supervise the construction of railways across Turkey (in 1899, the Deutsche Bank had obtained the concession to build the Berlin to Baghdad railway, the most ambitious railroad project of the age), and Germans should be the archaeologists digging among Hittite ruins. For his interest in archaeology, Kaiser Wilhelm II is said to have ruled "with a scepter and a spade," but the Kaiser's interest was not purely scientific. His foreign policy resulted from a mix of patriotism, thirst for power, and colonial ambition. No other monarch has linked royal power, state funding, and archaeology to such a great extent.[11]

Despite the strong interest of the German public in the riches of Anatolia and despite the authoritative meddling of the Kaiser on the archaeological scene, Germany could not immediately obtain excavation rights for Boğazköy. The reason was the timing, which could not have been worse: at the end of the 1800s and beginning of the 1900s, Anatolia was going through one of the most brutal periods of its history.

Ottoman Sultan Abdulhamid II, who had been in power since 1876, certainly did not have an easy reign. When he came to the throne, the empire was already fragmenting and suffered social unrest caused by ethnic tensions within its borders and foreign interest in territories at the empire's periphery. One of the main problems was dealing with religious diversity within the empire. The Sultan wanted to impose Islamic law within its entire territory. Christian populations protested this imposition, but the Sultan suffocated their revolts in blood. Among the Christian communities within the empire, the people who went through the fiercest conflict against the Muslim central power were the Armenians.

Armenians had been Christian for sixteen centuries and simply could not accept the Sultan's request to pay tributes to be able to celebrate their cult. This led to unrest, and Abdulhamid chose to react with an iron fist. Acting by the adage "divide and reign," he created a special regiment of Kurdish warriors, the *Hamidiye*, with the task of policing their Armenian neighbors into subordination. The Sultan strategically allowed the regiment to act with impunity and harass the Armenians. Between 1895 and 1896, the empire saw widespread massacres; Ottoman soldiers killed at least 100,000 Armenians, incited the crowds to violence, and forced a large part of the Armenian minority to convert or emigrate. The site of Boğazköy was at the epicenter of this religious-ethnic conflict. As we saw in Chantre's account, the tension with the Armenians had been why his expedition was cut short: the Ottoman government was wary of Christian Europeans meddling with the Armenians to decrease the central power[12] and mistook Chantre for a spy.

At the beginning of the twentieth century, as the Armenian unrest was cooling down, German scientist and orientalist Waldemar Belck (1862–1932) made another attempt at digging at Boğazköy. His was a very short visit of just five days, during which he unearthed a few tablet fragments. On his return to Germany, he proposed to create an archaeological society dedicated to Anatolia. This led to the founding of the *Deutsche Gesellschaft für die Wissenschaftliche Erforschung Anatoliens*, or German Society for the Scientific Exploration of Anatolia, in February 1902, which primary agenda point concerned an expedition to dig at Boğazköy. Belck never succeeded in this intent, probably because the German government understood through diplomatic channels that the moment was very delicate and did not want to ruin the good relationships with the Ottoman Empire by forcing their way into a sensitive area such as Cappadocia.

Within a couple of years, the ethnic tensions in Cappadocia relaxed, and the negotiations to start digging at Boğazköy resumed. Hamdi Bey, who was firmly sitting on his chair as director of the Imperial Museum (a post he would keep until his death, even appointing his brother Halil Edhem Eldem as his deputy) and the main advisor to the Sultan in matters of archaeology, was good friends with Archibald Sayce, so he wanted the excavation rights to go to the British. Hamdi Bey estimated that a bid of 3000 pounds would win the *firman* and wrote letter after letter to Sayce urging him to put together this amount, warning him that he could not hold out much longer because the Germans were "knocking at the door." Sayce was a genius-level academician, but he wasn't cut out for politics; lobbying was not his talent, and he eventually failed at obtaining a sponsorship. On the other hand, the Kaiser lost no time: he immediately promised the money needed to start the work. Under such pressure, Hamdi Bey had to give in despite his friendship with Sayce: the concession finally went to the Germans.

Sayce's disappointment was profound: "I had already raised this subject with Professor Garstang, and we were hoping that the Liverpool Archaeological Institute Committee would provide funds for the excavation ... unfortunately, the Germans were on the same track, and they had managed to interest the emperor in the project. The German Ambassador was all-powerful in Constantinople; the English Ambassador was not concerned with these things."[13] Sayce saw this missed opportunity as a failure of diplomacy. In a private letter to his friend and illustrious archaeologist John Garstang (1876–1956), he put it even more plainly: "I wish we had a man like Layard at Constantinople now."[14]

The Germans were very satisfied. This expedition had the potential of opening a new chapter in the archaeology of the Near East, and it was time to find a leader for the campaign. The choice fell on Hugo Winckler, but not without controversy. Winckler was undoubtedly one of the leading philologists of his time, but he was also a man cursed with a highly unpleasant disposition. He had the ability to make an instant enemy of anyone he met and was known for being particularly ill at ease in foreign cultures. According to the late Professor Horst Klengel (1933–2019) of the Free University of Berlin, "[it was] not least ... the personality of Winckler which cast doubt on his ability to lead such a project." Klengel cites an expert opinion of the Royal Prussian Academy of Sciences, which described Winckler as an unsuitable personality and concluded that his dig in Boğazköy would likely end up having the character of "plunder excavations."[15]

The expert was referring to Winckler's absolute lack of regard for a system in excavations. The truth was that Winckler wasn't interested in the excavation. He wasn't an archaeologist and did not aim to become one: he was a genius linguist and a master of Akkadian but getting his hands dirty was not part of his understanding of his role. All the reports of the time describe him sitting at a table in the shade, far from the digging site, while assistants or workmen fetched him crate after crate of unearthed tablets which he peered at all day. Most archaeologists dedicated their lives to studying ruins of temples, palaces, or city walls; these, for Winckler, were mere physical obstacles between himself and more tablets to study.

German archaeologist Ludwig Curtius (1874–1954) recalls his first meeting with Winckler: "I had looked forward with great eagerness to working with an orientalist whom I could not help imagining as a much-traveled man of the world. I was consequently not a little surprised, upon meeting Winckler in Constantinople, to find an unimpressive-looking fellow with a brown, unkempt beard, wearing a sport shirt with red silk trim and conducting himself in a petty bourgeois manner little suited to the real Orient. There was nothing at all of the man of the world about him."

But for what Winckler lacked in charm, he could make up for in ambition and notoriety within the intellectual circles, so once the

5. Hattusa 61

excavation rights were granted and he was appointed leader of the project, it took him no time to obtain funding for a reconnaissance visit to Boğazköy. He turned to Wilhelm Freiherr von Landau (1848–1908), a German nobleman with the hobby of archaeology, who promptly put his hand in his deep pockets. "Baron von Landau immediately provided the means for a research trip when I presented the matter to him"[16]—he later wrote—and off he went to Cappadocia.

Although the expedition was German, the agreement was that it should be carried out under the patronage of the Imperial Museum at Constantinople, so Winckler wrote to Osman Hamdi Bey and asked to send someone to assist him in his visit. Hamdi Bey had to select a museum representative who could protect the Ottoman interests in Boğazköy. A young archaeologist of the museum stepped forward and wrote him: "Since there is no excavation this year in autumn, I request you to kindly allow me to go to Boğazköy with Winckler."[17]

The name of the young archaeologist was Theodor Makridi Bey* (1872–1940), and he knew Winckler well: they had worked together in Sidon, Lebanon, a year earlier, where Makridi had been one of the few people who managed to get along with Winckler. Makridi was a Greek-Ottoman citizen. His name is only rarely mentioned in the history of archaeology, despite having served in the Istanbul Museum for almost forty years from 1892 to 1930 and having participated in some of the most successful excavation campaigns in the Near East. The curse of his life was to be perpetually second to someone else. From Istanbul to Macedonia, from Lebanon to Syria, his name always comes after now a French, now a British, now a German professor.

The place reserved for Makridi in the history of archaeology is highly disproportionate to his work; it is almost on the level of denying his existence. When Makridi died in 1941, it took three years for the eulogy to appear in an archaeology journal. It was written on the *Revue Acheologique* by French archaeologist Charles Picard (1883–1965), who had worked with him in western Anatolia. Picard's belated eulogy is a metaphor for Makridi's life. In its two and a half pages, the character of this man is depicted rather unceremoniously: honest but self-doubting; zealous but inconspicuous. The Muslim elite of Constantinople loathed him because he was Christian, and the archaeologists of the sites he worked at scorned him because he did not belong to the European Academia.

Year after year, Makridi reluctantly adapted to minor roles: the

---

* This is the spelling of his last name he used in publications, and which will be used throughout this book. However, in personal correspondence in the French language, Makridi would sign as "Macridy."

"hand" rather than the "brain," a "useful tool" more than a colleague: the man mediating with "the natives" and guiding the local workers through never-ending digs under the scorching sun rather than the fellow academician to discuss the findings with. "Makridi's great practical talent and his skill in dealing with people, especially with the simple country dwellers, enabled him to a particularly high degree to take part in excavations and expeditions."[18] It is precisely with these words that Kurt Bittel (1907–1991), later to become the leading excavator of Boğazköy, unceremoniously remembered him in his necrology. Bittel almost implied that Makridi was taken along on archaeological missions for his organizational skills rather than for his knowledge and experience.

Even Makridi's loyalty to the Imperial Museum, to which he dedicated his entire life, was misunderstood: "Macridy-bey"—Picard wrote—"made boundless efforts to collect and save the antiquities to which he fiercely attached the spirit and instinct of his race."[19] With these words, Picard almost depicted him as some kind of xenophobe or nationalist fanatic rather than a conscientious worker. Makridi was deeply misunderstood: he was trying to protect the interests of his beloved Museum from the bad old habit of smuggling artifacts to expand the collections of wealthy Europeans.

Makridi was born the son of a respected doctor and amateur numismatist who liked to call him by the affectionate nickname "Todoraki" and transmitted to him a passion for ancient history. When he was just eighteen, Todoraki started to work as a clerk in charge of French correspondence at the Istanbul Museum. In time, his loyalty and honesty shun through. From this desk job, he went on to participate in archaeological expeditions, especially in Lebanon and Palestine, in the capacity of inspector on behalf of the museum. His was a job of responsibility: he had to ensure the flow of artifacts to the museum and prevent the damaging or smuggling of the finds. He was a man on the frontline, ensuring the hard work would be done, never stepping into the limelight. "I must say that archaeology is a wonderful thing, but it starves me," he once wrote.

Makridi's devotion to Winckler was almost religious. He respected him and admired him. He never stopped addressing him as Professor, even when talking about him to others in his private correspondence, even after many years of friendship. "I work for the glory of Professor Winckler," he added. The good feelings were largely and uncharacteristically returned by Winckler, although it took a good deal of time for this to happen. In the report of his first trip to Boğazköy, which was just a three-day visit in October 1905, the mention of Makridi amounts to a total of one line: "...and so in October 1905, accompanied by Makridi Bey, I reached the ruins."[20]

5. Hattusa

The story of this expedition has almost comedic tones. It was organized in a rush and at an unsuitable time (too late in the year, too close to the rainy season). Winckler and Makridi reached Ankara (then a tiny and poor village) under the impression that they could collect all the needed gear there. They had a hard time finding anything suitable. Winckler complained about everything: he was too hot in the day, too cold at night, and exasperated by the haggling. From Ankara, they left for five days on horseback to reach Boğazköy. Winckler found the horses weak, the saddles hard, the beds of the caravanserais uncomfortable.

At Boğazköy, the conditions were slightly better because the local authority and landowner Zia Bey welcomed the archaeologist duo. Zia Bey was a Cappadocian *nouvelle riche*, his manners a mix of twentieth-century sophistication and countryside crudeness. He genuinely revered his guest academicians and treated them with the highest honors; however, Winckler still found reason to complain about the bugs which infested the silk mattresses on which he was supposed to sleep.

The visit was short: Winckler had to end it after just three days due to the weather. The incessant rain had made the terrain too muddy. But the visit was very successful, too: Winckler returned with thirty clay tablets inscribed in Hittite cuneiform, which amounted to more Hittite than the world had ever seen before. From that moment, two things were clear to all European scholars: that Boğazköy was a gold mine of Hittite findings and that the Germans would lead the development of Hittitology.

Within twelve months, in 1906, with great enthusiasm, Winckler started a larger-scale excavation. This time the funding was a mix of private and public, from the Georg and Frida Hahn Foundation, the *Vorderasiatische Gesellschaft,* and the *Orient-Comité*. It lasted less than four weeks, from July 21 to August 18. Boğazköy is no small archaeological site, and approaching it must have been intimidating. At its peak in Late Bronze Age, the place was home to almost 50,000 people, a considerable number for the era. Nearly eight kilometers of monumental defensive wall surrounded the entire territory of the city. The wall was composed of two layers, each three meters thick, separated by a two-meter passageway.

Besides the main wall, a smaller internal wall divided the upper city from the lower city. The upper city was built with great ambition. It contained a majestic royal palace and as many as thirty temples. The wall which surrounded the upper city, where the precinct of the royal palace lay, comprised almost a hundred watchtowers and five gates, of which three were monumental: in the south-west, the imposing Lions Gate, which takes its name from the two stone lions which guard it. This was probably the primary access to the city and the formal entrance for official visitors. In the southeast, the so-called King Gate, adorned by the statue of a deity, was likely used as the main exit from the city. Finally, to the south, the Sphinx Gate, with two massive stone sphinxes on each side, and likely used for religious processions.

From the moment Winckler set foot at Boğazköy, the goal of his first full-fledged archaeological expedition was clear: finding the largest cache of clay tablets and bringing home as many as possible. Thus, Winckler decided to dig where the only previous expedition, Chantre's, had discovered the tablets over ten years earlier, namely on the hillside of the royal citadel, known in Turkish as Buyukkale (Great Fortress).

Clay tablets are the primary archaeological remain of both Mesopotamian and Anatolian ancient history. At the time of the Sumerians, scribes realized that cheap and readily available clay was a practical support to write on by incising with reed sticks. The reed pen they used to impress signs on the clay influenced the appearance of their writing system. By pressing the edge of a reed stick, the sign which results on a soft surface is wedge-shaped. The word for "wedge" in Latin is *cuneus*, from which we get "cuneiform," and the cuneiform writing system became the standard of writing on clay.

If the text was definitive, the clay tablet could be baked to enhance its durability. Unfortunately, not all tablets underwent this treatment (essentially to allow for recycling), meaning that most tablets' destiny was to be destroyed by the passage of time. Archaeologists today are convinced that only a tiny fraction of the tablets ever written have withstood the test of time. Of those tablets which survived, only a tiny fraction have been unearthed. Danish Assyriologist Aage Westenholz of Copenhagen University hypothesizes that just about one tablet of every twenty thousand ever written may have reached us.

Besides clay, we know of cuneiform writing on other supports such as stone, metal, wood, and waxed tablets. Wood, especially, was quite popular among the Hittites, to the point that the Hittites had a name for the category of scribes who specialized in writing on wood rather than clay. There is even archaeological evidence of tools that seem to have been specifically used for writing on wood rather than clay, and at least one artistic representation of a scribe who appears to be holding a wooden writing support rather than a clay tablet. Records show that, at the apogee of Hittite power, 52 scribes were working at the Great Temple of the capital city; however, 33 were wood scribes, not clay scribes.

This proportion suggests that as much as 60 percent of the Hittite written record may have been recorded on wood. Unfortunately, wood is not a durable material and is unlikely to last millennia, so today, we have very little evidence of Hittite writing on wood. Metals are durable, and we have examples of Hittite texts written on metal that have been preserved to our day. Unfortunately, metal is a costly medium; therefore, very few documents—and only the most important, usually royal pronouncements—would be impressed on metal.

Winckler's team was small: the party of scholars found accommodation in the guest house of Zia Bey. They had arrived with their personal cook, a Bulgarian hired only because he spoke a little German, but this didn't stop Winckler from complaining about the food throughout their stay.

This time, Winckler was starting to warm up to Makridi. In his report, he described their companionship in almost poetic words: "So in the evening, we sat in the howling wind in front of our tent to eat our meal while our coats billowed out. By then, one was usually cool enough to crawl into the tent without too much formality, which was just enough space for two men who were undeterred at their work, and between them never an irritated word in this close togetherness or only an impatient thought arose, despite the fact that both of them suffered physically badly during this time."[21]

In less than four weeks, Makridi and his men unearthed an impressive volume of Hittite tablets for the joy of Winckler, who followed the works comfortably sitting in his room in the guest house. The Hittite language was not deciphered yet; luckily for Winckler, being this the royal archive, a good proportion of the tablets brought to him were written in Akkadian, the diplomatic *lingua franca* of the age. So Winckler, the first man to set eyes on this correspondence in over three thousand years, was able to quickly reconstruct chunks of Hittite history.

His main observation was that the territory where he had found the tablets was referred to as the "Land of Hatti" and the city in which he found them was referred to as Hattusa. The etymology of the name Hattusa implied that the city was considered the center of the Land of Hatti. This was proof that the archaeological site they were excavating at Boğazköy was the capital city of the Hittite Empire.

Luck and serendipity have always influenced the history of archaeology, and the dig of Hattusa was no exception. Winckler had only been digging for a few days and uncovered a modest number of tablets when he found the single most significant one in Hittite history. Under just a shallow layer of dirt, nicely preserved and readable from top to bottom, was a set of three tablets that at once confirmed the glorious history of the Hittite Empire and taught historians about international relationships in the Late Bronze Age. In Winckler's own words, the finding was:

> ... a marvellously preserved tablet which immediately promised to be significant. One glance at it and all the achievements of my life faded into

insignificance. Here it was—something I might have jokingly called a gift from the fairies. Here it was:

Ramses writing to Hattusili about their joint treaty ... confirmation that the famous treaty which we knew from the version carved on the temple walls at Karnak might also be illuminated by its counterpart. Ramses is identified by his royal titles and pedigree exactly as in the Karnak text of the treaty; Hattusili is described in the same way—the content is identical, word for word with parts of the Egyptian version [and] written in beautiful cuneiform and excellent Babylonian.... As with the history of the people of Hatti, the name of this place was completely forgotten. But the people of Hatti evidently played an important role in the evolution of the ancient western world, and though the name of this city and the name of the people were totally lost for so long, their rediscovery now opens up possibilities we cannot yet begin to think of.[22]

This finding could elicit excitement even in the coldest of archaeologists: it was the Hittite version of the peace treaty which Champollion translated at Karnak in Egypt, the first evidence of the existence of the Hittites found in Egyptian sources. It made a sensation worldwide: the oldest peace treaty in history, the first example of an ancient document in two copies, one for each signatory nation. A hundred years after its discovery, the treaty does not cease to fascinate the public. The tablets can be admired in two of the most prestigious museums in the world (two tablets in Istanbul Museum, one in Berlin Museum). A copy of the treaty is seen every day by thousands of visitors to the United Nations Headquarters in New York, donated by the government of Turkey as a symbol of friendship between nations. Winckler could not know it, but what he found was a copy. References from other sources suggest that the original Hittite version of the treaty was not written on clay tablets but silver plaques. The silver plaques have never been found; Still, the treaty is sometimes referred to as the Silver Treaty.

The 1906 campaign was a turning point in Hittitology and a happy moment in the career of Winckler and Makridi. The German professor was starting to warm up to his loyal assistant. "His cautious zeal and his unique ability to lead the people contributed most to the success of these initiatives"—he wrote in his report (once again stressing his operation capacity rather than his academic merits)—"I am deeply indebted to him, his kindness, and his friendly loyalty"[23] he added.

Winckler returned to Berlin acclaimed as a star. Makridi returned to Constantinople with less fanfare but was still praised for his work. Winckler translated all the Akkadian text he could find among the Hattusa tablets and wasted no time planning a second, more extensive campaign. This campaign took place a year later, in 1907, under the direction of the German Oriental Society, but once again backed by private money through the generous donations of a German philanthropist and art collector, Henri James Simon (1851–1923)—one of the founders of the Society. Simon was a successful entrepreneur and an extremely wealthy man who belonged to the closest circle of friends of the Kaiser. He was passionate about antiquities and had previously financed the German expedition to dig at Tell el Amarna, in Egypt. Later, Simon donated most of the antique artifacts of his collection to the Berlin Museum, where they can still be admired. It is ironic and maybe also a sign of the times that a staunch anti–Semite like Winckler would be financed by Simon, who was a Jew.

By now, the German Oriental Society had realized that Winckler's methods would make them rich in tablets but would not significantly advance any other archaeological discovery at Hattusa. Thus, a decision was taken to flank Winckler and Makridi with several archaeologists in a joint venture which marked the collaboration between the German Orient Society and the German Archaeological Institute. The intention was good, but the result was a catastrophe. A mix of personalities that were almost theatrically different, each following their agenda and nearly turning the expedition into a full-fledged riot.

The first to arrive at the site was Makridi in mid-spring 1907. From the moment he set foot in Hattusa, he constantly communicated with his superiors at the Imperial Museum to keep them updated about the campaign. In his letter dated May 27, a joyful Makridi is enthusiastic about being alone at the site. He never had the opportunity of working independently before: he describes how hard he works, but how free he feels, how proud he is of finding many tablets in the big trench he dug south of the palace where he had already wanted to dig the year before (but the professor had not allowed him). In preparation for the arrival of the rest of the team, Makridi even supervises the construction of a larger guest house for the accommodation of the Germans.

It must have been a happy time for Makridi, but his dream ended very soon. When Winckler arrived at Hattusa shortly after and took command of the operations, he re-established the old hierarchy. In June, two more classical archaeologists joined the party. They were Ludwig Curtius, the one who described Winckler as "unimpressive" in his memoirs, and the only slightly less prejudiced Daniel Krencker (1874–1941). It was agreed from the beginning that the two would concentrate on a different area of the site and with different aims, studying the building and artifacts rather than searching for tablets. However, despite this understanding, the frictions began.

Makridi knew Krencker since a German campaign in Baalbek, Lebanon, three years prior, where the two had been in constant disagreement.

The newly arrived German duo expressed the unilateral aim to stay in Hattusa for five to six months. This was longer than Makridi's mission on the site, and he immediately replied that this was unacceptable. Makridi came from an entire career of supervising foreign excavations in the Near East, and his *modus operandi* was simple: arrive before the foreigners and leave after them. His understanding was that whoever was on the site by himself was the director, and he simply could not allow the Germans to act independently. "When a German is involved, it immediately turns into an invasion"—he wrote in a summary tone on June 23—adding: "Since last year's excavation was a brilliant and decisive success, they are attacking us like birds of prey."

In July, starting to feel like a very hot summer, two more German archaeologists arrived at the site: Puchstein, who had recruited the team, and Heinrich Kohl (1877–1914). Puchstein was immediately enthusiastic about the place. On July 21, in a letter to his friend, German archaeologist Alexander Conze (1831–1914), he wrote: "What is amazing about the site, beyond all expectations, are the fortifications, the various colossal escarpments topped with walls, the Cyclopean posterns, the gates, the towers, and other things still unknown" and "The buildings were large and monumental, and they teach us to know, so to speak, a new style in oriental architecture" and concluding pointing out—if ever needed—with a touch of polemic, the difference between the archaeologists, interested in monuments, and the historians interested in documents: "...and that's for the archaeologist almost as surprising as the discovery of documents in cuneiform is for historians."[24]

Puchstein was a mild-mannered man, and his reports contain one of the few kind words tributed to Makridi: "The study of the ruins unearthed by Makridi on the hill known as Büyükkale is very useful for understanding the general features of the Hittite architecture." As for Makridi, he respected Otto Puchstein more than admired him and helped him as much as he could.

While Makridi also respected Kohl, whom he defined as "a sane boy" (though only five years his junior), he loathed Krencker. Writing to his superiors, he described him as "an altar boy with the rude manners of a soldier" or "inexperienced but stubborn." He declared to his face that if he had known that Puchstein had chosen him, he would not have joined the expedition.

Curtius, meanwhile, showed almost unchecked contempt towards Winckler. He described him sitting all day at his desk, far from the excavation site, waiting for his trusted laché Makridi, whom he dubbed *Iago*,[25] and his Kurdish assistants to dig tablets like they were "peasants harvesting potatoes."[26] Of Makridi, whom he loathed, Curtius wrote that he was "the most curious mixture of half-taught dilettante and passionate enthusiast."

Makridi reciprocated the feelings. In another letter, he wrote "There is a pottery specialist, Curtius; he is trouble. He eats like four, drinks like six, learns Turkish, goes into the water, picks flowers, reads poetry, sends mail. He writes 27 or 30 letters. Parasite. The scumbag of the team! Nasty sycophant." While taking more than his portion of food and water can be an understandable reason for being called a parasite, and while the animosity between the two was evident, it is not quite clear why Makridi was so incensed about Curtius learning Turkish or "going into the water." Probably, the reasons for this hatred were more deep-rooted and may have had to do with Curtius' attitude towards the locals.

In a different letter, Makridi wrote to his superiors: "you know our people well enough, they do everything, but they are also hostile to foreigners who want to undertake non-archaeological excavations" suggesting that Curtius may have acted in ways that could provoke the local people, following his agenda. "I cannot understand how Puchstein could trust those men who lack the slightest decency"—Makridi added–"From where did he gather all this zoo?"

The archaeologists were trying to stay away from each other as much as possible; however, this was not always possible. One morning Curtius noticed Winckler's main foreman, a young Kurdish man named Hassan, leaving Winckler's room armed with a basket and pickaxe and reaching the ruins of Hattusa's main temple, where dozens of clay tablets could be seen protruding from the dirt in neat rows. Hassan would attack them casually, breaking them, or collecting them without any order whatsoever in his basket, until it was full, then would return to Winckler and Makridi, emptying the content of the basket on their table. Curtius was shocked by this carelessness and offered Makridi to supervise their Kurdish assistant under the pretense of collecting ceramic artifacts, hoping to make him collect the specimens in a more orderly fashion. Makridi did not even listen to him; he dismissed the German and reminded him he had no business in that room of the temple.

Needless to say, the climate was heated. The never-ending conflicts impacted the quality of the excavations, which quickly degenerated. The local staff couldn't wait to go home and hardly tolerated the squabbles between the scholars. No one was really at ease. Even a very generous dinner thrown by Zia Bey in honor of the scientists turned into a nightmare, at least according to Curtius' account. In keeping with Turkish hospitality customs, Zia Bey served gargantuan amounts of food on three-meter-long trays, including a whole sheep roasted on the spit. Local religious authorities and clan members were invited, and the cook was ostensibly tasting all dishes before the guests to demonstrate that they were not poisoned. The Europeans had difficulties coping with the Turkish tastes, the cooking in fat, the spices used, and the local etiquette. They recoiled in horror when the food was served to them by the hands of their host, especially when whole chunks of sheep fat were ripped from the tail of the roasted animal and put straight on their plates as a sign of reverence.

In such miserable circumstances, there was not much left to do but make the best of the short remaining time, wrap up the expedition, which Makridi defined as "an invasion, rather than a cooperation" and start planning for a team with better chemistry to continue in the next campaign, which was supposed to start a few months later in 1908.

But that expedition never took place. In 1908, a crisis hit Turkey. In 1878, just two years into his reign, the Sultan suspended the parliament and centralized the political power in the hands of himself and a small circle of associates. He introduced internal espionage and censorship. Thirty years into this rule, the protest was ripe. In July 1908, a coup took place. The perpetrators were disgruntled fringes of the army; however, behind the coup was the group called Young Turks, a movement of liberals and unionists. The coup led the Sultan to release all power, and after a desperate and fruitless attempt to countercoup, he ended up in forced confinement, initially in Greece, then near Constantinople. The Sultan would end his days ten years later, still in custody. As with every situation of political instability, the coup disrupted the archaeological activities within Ottoman territory and the German plans to excavate Hattusa. German archaeologists had to wait until 1911 to return to Anatolia.

Meanwhile, Winckler had fallen ill, and the publications of his results slowed down. The last campaign was organized in 1912. Winckler was so severely ill he had to be constantly attended by a nurse, whom he gave out to be his wife so as not to upset the austere morality of the Ottoman government; at the same time, Makridi too fell ill. It was a short and unlucky campaign with little outcome. However, between 1905 and 1912, Winckler supervised the translation of all the Hattusa tablets written in Akkadian. Based on these texts, he could outlay an overview of the Hittite history, complete with the first list of kings.

Not long after his last expedition of 1912, Winckler started to receive stark criticism about his work. His linguistic abilities were not in discussion, but his archaeological method was. It is true that Winckler single-handedly unearthed 30 percent of all the Hittite corpus found to date; however, there are serious doubts regarding the excavations, which have been defined as of "dreadful quality" even by the standards of the day.[27] The main problem was that Winckler and Makridi did not keep any record of where precisely the tablet fragments were found. With some tablets

5. Hattusa

broken into dozens of fragments, it was not enough to note that they were found in a room of the temple: where exactly in the room they were found was as noteworthy. Curtius' eyewitness report of the young Kurd Hassan excavation technique is unforgiving. What is more concerning is that in his report to Puchstein, Winckler wrote that the tablets were highly fragmented and in disarray because they had been used as rubble to fill the walls. This version highly contrasts Curtius' memories and greatly shadows Winckler's reliability.

Attempts to put together the immense jigsaw puzzle of 28,000 tablet fragments go on to this day, and researchers are still cursing Winckler and Makridi for not keeping adequate records. Makridi even promised a belated but detailed publication of the results of his and Winckler's work. He claimed the manuscript was fully completed

Professor Hugo Winckler (1863–1913) of Berlin University in Germany. Winckler led the first large-scale excavation of the Boğazköy archaeological site, later identifying it as the Hittite capital Hattusa. Unknown author, Public domain, via Wikimedia Commons

and had notes, drawings, and plans from their earliest excavations. Sadly, in 1935, only a few years before he died, he confessed to German archaeologist Kurt Bittel that he had nothing of the sort.[28]

While succumbing to his illness, Winckler wrote a passionate, autobiographic report of his years at Hattusa under the title *Nach Boghasköi* (*To Boğazköy*). He did not manage to finish the book before his death; however, it was published posthumously and became very popular.

With Winckler's death in 1913, another chapter of Hittitology ended. It was the chapter of the first excavations of Hattusa, the glorious capital of the Hittite Empire. It was a time when the important, never obtained

The Lions' gate, the main of the three monumental entrances to the Hittite capital of Hattusa. Bernard Gagnon, CC BY-SA 3.0, via Wikimedia Commons

information on Hittite history started to surface. Suddenly this previously unknown civilization was taking shape. The names of the Hittite kings were no longer a mystery; bits of Hittite history were being reconstructed. The time was ripe for bringing the research to a new level: more excavations at Hattusa were needed, and the language of the Hittite tablets had to be deciphered. However, the appointment with the decipherment had to be postponed because Europe and the entire world were about to enter one of their most tragic times: the First World War.

6

Eat Bread, Drink Wine

It was mid-1914 when the Great War broke out after Archduke Franz Ferdinand, heir to the Austro-Hungarian throne, was assassinated in Sarajevo, Bosnia-Herzegovina. The incident was bloody and despicable, but no one expected it would carry the entire world into a spiral of violence that cost over twenty million deaths. When two blocks of European superpowers—on one side, the *Triple Entente* of France, Russia, and Britain, and the other side, the *Triple Alliance* of Germany, Austria-Hungary, and Italy—started the hostility, it was just the beginning. Soon, many more countries joined the war, some even changing sides mid-conflict. When the Ottoman Empire joined the war in alliance with Germany, Austria, Hungary, and Bulgaria, it had to fend off attacks from all sides.

Excavation sites turned into bloody battlefields. From archaeology to war. The spade was abandoned to embrace the rifle. No one better embodied this transition than British Officer Thomas Edward Lawrence (1888–1935). Until 1911, he, an Oxford-trained archaeologist, was digging at Karkemish for a British Museum expedition, but in 1916 he became an infiltrated intelligence agent and, under the famous moniker of "Lawrence of Arabia," he was the main orchestrator of a sanguinary revolt of the Arab peoples which severely wounded the Ottoman Empire. By the end of the Great War in 1918, the Ottoman Empire was utterly defeated and forced into an armistice. Two years later, some of the winning powers (France, the United Kingdom, Greece, and Italy) sat down to carve it up and divide its territories in the so-called Treaty of Sèvres.

The Great War completely disrupted archaeological research in the Near East. Sadly, this was bound to become a recurring theme for the coming hundred years, down to the present. Whether it is the destruction of the Temple of Baalshamin, at Palmyra, in Syria, in May 2015,[1] the blowing-up of the Buddhas of Bamiyan in Afghanistan in 2001, or the looting of the Baghdad Museum in 2003, the conclusion is always the same: war is not good for anything, archaeology included. But while Europe was plunging into the abyss of the Great War, thanks to an exceptionally talented and dedicated scholar, efforts to decipher the Hittite language did not come to a complete stop.

Bedřich Hrozný (1879–1952) was born the son of a reformed evangelical pastor in Lysá nad Labem, in Czechia, and, wanting to follow his father's steps, moved to Vienna to study evangelical theology. In Vienna, he saw a copy of the Old Testament in Hebrew and fell immediately under the spell of a fascination for ancient languages. This fascination lasted throughout his life and made him one of the central figures of twentieth-century linguistics. He mastered Hebrew, then moved on to Arabic, Egyptian, Ethiopic, Sanskrit, and Aramaic. He relocated to Berlin to study Akkadian under Winckler and to London to learn Sumerian. His talent for translating ancient languages made him famous, and he was invited to participate in a prestigious archaeological expedition in Megiddo, Syria. When he finally settled down in Vienna, he became an associate professor at the university, but, in his typical humbleness, he worked as a librarian as well.

While Hrozný, thanks to his talent for translation, was making a name for himself in the archaeology circles, the German Oriental Society was eager to attempt to decipher the Hittite language in the tablets unearthed by Winckler at Hattusa. However, with the Ottoman Government refusing to send the tablets to Europe, it became necessary to send someone to Constantinople, someone skilled enough to make high-quality copies of the tablets. In 1914, the choice fell on Hrozný. Commissioned by the Society, he traveled to Constantinople, where he spent days and nights at the Museum, obtaining copy after copy of the precious tablets until his work was suddenly interrupted by a telegram he received from Vienna. The Great War had broken out, and Hrozný was called back to Austria to fight.

When the Vienna Home Regiment drafted him in February 1915, Hrozný was crestfallen: he had the copies of the tablets in his hands and could start to decipher them when he had to stop to be enlisted. But luck was on his side, and he was immediately dismissed due to strong short-sightedness. He then started working and made his way through the texts for another half year, when the bad news reached him again: with the advancing of the war, all able men, including the short-sighted ones, were desperately needed, so Hrozný was re-drafted in December, to serve as a scribe for an indefinite time.

Once again, this time even more disheartened, Hrozný put the uniform on and joined the army. But it was there he was met by luck again. This time chance came in the guise of a Viennese lieutenant: A. Kammergruber (fl. 1920). The officer got to know Hrozný and realized that the talent of a man who could translate from half a dozen ancient languages was

6. Eat Bread, Drink Wine 75

probably wasted sitting at a desk writing letters under dictation, so he allowed Hrozný ample time to study the copies he had with him.[2]

We do not know what happened to Lieutenant Kammergruber of Vienna, but this man, generously giving Hrozný time to study, serendipitously earned a special place in the history of archaeology and linguistics because it was during this time that Hrozný came to an illuminating realization, a turning point similar to the one of Champollion when he solved the mystery of the Rosetta stone.

It happened as he was attempting to read the text of a tablet, which later turned out to be a religious text, a collection of rules and instructions for priests and temple officials. In one line of the tablet, Hrozný read: *nu ninda-an eizzaateni waatar-ma ekuutteni* and promptly identified the word *ninda*, a so-called Sumerogram, a Sumerian word borrowed by Hittites. Hrozný knew that *ninda* meant "bread." Since the sentence discussed bread, Hrozný guessed that the word *waatar* would mean "water." His guess was quite a wild one. The thought that the word for water in a 3000-year-old Anatolian language was almost identical to modern English was almost frivolous. But Hrozný, undeterred and open-minded, went on.

He had previously thought that the endings *-an* attached to *ninda* and *-ma* attached to *waatar* could be markers of the accusative case, which means the noun is the object of an action in the sentence. Also, based on other Akkadian words inserted in the Hittite text, which are called Akkadograms, he knew that the ending *-teni* was probably marking the second person plural in verb conjugation, so he identified *eizzaatteni* and *ekuutteni* as verbs.

Then he asked himself: If bread and water are mentioned in a sentence, what could the verbs mean? He noticed that the verb root *eizza-* sounded a lot like the German verb "to eat": *essen*. For the verb root *eku-*, he saw a resemblance with Latin *aqua,* which means "water," and he thought it might mean "to drink" (this turned out later to be incorrect). As for the initial word in the sentence, *nu*, Hrozný knew that almost every written Hittite sentence started with *nu*,* and concluded it may mean "now." So, he translated the whole sentence as "Now you will eat bread, then you will drink water."

His translation was perfectly correct (to be precise, the sentence could be translated in the present tense as well because Hittite does not differentiate between present and future tenses). Thanks to the ingenuity of this

---

* The actual meaning of *nu* is not fully understood. It is clearly a sentence connector, is often translated as "and" or "so" and it is sometimes omitted in translations. The word may derive from the same proto-Indo-European root which lead to Latin *nunc* and Ancient Greek νυν (nun) from which the word "now" comes.

placid Viennese scholar, who himself had been a skeptic of Knudtzon's theories on the Indo-European origin of Hittite, and who freely admitted that Indo-European languages were not his strong side, for the first time, the world could read a sentence in Hittite.[3]

Hrozný was thrilled. He traveled to Berlin where, on November 24, 1915, in front of the members of the Near Eastern Society of Berlin, he delivered a historical lecture on his discovery. His surprising conclusions were initially met with cautious criticism by the scientific community (by then, most philologists assumed that Hittite could be Caucasian or Georgian-related). Still, his lecture was repeated just three weeks later, on December 16, at the University of Vienna at the *Eranos Vindobonensis*, the yearly meeting of a club of Austrian academicians who promoted the exchange of knowledge in the field of classical studies.

The lecture was a success. Before the end of the year, his lecture was published in the "Reports of the German Oriental Society." The paper, called *Die Lösung des hethitischem Problems* or "The solution of the Hittite problem" is a thirty-three-page excursus, a milestone in the history of linguistics.[4] It is a highly sophisticated work, including advanced glottology and comparative grammar, with countless examples from the Hattusa tablets, offering an attempted translation of many passages.

Hrozný's analysis of the undeciphered texts started with observing the opening of the sentences. He was the first to recognize that Hittite sentences began with a series of repetitive, almost formulaic monosyllabic words, today referred to as "clitics." This is a peculiarity of the written Hittite language: nearly every sentence is introduced by particles that carry semantic meanings; for example, they can convey the type of sentence, presenting a discourse or finalizing it, or they could express causality in a sentence, or imply the sentence is a direct quote and so on. Not unlike the conjunctions "then," "thus," and "since" in English, however, organized differently, their uniqueness lies in the fact that they were often lined up one after the other in long strings of particles at the beginning of a sentence. Still today, it is debated whether these particles were confined to the written language or used in the spoken language as well.

At the same time, Hrozný expanded on the work of Winckler and Knudtzon on pronouns, especially possessive pronouns, which, as we have seen in Chapter 4, are usually attached at the end of words. Looking at verb conjugations, Hrozný was the first to point out the similarity between the Hittite participles ending in *-anti* and their Latin and Ancient Greek counterparts *-antes* and *-οντες* (*-ontes*). In noun declension, he correctly identified almost all case endings, such as the *-aš* characteristic of genitive and *-i* of dative (which bears similarity to Latin).

It is a disappointment that, of all this magistral work, only the translation of the sentence about bread and water is widely reported and remembered. On the other hand, it is natural that that particular sentence attracts the public. Being so simple, almost banal, it speaks to the code-cracker in all of us. Hrozný's intuitions make us almost feel like *we* could have worked out the mystery of the Hittite language. Without knowledge of syntax or grammar, just thinking of bread and water in a sentence. Hrozný highlighted how something written in a dead language over three thousand years ago can be so similar to the language we speak today. This seemingly insignificant sentence, so familiar it could be in a lesson in a modern-day book to learn a foreign language, in its simplicity, makes perfect sense to all of us. For thousands of years, the Hittite language had been a mystery. Forgotten, unknown to man. Now, at the hands of a humble Czech academic, this language opened the door to an entire civilization.

The news of Hrozný's discoveries made an impact on public opinion. The first communication of his study happened in late November 1915. By mid–December, all the leading newspapers in Austria and Germany, from *Neues Wiener Journal* to *Frankfurter Zeitung*, were celebrating him,[5] in some cases with words of pure, enthusiastic admiration: "'During the war, art and science rest'… Recently, however, a science that has nothing to do with war, that lives far from the noise of battle in the scholar's study, has celebrated a triumph."[6]

It is possible that the interest that Hrozný's discoveries sparked in journalists of the day was colored by racial pride. Thus the article on *Provinzial-Zeitung*, commenting on Hrozný's research: "In addition to the two powerful kingdoms of the ancient Orient of biblical times, Babylonia and Egypt, there were in the second millennium B.C. a third flourishing empire, that of the Hittites…. Hrozný was able to provide eminent proof that the Hittites mentioned in the Old Testament were Indo-Germanic," implying the contrast between the newly re-discovered Indo-European people against the well-known Semitic populations in the early history of human civilization.

In scholarly circles, the acceptance of the theory of the Indo-European origin of Hittite was slow but ended up being nearly unanimous. Indeed, initially, Hrozný faced the same opposition that Knudtzon faced. Renowned linguists like American Carl Darling Buck (1866–1955) and Germans Otto Schroeder (1887–1928), and Ernst Weidner (1891–1976) were quite dismissive in their reviews of his work. Weidner, in particular, had a different theory altogether. Two years after Hrozný's publication, he still maintained that the Hittite language belonged to the Caucasian language family.

Hrozný, however, was unperturbed. Working incessantly, he

reconstructed a language from nothing. In twenty-four months, he mastered Hittite, and in 1917, he published a comprehensive grammar. The grammar pointed out in its title *Die Sprache der Hethiter, Ihr Bau und Ihre Zugehörigkeit zum Indogermanischen Sprachstamm*[7] that Hittite is an Indo-European ("Indo-Germanic" for the German audience) language, now as a *fait accompli*.

Hrozný even remembered the then-famous Lieutenant Kammergruber, acknowledging him in the preface for his "understanding consideration of the author's work."

Immediately afterward, having become the leading name in Hittitology, he proceeded to a systematic translation of some important religious and historical Hittite texts, which essentially confirmed the correctness of his theoretical conclusions. This work was published in Leipzig in 1919 under the title *Hethitische Keilschrifttexte aus Boghazköi. In Umschrift, mit Übersetzung und Kommentar* or "Hittite Cuneiform Texts from Boghazköi in Transcript with Translation and Commentary" and represented his *opus magnum*, his solution to the Hittite riddle.[8]

In the world of academia, often, the recognition of a new theory comes when a renowned authority puts its "stamp of approval" on it. For Hrozný's Indo-European theory, the stamp came from German comparative language scientist and philologist Ferdinand Sommer (1875–1962). Sommer was intrigued by the discovery of the oldest Indo-European language ever known, developed an interest in it, and started to study Hittite intensively. In 1920, Sommer, who was hugely respected, took a stance and supported the uncomfortable thesis of the Indo-European origin of Hittite.[9] In the eyes of German philologists, all doubts and objections to the "solution" were dispelled.

The reason why Hrozný's theory won the acceptance of scholars initially in Germany, then across Europe, whereas Knudtzon failed, is largely to be found in the increasing body of documents unearthed at Hattusa. In 1902 Knudtzon had access to a grand total of 63 lines of Hittite from the two Arzawa letters, while Hrozný, thanks to Winckler's work, had copies of a large number of tablets.

Unfortunately, the difficulties of understanding the Hittite language did not end with Hrozný's pioneering decipherment. Linguists eager to learn more about Hittite clashed against a problem we still have today: the body of the language, the so-called *corpus*. The corpus of the Hittite language is quite limited. Excavations in the last hundred years have brought a total of approximately 30,000 clay tablets (primarily from Hattusa), while other forms of writings, like inscriptions on rocks or buildings (called epigraphs), are especially scarce. Many of the tablets excavated by archaeologists are fragmented and incomplete, not fully readable, or extremely small—some no larger than a credit card—and containing just a handful of out-of-context words.[10] the entire corpus of the Hittite language available to modern scholars is estimated to amount to about fifty-thousand words. This wouldn't be much more than the corpus produced by *one single* Latin author like Cicero.

Moreover, the corpus of the Hittite language is not very diverse. Of the 833 texts listed by German scholars in the largest existing catalog of extant Hittite texts, a quarter represents festival instructions like rituals. Among the remaining texts, there are prayers, spells, vows, hymns, and everything connected to the Hittite religious cult. Approximately 7 percent belong to the category of historiography, like *res gestae*. A few texts are technical, and only a tiny fraction can be considered literature in the sense of creative writing[11] (none of the poetic type, at least none written in meter). The result is that there are only a few colloquial expressions within the entire extant Hittite production. Thus, even experts of the Hittite language would struggle to translate a conversational sentence into Hittite: we have a very limited understanding of how Hittite people spoke to each other.

Another problem that stems from the limited corpus and the fact that the Hittite language was not spoken past antiquity is that we cannot know what Hittite sounded like or how the words were pronounced. Scholars can make educated guesses but will probably never know with certainty. For example, there is no certainty on what syllable of a word the stress should be. Also, we know that the Hittites had only one sign for the letter *s*, but we are unable to tell if they pronounced it < s > as in "sip" or < ʃ > as in "shoe."

For Hrozný, figuring out the grammar was just the beginning of the journey. The hardest part was figuring out the meaning of each word. Scholars of Akkadian had been able to reconstruct the Akkadian vocabulary because Akkadian was the *lingua franca* of diplomacy, and they found word lists, sort of small vocabularies from other languages—predominantly Egyptian—used by scribes to translate diplomatic correspondence. Word lists Hittite–Akkadian, on the other hand, are extremely scarce.

The Institute for the Study of Ancient Cultures of Chicago has collated all documented Hittite words in a comprehensive dictionary.[12] Still, hundreds of entries within the dictionary are marked with "meaning unknown." For some words, all the philologists can do is guess the meaning based on the context: "a proper name" or "a type of vegetable" or "a magic word," but, unless substantial new findings happen, the meaning of many Hittite words will forever remain unknown to us.

This is partly due to how Hittite came to be committed to writing.

Akkadian, the primary language of Mesopotamia, took its writing system from Sumerian. But while Akkadian was written already by 2500 BCE, according to Professor Van den Hout of the Institute for the Study of Ancient Cultures at Chicago: "writing came relatively late to the Hittites. Anatolians ... must have been familiar with the Old Assyrian cuneiform of the merchants from Assur during the first two centuries of the second millennium BC; however, they never took the step of adopting their writing system for internal purpose."

Indeed, there is evidence that, until well into the 1500s BCE, rather than writing in their language, Hittites would use the Akkadian language for written communication. Once the Hittites expanded militarily outside Anatolia and into Syria around 1650 BCE, they started employing local Syrian scribes for occasional tasks. Over the following century, their writing evolved into what we call Hittite cuneiform by the middle of the sixteenth century BCE.[13] As opposed to Akkadian writing, Hittite writing began to become the custom early in the fifteenth century BCE, and by 1400 BCE Akkadian was no longer used for internal purposes.

Once Hittites adopted it to write their language, cuneiform came with its own "heritage" of Akkadian and Sumerian. A well-established partnership between two languages suddenly became a tumultuous "ménage à trois." So, while Hittites kept speaking their Indo-European language among themselves, the moment they wanted to write down their thoughts, they did it through a writing system that showed a sophisticated interplay of Hittite words, Akkadograms, and Sumerograms.

When a Hittite scribe would write down a letter for their king, they would listen to the king speaking Hittite. Each word pronounced by the king would be written down in the cuneiform characters they had borrowed from the Akkadians. However, to do so, the scribes had to make several changes to adapt the cuneiform signs to Hittite phonology. This is because cuneiform characters do not exactly work as an alphabet. In an alphabet, each letter represents a sound like *b, t,* or *s*. The cuneiform writing system the Hittites adopted is a syllabary rather than an alphabet. This means that, although some single letters occur (like the vowels 𒀀 *a* or 𒄿 *i*), most signs represent groups of two letters, like 𒆷 *la* and 𒈬 *mu*, or groups of three letters like 𒋻 *tar*.

This system was suitable for Akkadian; however, many Hittite words were incompatible with this syllabic breakdown. For example, the Hittite word for "pin" is *špikušta*. In the cuneiform syllabary, there were no signs for a consonant without a vowel; therefore, *špikušta* had to be spelled with some extra letters as 𒊺𒉿𒅅𒆪𒍑𒋫 "*še-pi-ik-ku-uš-ta.*" However, when reading these signs, the reader would still pronounce *špikušta* because that is how the word was used in the spoken language. This is not unlike current English, in which written words are commonly spelled with "silent" letters, which are ignored when reading.

The Hittite scribes developed a habit of finding the most similar-sounding group of cuneiform characters to make whoever was reading understand this adaptation, but unfortunately, they were not always consistent. For example, the name of the neighboring state Mitanni could be spelled differently as 𒈪𒋫𒀭𒉌 *Mi-ta-an-ni* or 𒈪𒀉𒋫𒉌 *Mi-it-ta-ni*, but it would be pronounced in the same way when a Hittite would read it.[14] Alternative spellings, especially for foreign words, are a common occurrence even in current English. The inconsistency between spelling and pronunciation made the philologist's work more complicated.

Another aspect of written Hittite that favored the philologists who first approached the Hattusa tablets is that Hittites used word separation in their texts. This is not a given because most languages of antiquity, including Akkadian, used to some extent the *scriptio continua*, which implies that words are written without spaces between them, as a continuous flow of signs.

Unfortunately, however, further levels of complexity awaited the decipherers. Hittites used plenty of Sumerograms and Akkadograms in their writing. However, when reading their writing, some of the Sumerograms would not be read at all, while for other Sumerograms and Akkadograms, the Hittites would read the corresponding Hittite word. These two concepts require some explanation. Several Sumerograms were used as "determinatives"—ideograms used to mark categories of words. For example, the ideogram 𒁹 was used to indicate that whatever followed was a proper male name, while the ideogram 𒄑 was used to indicate that whatever followed was an object made of wood. These two ideograms carry their phonetic value, which means they could be, in theory, read as *diš* and *iz*, respectively. However, they were not thought to be read. Instead, they were just used in the written text to convey meaning. The concept may sound foreign initially; however, it is not extraneous to our way of writing in modern English. For example, in written English, proprietary brands' names are followed by the symbol "™" in some contexts. This symbol, which is short for "trademark," could be, in theory, read out following the brand's name; however, in practice, it is not. It is put there only to make readers aware that the proper name they just read is a trademark.

On the other hand, some Sumerograms or Akkadograms were read, but they were read with the corresponding Hittite word. Again, this feature may sound bizarre initially but can be found in modern-day writing. The percentage symbol "%," for example, is used in most languages to convey an idea—the idea of a percentage. However, when it is read out loud, it is read in the reader's language. Thus, in an English text, "%" is read as "percent," but a Swedish reader in the context of a text written in Swedish would read it *procent,* and a Spaniard in the context of a text written in Spanish would read it *por cien.*

So, the Hittites would write the word king using the Sumerogram ⌘, which represents the Sumerian sign for LUGAL and literally means "big man" (by convention, Sumerograms are written in capital letters) and uses the stylized shape of the head of a man wearing a crown. However, when reading it, the scribes would recognize the LUGAL Sumerogram and read it with *their own* Hittite word for king, which is *ḫaššuš*. Same thing for Akkadograms.

In some instances, for example, in composite words like "horseman," the scribe would even mix a Sumerogram with an Akkadogram but still read it with the corresponding Hittite word for horseman.

Linguists have speculated a lot on the reason that led the Hittites to write the word king with the Sumerogram LUGAL rather than just spelling out *ḫaššuš,* and no clear conclusion has been reached. Probably, the fact that the writing system was adopted by scribes who were already versed with Akkadian (and therefore made ample use of Sumerograms) brought them to take shortcuts and use signs which were, for them, more recognizable and, thus, less laborious than spelling out the Hittite words. In any case, this shortcutting was so habitual that some words were *always* written with Akkadograms or Sumerograms, to the point that still today, philologists do not know what Hittite is for such common words as goat, son, or woman.

The matter is complicated by the fact that in the Hittite language,

Professor Bedřich Hrozný (1879–1952) of Vienna University, in Austria, the linguist who deciphered the Hittite language in 1915. Volné dílo, public domain, via Wikimedia Commons.

6. Eat Bread, Drink Wine

like Latin and Ancient Greek or, in current times, Russian, the endings of nouns, pronouns, and adjectives change according to the function of the word. They change through something called a "desinence." For example, if the noun is the subject (nominative case) or the object of an action (accusative case). For reasons not fully understood, Hittite scribes sometimes chose to use a Sumerogram or an Akkadogram to express a word in the nominative case, but the Hittite version of the same word for the accusative case. Other times, scribes would use a Sumerogram, but with a Hittite desinence or even an Akkadian *and* a Hittite desinence. This mix of two languages is not uncommon in modern English: consider the word "pizza," loaned from Italian. The plural of "pizza" in Italian is *pizze*, whereas, in English, it is "pizzas." So, essentially, modern English writers do the same thing Hittite scribes did, attaching a desinence from their language to modify a word loaned from another language.

On the other hand, the translator's work was made easier by the many Hittite words similar to the corresponding words in other Indo-European languages. We have seen how Hrozný intuited the similarity of *wataar* to "water." In this same chapter, we looked at the word *špikušta*, which means "pin"; it is easy to notice the similarity of *špikušta* with the Swedish word

Stele commemorating Bedřich Hrozný in front of his home in the town of Lysá an Labem, in the Czech Republic. At the top of the stele, the famous line "Eat bread, drink water" in Hittite cuneiform. Barocco, CC0, via Wikimedia Commons.

for "nail" *spik*, and the English word "spike," all words which design a pointy object. There are many other examples; take, for instance, the word for "new": *newa,* which is almost identical to modern English, or the word for "puppy": *ḫuelpi,* highly reminiscent of the English word "whelp," or the verb "to grind": *malla,* almost identical to Swedish *mala,* or the word for "heart": *karz* very similar to German *Herz,* and the list could go on and on; there are countless similarities between Hittite, spoken over three thousand years ago, and current European languages: a source of true delight for etymologists.

These vocabulary similarities were helpful, and the vast number of Sumerograms and Akkadograms were valuable in interpreting texts because they were known to scholars from the study of Sumerian and Akkadian. On the other hand, the limited corpus, the phonological uncertainties, and the spelling inconsistencies made Hittite a giant riddle for the philologist. Translating the Hattusa tablets required a skilled, dedicated researcher willing to plunge into the unknown of a language just being uncovered after three thousand years of silence. Luckily, that man was there, in the right place and at the right time, ready to take on the job.

7

The Hittites Start to Tell Their Story

The destiny of some people is written at birth. For others, a single moment, a turning point in their lives, shapes their existence. Both things probably happened to the Swiss philologist Emil Forrer (1894–1986). He was born in a Swiss family in Strasbourg—then under German rule—the third son of a man who was a giant in the field of history and archaeology, one of those scholars whose work created an entire school of thought and is still read a hundred years later. The destiny of Emil at birth was to get from his father the passion for the past (as well as the unusual middle name Orgetorix in honor of an obscure Helvetian chief who had aspired to conquer the whole of Gaul at the time of Julius Caesar).

At eighteen, fresh out of high school, young Emil started his studies in history at Strasbourg. When his talent shone through, he was soon recruited for a doctorate in Berlin under the mentorship of renowned German orientalist Eduard Meyer (1855–1930). At Berlin University, Forrer's unusual talent for translating ancient languages made him a bit of a celebrity, but luck was also on his side. His timing couldn't have been better: he was the right man at the right time: the end of his doctorate in 1917 coincided with the arrival to Berlin from Constantinople of the whole collection of tablets excavated at Boğazköy by Winckler. It was a short-term loan, an achievement of the then curator of the Berlin Museum, Otto Weber (1877–1928), who had the difficult task of persuading the vice-director of the Imperial Museum at Constantinople, Halil Edhem Eldem (1861–1938).

Eldem was the younger brother of the legendary museum director Hamdi Bey and had previously been very rigid in loaning out museum collections to European institutions. Perhaps he should have kept his rigid attitude: the tablets were supposed to be returned after publication; in reality, it took almost twenty years to return just a third of them, and the other two-thirds weren't returned until 1989. Anyway, for German scholars, this loan was an opportunity not to be missed if they wanted to get a head start on the rest of Europe in the field of Hittite philology.

Once the tablets arrived in Berlin, it was immediately evident that translating them would be a considerable challenge. It was a mastodontic volume of tablets in cuneiform Hittite, primarily fragments, an immense jigsaw puzzle, a job of maddening difficulty yet of inestimable value for the progress of Hittitology. Weber, the curator, and Meyer, the professor, were looking for someone who could take on the transcription and translation project, and they agreed that there was no better person for this than the young and promising Forrer.

When this job was proposed to him, Forrer was hesitant: he felt that, within the academic circles, a slight prejudice against Hittitology was still clinging, and he would have had to set aside his successful research in Assyriology to plunge into the unknowns of Anatolian languages. However, he decided to accept the challenge, and once he did, he wholeheartedly dedicated himself to it. For almost three years, he worked incessantly on the tablets, becoming the first scholar to have a comprehensive, total knowledge of the Hittite literature available at the time.

The job he embarked on became of colossal proportions. By 1920 he had supervised the publication of the entire corpus in several volumes. Forrer could have made his work much easier if he had just photographed the tablets and published the images, but the cost of such a production, at that time, was considered prohibitive. Instead, he resorted to spending days and nights at his desk, beautifully crafting hand-drawn copies of the over 300 tablets: a monumental endeavor. The result is impressive. Thousands upon thousands of lines of neatly copied cuneiform characters, which are still, a century later, the central resource for Hittite cuneiform studies.[1]

Maybe because the job absorbed him wholly, maybe because of bad luck, in the same year, Forrer failed the test he most desired to pass: the exam to become a professor. This was a nasty blow for young Forrer, but within a few more months, something even more impactful happened in his career, a seemingly insignificant incident, a single exchange that changed his life.

It was the summer of 1921 when Forrer, fresh from his disappointment of failing the exam to become a professor, received a letter from one of the Assyriologists he most respected, Bruno Meissner (1868–1947) of Breslau University. Meissner, who was helping in organizing the "German Orientalist Day," a symposium of oriental studies to be held at Leipzig in late September, proposed that Forrer would participate in a break-out session on Hittitology.

The leader of the symposium was Ferdinand Sommer, the philologist of the University of Jena who, as we saw in the previous chapter, with

7. The Hittites Start to Tell Their Story

his endorsement, had helped Hrozný's theories gain ground in German academia. Sommer was twenty years senior to Forrer and considered authoritative and authoritarian. Forrer was enthusiastic about Meissner's suggestion of participating in the symposium and wrote a respectful letter to Sommer, proposing himself as a speaker for the session. He was accepted and traveled to Leipzig carrying with him his notes.

When he stepped on the podium to discuss Hittitology in front of the crème of German oriental studies, he was happy and excited. His fame as the foremost translator of the Hittite corpus preceded him. In a letter to his father, he would later recall that when the moderator announced that it was his turn to intervene, "a murmur went through the auditorium."[2]

"Not that it would mean anything for me…" he added in the same letter, but his pride in talking about this tiny bout of fame to his beloved father (who had even lent him money to travel to Leipzig) was palpable. But academia can be treacherous to navigate, and sometimes, behind a façade of friendship, bloody turf wars are going on. Forrer could not know it, but Sommer was fighting his own battle. He had recently attained a prestigious position within the German Oriental Society, and his ambition was to make himself a name within Hittitology, which he saw as a promising, emerging niche. After the debate, armed with his agenda, Professor Sommer approached Forrer in the auditorium's foyer in front of several other scholars.

Forrer's immediate impression of Sommer was not that of a pleasant man: "Majestic, imposing and arrogant" he wrote in his memoirs. Sommer informed Forrer that Hittitology would soon be the subject of a break-out session that he would lead at the upcoming national meeting of philologists, which would take place at his University, Jena. Clearly, he wanted to mark his territory, announcing rather than discussing his leading role in the field with Forrer. "He talked to me in the tone of an officer addressing an infantryman," wrote Forrer later, describing the exchange to a friend. But Sommer did not stop there.

Unilaterally imposing his presence on the scene of German Hittitology was evidently not enough for him, so he pointed out what he unceremoniously defined as weaknesses in current Hittitology, such as inconsistencies in text transcription. Forrer was appalled; he felt the criticism was not even veiled and directed at him and Hrozný. Finally, Professor Sommer added with a complacent tone that he would "agree to take over the leadership and try to give Hittitology the foundation it lacked." Forrer was beside himself and did not pull punches. "With all due respect," he asked "do you think you could manage this at all? As far as I know, you are an autodidact in the matter of cuneiform writing and still very fresh in these subjects."

The candid reply did not sink well. "I confess that I have probably overdone it a little," wrote Forrer to a friend recalling the incident. Sommer was furious: "You disrespectful little doctor!" he shouted in front of all the other scholars. "Your insulting and shameful disrespect could not be forgiven even on account of your youth!" and left.

Forrer was secretly proud of standing up against the pompous and arrogant academician. Still, he got a hint of how deeply in trouble he was when he met his mentor, Meyer, in the next room at the symposium and told him about the altercation. Meyer threw a "Forrer, you fool" at him, shook his head, and hurried off. Minutes later, Meyer was seen in a corner with Sommer, trying to calm him down, but to no avail. He reached Forrer in the foyer and informed him that Sommer had just declared him *persona non grata* within the German Oriental Society. He advised him: "Write Sommer a letter, urgently. Write humbly in style and wording and apologize." We do not know if Forrer ever wrote that letter. He probably didn't. What we know is that, from that moment, Forrer's career was marked. He became a pariah within the Society, and his future work would be met with prejudice in the circles in which Sommer exerted his unchecked power when not met with open, public critique by Sommer himself.

Within two years of the incident, Forrer made a new attempt at the test to become professor and failed for a second time. We will probably never know if his conflict with Sommer influenced this result.

Despite Forrer's failure at attaining higher academic status, his contribution to Hittitology cannot be overstated. His patient work made the Hattusa tablets available to the academic world. Any researcher could quickly obtain copies, arm themselves with the newly published Hrozný's grammar of Hittite, and attempt translations. Translating from Hittite became popular among orientalists. In the following years, not a month would go without a new translation being published, adding piece after piece to the Hittite puzzle.

While reconstructing the history of these people, however, it became apparent that no text source could answer the question of how the Hittite civilization originated. Hittitologists were asking themselves where the Hittites came from and when they appeared in Anatolia, but no answer could be found.

Philologists had recently agreed that Hittites spoke an Indo-European language, making them related to people as diverse as the Celts or the Iranians. Still, the history of how Indo-Europeans migrated through Europe was far from being understood.

A Hittite religious ritual from 1300 BCE reads: "Sun God of Heaven, shepherd of man, you rise from the sea."[3] When scholars translated this line, they were puzzled. In no part of central Anatolia can the sun be seen rising out of the sea. The words in the ritual could be a memory of the time when the ancestors of the Hittites were migrating toward Anatolia. The sea mentioned in the ritual, from which the sun is seen rising, would then be either the Caspian Sea (if the migration happened through the Caucasus) or the Black Sea (if the migration happened through the Balkans).

The existence of a people called Indo-Europeans, who had spread over most of Europe and a large part of Asia, bringing along its distinctive language, has fascinated scholars for over two centuries. For most of this time, the discipline which helped trace this people's history was linguistics, followed, by distant second, archaeology. Since the 1950s, one theory on the origin of the Indo-Europeans has prevailed over the others. This theory is commonly referred to as the "Kurgan Hypothesis" and is associated with the Lithuanian American scholar Marija Gimbutas (1921–1994).

Gimbutas is one of the most influential figures in the history of archaeology, one of those unique scientists who create a whole new field of studies: archaeomythology: the understanding of the past through the study of mythology. Gimbutas' Kurgan hypothesis takes its name from the *kurgans*, burial mounds characteristic of the steppes north of the Black Sea. For Gimbutas, this is the area where Indo-Europeans originated in the first half of the 4th millennium BCE. Following at least three waves of migration, the Indo-Europeans would have spread to a large part of continental Europe, the Caucasus, and Anatolia.[4]

According to this hypothesis, the people who then became Hittites would have entered the Near East stage and conquered their place there, at the expense of the local, autochthonous populations, around the mid-third millennium BCE. Like every innovative theory, Gimbutas' ideas were strongly criticized; numerous counter-theories were put forward, including a view that put the origin of the Indo-Europeans right in Anatolia. Gimbutas' Kurgan hypothesis went through decades of modification and elaboration, widely accepted or dismissed by different factions of archaeologists.

Although a shy speaker, Gimbutas had a gift for engaging the masses through her writing: in the 1970s, her books, intended as academic works, attained mass popularity and even obtained the probably unwanted interest of the feminist movement, which joined the diatribe having partly misinterpreted Gimbutas' work[5] and asserting that the Indo-Europeans, who had a patriarchal, male-dominated culture had expanded at the expenses of "Old Europe" civilizations who had a matriarchal, female-centered culture. In the last two decades, the debate about the Indo-European migrations shifted from a purely linguistic and archaeological study to a debate in paleogenetics, the science which studies the past by examining genetic material. While the debate is ongoing, most of academia sides with Gimbutas' Kurgan Hypothesis.

Whichever way they arrived in Anatolia, this Indo-European people—which we would later call Hittites—started to expand at the expense of other local, non–Indo-European groups, like the Hattians. The latter were autochthonous and had developed along the river Halys, in Central Anatolia, during the second half of the third millennium BCE. Evidence of fires and other destructive events in prehistoric Anatolian settlements confirms this hypothesis. Through the centuries, Hittites partly expelled and partly assimilated with the Hattians. The Hattian civilization left some remnants of their language in the Hittite texts: scattered words marked by the Hittite expression *hattili,* which means "in Hattian." Whatever balance they reached, within about 400 years, the Hittites ruled over urban Anatolian centers which were previously Hattian. These new-founded Hittite cities were independent of each other, thus not yet the unitarian Hittite Kingdom.

At that time, Assyrians, the more commercially evolved population, opened prosperous commercial routes from Mesopotamia to Anatolia. The routes were used to exchange goods, especially metals, of which Anatolia was richer than Mesopotamia; there are examples of entire Assyrian tribes from Mesopotamia who relocated to Anatolia, and through the years between 1950 and 1750 BCE, Assyrians established a sophisticated network of trade posts. The trade posts are known as *kārum* and host large communities of Assyrian merchants. The karum had the purpose of overseeing commerce over territories (called *mātū*) through a network of subsidiary posts.

Anatolian rulers established agreements with the Assyrian merchants, taxing their caravans and regulating their trade, and each kārum was allowed to preserve its extraterritoriality. The largest Assyrian kārum, a true metropolis for the age, located in the heart of Anatolia, was called Nesa or Kanesh (modern-day Kültepe). At the time, the Assyrian civilization was more advanced than the local Anatolian population, so Nesa was probably the most magnificent of the cities in Anatolia, with paved streets, aqueducts, a sewage system, and houses ornate with fine ceramics.

The Hittites were not yet organized in a territorial state; they operated from several independent city-states. Hittite King Pithana of the neighboring city-state of Kussara coveted the riches of Nesa, attacked it, and conquered it around 1750 BCE. This is the first example of a Hittite king reigning over a territory rather than a city-state. Pithana passed on his kingship to his son Anitta, who shared his father's appetite for military campaigns.

Among the texts Forrer translated back in 1922 was a small and

7. The Hittites Start to Tell Their Story 91

poorly preserved tablet that came to be known as the *Proclamation of Anitta*. Unbeknownst to Forrer, the text was not the original one but rather a fourteenth century BCE copy of the original. This text is a foremost example of the Hittite style in historiography: the "justification." The king, who speaks in the first person, wants to justify his actions in front of all men and what led him to wage war, campaign, or create alliances. The king is seen as more potent and courageous than anyone else, but still a man. Later, Hittites would see kings being exalted at the time of their deaths, becoming gods, to the point that in later literature, "he became a god" would be used as a euphemism for "he died."

The text briefly describes how Anitta's father Pithana conquered the city of Nesa "but did not do any harm to the habitants of Nesa" and how he subjected communities of indigenous Hattians. Anitta continued his father's territorial expansion by conquering the city-state of Hattusa sometime between 1740 and 1720 BCE. The conquest of Hattusa was not benign like his father's conquest of Nesa. Anitta destroyed the city and its crops (onto which, he declares, he sowed weeds) and cursed whoever would later become its ruler. Ironically, no more than a hundred years later, this cursed city would become the capital of the Hittite Kingdom. Archaeologists would have to wait until 1954 to find corroborating, material evidence of the power of King Anitta.

In that year, Turkish archaeologists Tahsin Ozguc and Kemal Balkan were excavating at the archaeological site of Nesa when they came across the ruins of a large building that had been destroyed and burned. In one of the main rooms, amidst smashed metal vessels, they unearthed a well-preserved bronze dagger which immediately became a milestone in the history of Indo-European languages owing to the inscription on it. Short, but very significant, it read: "Palace of Anitta, the king."[6] These five simple words represent the earliest extant sentence written in any Indo-European language and corroborated beyond doubt the historical sources written later by the Hittites.

The embryonic kingdom created by Pithana and his son Anitta was very short-lived: soon after Anitta's death, it disintegrated. Each city carried on independently, and between 1750 and 1680 BCE, constant warfare and divisions plagued Anatolia. Nevertheless, the conquest of Nesa left an essential mark in Hittite history. Once the Hittites unified, for centuries, they called their own language *Nesili,* which means "from Nesa." When scholars like Forrer started translating Hittite and noticed that it was called Nesili by the Hittites themselves, they began to refer to it as Nesite, or sometimes Kaneshian, as Kanesh was the Akkadian name for Nesa. The word Nesite never caught on, and today the language of the Hittites is still called Hittite. On the other hand, the Hittites referred to themselves as "men of Hatti," borrowing the name of the land from the indigenous Hattians, so the name Hittite is not a complete misnomer.[7]

As he waded through the hundreds of fragmentary texts recovered at Hattusa, Forrer was bewildered by the language variety he encountered. In 1919 he famously published a 96 page paper listing "the eight languages of the Land of Hatti," all written in cuneiform.[8] Besides Hittite (or Nesite as he kept on calling it), it was natural to see Akkadian and its "baggage" of Sumerian as it was used for diplomatic correspondence with Mesopotamian kings. Nor was it surprising to find, also for reasons of diplomatic correspondence, some texts in Hurrian, the language of the people of the kingdom of Mitanni, Hittites' southern neighbors. As noted before, one of the three Amarna Letters not written in Akkadian came from the kingdom of Mitanni and was written in Hurrian.

Hattian, the non–Indo-European language spoken by the autochthonous people of Anatolia before the arrival of the Hittites, appeared sporadically, especially in ancient religious rituals. Like Sumerian, Hattian is a language isolate, unrelated to any other known language. Then there were two more languages, both Indo-European, which were used by peoples who likely migrated into Anatolia at the same time as the Hittites but were later conquered by them. One is Palaic, the whole corpus of which consists of just five tablets; the other, much more common, Luwian, which would later become very important in understanding the Anatolian hieroglyphs (see Chapter 12).

To complete the list, Forrer identified a handful of words (mainly names of gods) that, he maintained, were Sanskrit in origin and which he dubbed *Urindisch*. It is clear from Forrer's research that ancient Anatolia was a melting pot of people, some Indo-European, others not, which had a symbiotic relationship with the Hittites, whose military power was growing.

We left the Hittite society organized in a collection of city-states after Pithana and his son Anitta's attempt to unify it between 1750 and 1720 BCE. The details of what happened next are hazy; however, later sources show that the city-states were unified by another conquering king named Labarna (sometimes called Tabarna in the ancient sources) at the beginning of the 1600s BCE. Unfortunately, the sources are so limited that the actual existence of this king has been questioned. It is possible that, rather than a real person, Labarna was a title that Hittites gave to the first king who unified the territory, which in such case would be Hattusili I, of which we have a better record.

In his time, Forrer could not accurately reconstruct the age of King Hattusili, who reigned from approximately 1650 BCE, according to current dating. The main document with an account of Hattusili's kingdom called

7. The Hittites Start to Tell Their Story

the *Annals* of Hattusili was found only years later and consisted of one larger tablet with text in Akkadian and several highly fragmented copies of the corresponding text in Hittite. Only in 1957, when German Hittitologist Heinrich Otten (1913–2012) produced a preliminary translation of the document,[9] the world learned about King Hattusili.

The *Annals* of Hattusili recovered were not original but a copy from 400 years later. A careful reading of the text revealed that the original must have been written on a gold plate and was associated with a statue of King Hattusili. It is unclear whether the gold plate would have been on the statue itself or close to it; however, this precious artifact must have been highly tempting for looters because, to date, neither the plates nor the statue has been found. The *Annals* tell how Hattusili made Hattusa the capital of the unified kingdom and took his crown name from it (previously known as Labarna) and how he conquered territories in northern Syria and west Anatolia, "extending his domain to the sea."

This meant that by the end of the 1600 century, the Hittites reigned over most of Anatolia from its west coast on the Mediterranean to the eastern mountains and reigned over a portion of the Levant, namely the northern portion of Syria and its coastline. In west Anatolia, the Hittite dominion bordered the land of Arzawa, where the famous letter translated by Winckler originated. More than a single kingdom, the Arzawa was a coalition of small kingdoms, largely city-states; according to the Hittite sources, its largest city was Apasa, on the site that centuries later came to be known to the Greeks as Ephesus. This city enjoyed high commercial and cultural status throughout antiquity and lies near modern-day Selçuk in the Province of İzmir.

Besides greatly extending Hittite dominion over Anatolia, Hattusili wrote the first Hittite law code and created a judicial body called *pankus*. The pankus was an assembly of elders of the royal entourage which would "witness and enforce agreements and royal proclamations and try criminal offenders of particularly high status."[10]

At the end of his thirty year reign, around 1620 BCE, Hattusili fell severely ill, and on his deathbed, delivered a speech recorded by his scribes. The speech, called *Testament of Hattusili*, was discovered in 1937 as a well-preserved bilingual (Akkadian and Hittite) copy from some centuries later.[11] The Testament of Hattusili is the king's message to dignitaries and warriors of Hatti about appointing his grandson Mursili as heir to the throne. King Mursili continued the tradition of expansion of his predecessor, invaded Syria, and, in 1595 BCE, carried out a military operation that made him legendary: he led the invasion and sacking of Babylon.

The feat is impressive even by modern standards: Babylon lay in southern Mesopotamia, just south of modern-day Baghdad, 1500 kilometers away from Hattusa; it had been one of the leading centers of culture in Mesopotamia and one of the largest cities of the ancient world and was then an independent city-state under the rule of a people called Amorite; the city was strongly fortified and well-defended. The Hittites did not invade Babylon to occupy it; after all, the city was very far from the borders of their kingdom, so the intention was not to extend their power over this region but rather to "show the muscles" to the neighboring powers. After the Hittite sack, Babylon would never be the same again, and it would take several centuries to return to its splendor.

The event has enormous historical importance also because it allows us to shed some clarity on the chronology of the Hittite kingdom, which is otherwise highly uncertain. Ever since Forrer started to trace the history of the Hittites, he was frustrated in finding how limited the sources were. The Hittites did not leave lists of kings with the duration of each reign as the Egyptians did; nor did they count the years from a single event in the remote past like the Ancient Romans, who used the year of the foundation of Rome. A chronological system was needed to trace the early history of the Hittite Kingdom more accurately. To put events in order, the only solution was to look outside Anatolia.

Significant help in establishing a chronology not just of the Hittites but of the Ancient Near East at large was provided by Sir Rawlinson himself. In 1870, Rawlinson (assisted by a young Smith before he became famous for the Gilgamesh texts) published a translation of some obscure texts of Babylonian astrology. One of them, the so-called "Venus Tablet of Ammisaduqa," recorded the conjunction of the rise of the planet Venus with the new moon during the eighth year of the reign of Babylonian King Ammisaduqa.[12] Because astronomers can retrace the position of the planet Venus in relation to the moon's phases at any point in the past, they could pinpoint that year on the calendar. Scholars knew the names of Babylonian kings before and after Ammisaduqa and the duration of each of their reigns, so they could work out a chronology of Babylonian kings.

The main issue with this clever system is that the phases of the planet Venus follow a cycle of length that varies between 56 and 64 years. Because the document translated by Rawlinson did not provide other occurrences that correlate with the phases of Venus, it follows that Babylonian King Hammurabi's ascension to the throne may have happened in 1848, 1792, or 1736 BCE. The chronologies that stemmed from these four dates differed by 56 years and were called High, Middle, and Low Ancient Near East Chronology. A vast body of research aims to establish which chronologies are more accurate, and scholars from all disciplines have contributed with data.

Currently, most historians favor the Middle Chronology; however,

7. The Hittites Start to Tell Their Story

there is still no final answer on which one is the correct one. After the Ancient Near East Chronology was established, in three possible versions, historians based themselves on an historically known moment of contact between the Babylonians and the Hittites to work back the Hittite chronology. The choice fell on the sack of Babylon by Mursili's army, and it is mainly by leaning on the proposed date of this event that the timeline of the first centuries of Hittite history was reconstructed.

Having put their hands on the city of Babylon, it seemed the Hittites were projected to reign undisturbed over most of the Near East. However, one recurring theme in the history of these people emerged: bad planning of succession in leadership brought internal conflict, which ultimately weakened the kingdom. Thus, after Mursili was assassinated by his brother-in-law Hantili, who seized power and reigned until about 1560 BCE, for the following forty years, internal conflict dominated the history of the Hittites. A stable leadership was only restored with the accession to the throne of King Telipinu in approximately 1525 BCE.

Telipinu's reign started with the intent of restoring order after the years of the mayhem of Hittite royal succession. Even Telipinu's name itself may have been chosen for the purpose. His was not a usual name as it was the name of a Hittite god who served as a patron of farming and agriculture. It is possible that he chose this name as a symbol of the deity who cyclically returned from his absence and carried fertility and prosperity to the fields.[13]

Like kings Anitta, Hattusili, and Mursili before him, Telipinu left a document about his years in power. This one, rather than a *res gestae*, was in the form of an edict to establish rules of succession to the throne. Archaeologists never found the original of the edict. Instead, they had to rely on seven copies written in the fourteenth century BCE, over a hundred years after Telipinu's death, on twenty-four tablets in different states of preservation, published in 1935.[14]

The edict provides an account of the dark years of chaos that followed the assassination of Mursili. Telipinu gives another example of Hittite "justification": a story of violence, deceit, parricide, and a succession of coups that seem never to end until he accedes to the throne.

The Edict introduces laws of succession, which Hittites did not have yet, and rules for safeguarding the throne's stability, basically sanctioning with capital punishment any attempt at disturbing the kingship. Despite Telipinu's effort to regulate royal succession, his work failed to bear immediate fruit, and he died without heirs. The 70 years following his death, from 1500 to 1430 BCE, are only poorly attested. This period has been defined as the "Dark Ages" of the Hittites. During the Dark Ages, the Hittite kingdom suffered attacks from neighboring people, among them the notorious Gasga, or Kaska, a non–Indo-European people from northern Anatolia and other populations in western Anatolia.

Thus, early Hittite history is characterized by military success and expansion from its beginnings around 1750 BCE to the death of Telipinu around 1500 BCE. After this time, the Hittite kingdom plunged into a downward spiral of political unrest, which led to a contraction of its territory lasting until the second half of 1400s BCE, when the Hittites underwent a phase of renewed growth called the New Kingdom, which brought them to become a full-fledged empire.

At the beginning of the New Kingdom, between 1420 BCE and 1344 BCE probably four kings ruled over the Hittites. The word "probably" is necessary because, as seen in the previous chapter, it is uncertain whether just one or two kings named Tudhaliya existed. The existence of a king named Hattusili II is disputed as well.

While huge credits for making a vast body of Hittite sources available go to Forrer, history is not the only discipline enriched by his translations. One of Forrer's discoveries soon changed our understanding of classic literature.

Old Kingdom

Labarna I	1680 – 1650
Hattusili I	1650 – 1620
Mursili I	1620 – 1590
Hantili I	1590 – 1560
Zidanta I	1560 – 1550
Ammuna	1550 – 1530
Huzziya I	1530 – 1525
Telipinu	1525 – 1500
Tahurwaili	1500 – ?
Alluwamna	Uncertain
Hantili II	Uncertain
Zidanta II	Uncertain
Huzziya II	Uncertain
Muwatalli I	? – 1420

List of kings of the Old Kingdom. All dates are BCE and according to the Middle Chronology. Some scholars propose the term Middle Kingdom for the reigns of Tahurwaili to Muwatalli I.

8

Troy

Emil Forrer has a peculiar record, an unwanted accomplishment: he started one of the most protracted disputes in the history of literature: the "Ahhiyawa Question." Forrer was translating the *Annals* of Hittite King Tudhaliya I/II,* the king who emerged after the "Dark Ages" of the Old Kingdom, around 1400 BCE, at the start of the so-called "New Kingdom." Tudhaliya I/II was an important king, both politically and symbolically, as he was a direct descendent of Hattusili I. With his ascent to power, he brought back on the throne the original bloodline of the ancient family which had unified the Hittites centuries earlier.

Tudhaliya I/II was the first of the Hittite rulers in a long time to concern himself with the western periphery of the reign. Through a series of military incursions, he consolidated his power over the west coast of Anatolia. Because of their position, the lands on the west coast of Anatolia had strong ties with the Mycenaean civilization, the civilization which inhabited Greece during the Late Bronze Age. As we will see shortly, this connection puts Tudhaliya I/II's reign at the center of a critical debate within ancient history: whether (or how much) the Hittites interacted with Mycenaean Greeks.

Through his translations, Forrer repeatedly came across the name of a people called Ahhiyawa and references to places called Truwisa and Wilusa. These names immediately unleashed a series of thoughts and conjectures, leading him to an intuition that would revolutionize our understanding of ancient literature. To appreciate the magnitude of his discoveries, we need to take a step back to discuss the *Iliad*.

The *Iliad* is the main literary work of the Classic Age, a long epic poem that tells the story of the war of Troy. It is traditionally attributed to the blind Greek poet Homer, who may have lived in the eighth century

---

* Still today, there is no historical clarity whether there was one king named Tudhaliya or two kings named Tudhaliya, in rapid succession. For this reason, historians often refer to a Tudhaliya I/II.

BCE; however, the identity of Homer is not well documented. In any case, the poem is believed to have come to whoever wrote it through a very long oral tradition. In the *Iliad*, the city of Troy, also called Ilios, is described as being located somewhere on the west coast of Anatolia. The story retells facts that happened during the nine-year Trojan War, which was waged against the city of Troy by the Greeks—called Achaeans in the poem—after Paris, son of the King of Troy Priamus, took Helen from her husband Menelaus, king of Sparta.

The war is purported to occur sometime between the fourteenth- and twelfth century BCE, four centuries before the age of Homer; however, this dating is uncertain. It is impossible to overstate the *Iliad*'s impact on Western culture. From Greek tragedy and Latin epic, all the way to Shakespeare and modern times, twenty-eight centuries of literature have been influenced by this poem. Cicero knew the poem by heart, Napoleon held a copy of it on his nightstand, and four-time British Prime Minister William Gladstone proposed that Homer should be obligatory reading for all schools of England.

In the ancient world, the *Iliad* was so popular that people accepted the facts depicted in it as historically accurate. This belief was carried on well into the Middle Ages. However, by the seventeenth century CE, scholars had started to doubt that the Trojan war had ever occurred and considered it a fictional event. By the time the age of enlightenment swept through Europe, Troy had come to be regarded as an imaginary place and its story nothing more than a fable.[1] Some archaeologists, undeterred, kept on searching for the ruins of Troy and in 1870, when Heinrich Schliemann claimed he had discovered them, historians were divided. Schliemann had indeed found the ruins of a Bronze Age city, but there was no evidence among the unearthed ruins that the city was undoubtedly Troy, and there was no mention of Troy in any ancient source of any time or from any place before the *Iliad*.

Then Emil Forrer came along. In a groundbreaking 1924 paper,[2] he concluded that Ahhiyawa was the Hittite name for the Achaeans—the Greeks—and that Truwisa and Wilusa were nothing other than Hittite names for Troy and Ilios. The similarity between Wilusa and Ilios is better appreciated considering that Ilios was originally spelled with a letter called "digamma," but later dropped, which made it sound more like *Wilios*.

But he did not stop there. In another text he translated, Forrer found the poorly preserved treaty of alliance between a Hittite king and the city of Wilusa. The ruler of Wilusa was called Alaksandu, and he swore upon a god called Apaliunas. Forrer concluded that Alaksandu was the Hittite rendition of Alexandros of Ilios, better known as Paris of Ilios, one of the main characters of the *Iliad* and that Apaliunas was the Hittite name for the Greek god Apollon, according to the *Iliad*, the protector of the city of Troy.[3]

At the same time, Forrer translated a letter written by an unknown Hittite king, probably Tudhaliya IV, to an unnamed king of a land of western Anatolia. It is a diplomatic letter of cordial tone in which reference is made to two cities under Ahhiyawa control called Milawata and Atreya. Forrer worked out that Milawata was the Hittite name for the Greek city, Miletus.[4] This way, he confirmed that the Ahhiyawa were none other than the Achaeans, the collective name used by Homer to describe Bronze Age Greeks, with their central city at Mycenae. Moreover, in the *Iliad*, the kings of the Greek cities of Mycenae and Sparta (Agamemnon and Menelaus) are called "the Atreid" because they are children of the mythical figure Atreus. Forrer hypothesized that their family name may come from the name of the other city under Ahhiyawa control, which the Hittites referred to as Atreya.

In another letter, also translated by Forrer, another Hittite king (likely Hattusili III) writes to an unnamed Ahhiyawa king to request the rendition of a former regent of Wilusa, which was under Hittite control. The former regent had led an insurrection against the central Hittite government and was now hiding in Ahhiyawa territory. His name was Piyama-Radu. For Forrer, Piyama-Radu was the Hittite name for Priamus, the king of Troy in the *Iliad*. The brother of the unnamed Ahhiyawa king is also mentioned. His name is Tawagalawa, which according to Forrer, was the Hittite name for Eteocles, another king celebrated in ancient Greek literature and until then believed to be a fictional character, the son of Oedipus and Jocasta. Once again, the similarity between Tawagalawa and Eteocles is better appreciated considering that Eteocles was originally spelled with the digamma, which made it sound more like *Etewoklewes*.

Forrer's conclusions could not have been more sensational. In one single paper, he was alleging the first historical evidence that the city of Troy had existed *and* that some of the characters of the *Iliad* were not fictional.

But the most surprising of his conclusions came from one single line further down in the Tawagalawa letter. A few simple words which changed everything we know about the historicity of the *Iliad*. The Hittite king wrote: "Now, as we have come to an agreement on Wilusa *over which we went to war*...." In that sentence was the key to the mystery: the only supposed historical mention of a Trojan war to date.[5]

Emil Forrer's theories shook a centuries-old system of beliefs. The reaction from the community of classic historians, archaeologists, and classic literature experts was immediate. Dozens of articles were written, and meetings were held. Scholars were divided: some lamented that

Forrer's deductions were merely based on philological conjectures and tried to downplay them. In contrast, others were enthusiastic about the new concept and started to look at the *Iliad* with fresh eyes in search of confirmation of Forrer's theory.

Unfortunately, despite having been the inspirator of a new field of research, Forrer's career immediately went into an unpredicted downward spiral. Having failed his professorship exam for the second time, by 1925, he was without a job. He had to resort to a scholarship as a lecturer from the *Notgemeinschaft der Deutschen Wissenschaft* or Emergency Association of German Science, a sort of unionistic body that supported researchers facing difficulty.

In the years which followed, Forrer neither found a steady job nor reached any higher status in academia. He did short stints of everything: archaeological expeditions in the Near East, contract lecturing, guest research at several American institutions, temporary jobs at museums, and even a half-hearted collaboration with the Nazi party. It is not a long stretch to suppose that his conflict with Sommer had gotten him many enemies in academic circles and that it contributed to his misfortune. Forrer's hypotheses were controversial and received their share of critiques. Still, no reviews were as scathing as the ones he received from Sommer himself.

In 1932, in a publication weighing in on the Ahhiyawa question, Sommer literally bashed Forrer's work.[6] For years, Sommer's criticism of Forrer's theories was the mainstream, and demolishing Forrer's work became a common pastime among classicists. Many years later, in 1959, Sir Denys Page, professor of Greek at the University of Cambridge, published a leading work on the history of the Homeric *Iliad*. Its first chapter, dedicated to *Achaeans in Hittite Documents,* is almost entirely dedicated to ridiculing Forrer's interpretation of Greek names in Hittite sources (including the very notion that Ahhiyawa indicated Greece),[7] with a tone so condescending it is almost uncomfortable to read.

Sommer carried his strong opposition to Forrer's theory (probably as well as his grudge against him) to the grave: when he died in 1962, the rather partial, Nazi-sympathizing German linguist Johannes Friedrich (1893–1972), who had competed with Forrer in the translation of Hittite texts and had harshly attacked his theories in a couple of publications,[8] felt obliged to write in his eulogy that "caution and reluctance to face uncertain claims was one of Sommer's main virtues" and that "even if Sommer might have gone too far in his skepticism, he still has the merit of having neatly separated the safe from the uncertain and the perhaps possible,"[9] with explicit reference to Forrer and, interestingly, with a choice of words very similar to what Page (who had an almost extravagant devotion to Sommer's work) had written about Sommer in a book, three years earlier: "...distinguish what is known from what is hypothetical, or false, or simply unknown."[10]

After years of precarious occupations, Forrer grew tired of the German milieu. In 1947, aged fifty-three, he spent his father's inheritance to relocate to El Salvador in Central America with his fourth wife. In Salvador, he found what he was looking for. He finally obtained a stable academic career as a university professor, which he kept until retirement, and fathered another seven children. He had a good and long life and never stopped his research in ancient languages. He even gave it a curious spin when, in the 1970s, past retirement, he promoted a fanciful research field called "Meropis Research," based on the belief that in ancient times the Near East civilizations had come in contact with the South American civilizations, an idea which was later dismissed as unscientific, a pseudoscience.

Throughout his life, Forrer has always given the impression of a man searching for vindication. Without material archaeological evidence, his theories were doubted even by his strongest supporters.

This vindication did come, in part, in 1983, just three years before his death, when Dutch Hittitologist H.J. Houwink ten Cate translated a Hittite letter, the so-called "Manapa-Tarhunta Letter." The letter was written by Manapa-Tarhunta, the regent of a tiny vassal state within the Hittite Empire called the Kingdom of the Seha River in western Anatolia. Manapa-Tarhunta was writing to an unnamed Hittite king around 1295 BCE. In the letter, Manapa-Tarhunta laments that he has been trying to drive out the gang of the insurrectionist Piyama-Radu, who with his raids is wreaking havoc in Manapa-Tarhunta's peaceful land.

Manapa-Tarhunta has tried to fight him, but without success, and is now pleading with the Hittite king for military help. Until this letter was translated, the detractors of Forrer's theory argued that although Truwisa or Wilusa could be accepted as names for Troy, there was no evidence of *where exactly* Truwisa or Wilusa were located. But the letter changed this: in his plea, Manapa-Tarhunta sketches a plan for the Hittite army intervention and suggests camping at the Seha River before "marching west towards Truwisa."

Considering where the Seha River is located, the letter places Troy in the exact same area where Schliemann found his Bronze Age city. For the community of historians, this was corroborating evidence that the location of Wilusa was consistent with the archaeological site of Troy, suggesting that Schliemann and Forrer had been right all along.[11]

By this time, the tide on the Ahhiyawa question had started to change. In 1974, University of Pennsylvania historian James D. Muhly, writing on a publication of the Penn Museum, was probably purporting what most historians thought when he contemptuously dispelled Forrer's Ahhiyawa theory. He maintained that Ahhiyawa was not Greece and that the Hittites would not have had any contact whatsoever with Mycenaean Greece: "The Hittites had no interest in Mycenaean Greece. Why should they have concerned themselves with a primitive, rather barbaric, and mostly illiterate land, far beyond a sea they would never have dreamed of crossing? ... The Hittites had no cause to remember the Achaeans; they had never even heard of them."[12] But just a few years later, in 1982, considering the discovery of new sources, Hittitologist Hans Güterbock (see the next chapter) as a translator of key Hittite texts, could write, in a much more composed tone, that he thought that Ahhiyawa was, in fact, Greece: "I think one should draw the necessary conclusion from it. The Great King of Ahhiyawa ... ruled over mainland Greece."[13]

But persuading historians wasn't enough. For a complete vindication, archaeologists had to be shown evidence too: material evidence, the kind of objects put at the center of a museum for all to see and believe. Although one of the most extensively excavated sites in the world, no single artifact found at Troy could give a shred of persuasive, incontrovertible evidence that the Trojan War actually took place. The last piece of this three-thousand-year-old puzzle was found only in recent times. Oddly, the finding did not come from Troy: it came from Hattusa. And it was not the result of an archaeological excavation but a once-in-a-lifetime, serendipitous moment.

It was a hot August morning in 1991 when a Turkish builder was operating his digger on a side street near the Hattusa archaeological site, just 750 meters from the Lions Gate of the ancient city wall. Work was ongoing to widen the road which brought the occasional tourist to visit the main Hittite site in Turkey. While digging just ten centimeters deep in the dirt, the blade of the digger touched a metal object. The worker got off his machine and moved the earth with his hands to reveal an eighty-centimeter-long, seven-centimeter broad, flat, greenish metal object. He immediately realized the object was a relic from the past and brought it to the resident archaeologists at Hattusa.

The archaeologists were beside themselves. While they had carried out year after year of excavation with sophisticated modern techniques, painstakingly lifting dirt with spoon-sized tools, one of the most beautiful and best-preserved ancient artifacts was picked up by the blade of a digger. The metal object was a sword in an excellent preservation state. The archaeologists rushed to the site where the digger had found the sword and cordoned an excavation site in search of other artifacts. They dug for weeks but could not find any other object of relevance, nor any building or structure associated with the sword. It was a bizarrely placed and highly unexpected find.

A sword from a Hittite archaeological site is a remarkable object, undoubtedly worthy of being exposed in a museum, but this sword represented much more for two reasons. The first reason is that it carried a remarkably well-preserved inscription in Akkadian. The inscription read: "As Tudhaliya the Great King destroyed the country of Assuwa, he dedicated these swords to the Storm-God, his lord,"[14] which meant that the sword was part of a trophy of several swords (notice the plural in the inscription) taken from the defeated enemy during a battle in the country of Assuwa, brought back to the Hittite capital Hattusa and consecrated in a religious ceremony, presumably to thank the gods for the victory.

Who were those enemies in the country of Assuwa? From several sources, historians knew that Assuwa was a confederation of small kingdoms in the coastal region of western Anatolia, a mainly military alliance of countries. The name Assuwa survived long past the Bronze Age and became a name to loosely designate territories to the east of Greece, in Anatolia or beyond; later, the Romans borrowed this term from Greek, and "Assuwa" evolved into "Asia," to which we owe the modern name for the continent.

Hittite documents tell that around 1430 BCE, Hittite King Tudhaliya I/II received news that the Assuwa confederation was rebelling against the Central Government. Tudhaliya I/II rapidly converged onto Assuwa with his mighty army and suffocated the rebellion in blood. Hittite tablets list as many as twenty-two kingdoms in this confederation, including Truwisa/Wilusa. Because we know that Truwisa was one of the largest cities of west Anatolia, it is likely the main battleground for Tudhaliya I/II. This event is mentioned in another artifact of the age, an ornate silver bowl called the "Ankara Silver Bowl," on which an inscription translated in 1996 confirms that Tudhaliya I/II subjugated Truwisa.

Tudhaliya I/II's battle account is precise and breaks down in detail the booty of the campaign. He brought back to Hattusa: "Ten thousand Assuwan soldiers" (deportation of defeated enemies as prisoners was a common practice of the age), "six hundred teams of horses and their Assuwan charioteers," as well as the conquered population, including oxen and sheep.[15]

But for the archaeologists, the surprises were not over. The second reason for the uniqueness of Tudhaliya I/II's sword was the most sensational. The shape of the sword did not appear of typical Anatolian style. Experts around the world were asked to weigh in. At the time, Danish archaeologist Ove Hansen, based in Athens, was one of the foremost scholars of ancient warfare and an expert on ancient Mediterranean weaponry.

When asked to examine the sword, he had no doubt: it was a Greek sword, more precisely of Mycenaean origin.[16] That sword was the first material evidence of the military involvement of Mycenaeans in western Anatolia, which testimonies that Mycenaeans fought side-by-side with Assuwans against the Hittites, likely clashing against them at Troy.[17]

Today historians are still cautious about connecting the dots. Most accept that Troy existed and was not just a fictional place, that it used to be under Hittite control and that the city found by Schliemann at Hissarlik is likely what remains of Troy. It is also agreed that the Hittites and Greeks fought in the region of Troy. To what extent the facts narrated in the *Iliad* retell the story of one single conflict is still debated. The story of the *Iliad* is not limited to the nine years of the Trojan war. Through a series of digressions, the *Iliad* gives accounts of facts that happened long before the war. Maybe the Trojan war narrated in this epic poem is not a single event but rather an allegory for centuries of hostilities between Anatolians and Greeks.

After all, it is known that the *Iliad* speaks through allegories and various, sometimes cryptic, symbolisms. One of the stories, among many others, stands out as a potential symbol of the relationships between Greeks and Hittites: the story of Bellerophon.

In book 6 of the *Iliad*, the Achaean Diomedes and the Trojan Glaukos, enemies, have a conversation, and Glaukos tells the story of his mythical grandfather Bellerophon. Bellerophon represents the archetypical hero: he is exiled from his Greek hometown, goes on a journey, interacts with the gods, and accomplishes several acts of bravery. His main achievement is to slay the terrifying monster called Chimera.

Scholars have long been baffled by the etymology of the name Bellerophon and thought it could derive from ἑλλερον (*élleron*), a rare Ancient Greek word for "evil" and φονεύω (*fonéuo*) which means "to slay." Philologists have hypothesized that the Ancient Greek word *élleron* may, in turn, come from the Hittite name *Illuyanka*. The Illuyanka is a monster of Hittite mythology in the shape of a serpent; its name is a compound of two Hittite words for snake: *illu* and *anka*.*[18] If this etymology is correct, the myth of Bellerophon finds its roots in a prehistoric Indo-European myth of a hero who slays a serpent-shaped monster; it is an archetypical myth that seems to have spread to several traditions, including Middle-Ages European legends like the one of St. George slaying the dragon.

Even more interestingly, according to the *Iliad*, Bellerophon's journey took place long before the Trojan war, and after slaying the monster,

---

* *Anka* and *illu* merged are also believed to be the origin of the Latin word for "eel" *anguilla* and indeed the English word "eel" itself could derive from *illu*.

the hero resettled in Anatolia carrying a letter written on a tablet by a Greek King, Proetus. According to the legend, Bellerophon was not able to read the letter; however, when he showed the letter to the Anatolian king Iobates, *he* was able to read it. From the Hittite archives, we know that the Greek kings used to write diplomatic letters to the Hittite kings in the Hittite language, so the letter carried by Bellerophon could be yet another allegory for Greek-Hittite relationships.

The stories told in the *Iliad* span hundreds of years and are tales of a time about which we know very little. Even with the most serious scholarly efforts, reconstructing this long-gone past with limited historical sources and scant archaeological evidence is complicated. We will probably never know how much of the *Iliad* is truth and how much is a myth. Still, today we are sure that the most famous epic poem in history is more than just a literary work: it is a window that allows us to investigate the past.

With his intimate knowledge of the Hittites, Forrer was the man who made archaeologists look at the *Iliad* with different eyes, eyes that studied the tradition of Greece and Anatolia and its influence on the literature of several centuries later and mythology into the modern age.

A portion of the Tawagalawa letter (CTH181), one of the texts which led Swiss scholar Emil Forrer to formulate a theory about cultural and political interaction between the Hittites and the Mycenaean Greeks. Credit: hethiter.net/: fotarch B5009

Almost a hundred years after his historical paper, the Ahhiyawa question is still debated, criticized, and expanded. Most scholars agree that Forrer was right: Ahhiyawa was, in fact, Mycenaean Greece. The extent to which the Hittites and the Mycenaean Greeks interacted is still discussed; they certainly had multiple military conflicts, although it is not certain if one of them or a conflation of all of them may have inspired the narrative of the *Iliad*. They certainly entertained commercial and political relationships (as covered in the following chapters), and excavations at Hattusa have proven Mcyaenaean influence on Hittite art.

Most of this evidence is posterior to Forrer. When King Tudhaliya I/II's sword, one of the main pieces of the puzzle, was added, Forrer was already dead, so the Swiss scholar wasn't fully vindicated during his life, but Forrer's legacy goes beyond the Ahhiyawa question. A hundred years after his translation work, his copies of the Hattusa tablets are still the primary tool for Hittitologists.

Forrer had mainly worked on the tablets found during Winckler's expeditions before the First World War broke out. Once Europe and the new-founded nation of Turkey re-emerged from the Great War, it was time to resume the search for the Hittites.

9

Between the Two Wars

By the end of the First World War, and through a death toll of twenty million people, the political geography of Europe and the Near East had changed radically.

The Ottoman Empire was defeated, and the winning nations France, the United Kingdom, Italy, and Greece, tried to carve up the empire among them, purportedly to re-establish peace. The attempt, stipulated in the so-called Treaty of Sèvres, failed miserably because, instead of settling border disputes, it generated even more violence and a new, bloody conflict along the Greek-Ottoman border. The people of the Ottoman Empire were growing tired of continuous fighting. Years and years of war had left the land impoverished, and the trust in the central power was dwindling.

In 1920 several political forces united and created the Grand National Assembly of Turkey, led by the nationalist military leader Mustafa Kemal. In 1922, the long-awaited change finally took place. The Assembly stripped the Sultan of all his powers and declared the creation of a republic, with Kemal its president and Ankara its capital. Kemal immediately agreed to new terms with the European powers. Six centuries of Ottoman history were canceled almost overnight. From the ashes of the empire, a new nation was born, Turkey, over a territory corresponding almost exactly to the boundaries of Anatolia.

Kemal would remain in office until his death fifteen years later in 1938. He had such an essential role in creating the basis for a new nation that the Turkish Parliament bestowed upon him the moniker of Atatürk ("Father of the Turks"). Atatürk had a clear plan: he wanted to modernize Turkey and make it look towards the West, rather than the East, for international relationships. The most meaningful change was his decision that the Turkish language should be written in the Latin rather than the Arabic alphabet used for the previous thousand years.

The Ottoman Sultans had tried to unite numerous nations and cultures for centuries by imposing a theocracy. Atatürk aimed to obtain the exact opposite: one nation and one culture under a secular constitution.

He wanted to build a sense of belonging in a people disheartened by years of war. The Turks needed a past of which to be proud. Fascist dictator Benito Mussolini made the Italians celebrate the past glory of the Ancient Romans; Adolf Hitler in Germany created the myth of a made-up race of warriors called Aryans; and Atatürk chose the Hittites. This trend became the trademark of nationalist leaders well into the second half of the twentieth century: In the 1960s, Egyptian President Nasser appropriated the pharaonic past of Egypt; In the 1990s, Iraqi President Saddam Hussein chose the Neo-Babylonian Empire. Ethnically, neither had anything to do with the past civilizations they tried so hard to relate to.

Atatürk's choice was bizarre. Historians worldwide knew very well that the ancestors of the inhabitants of Turkey, the Seljuks, migrated from Central Asia into Anatolia in the eleventh century of the common era, which means more than two thousand years after the Hittite Empire had ceased to exist. This did not seem to deter Atatürk, who, in 1923, instituted the Turkish History Foundation to study Turkish history. Led by a State Committee for Research on Turkish History, a group of scholars characterized by a rather partial outlook on national history, one of the foundation's main aims was to celebrate the glory of the Hittite civilization. Within a few years, the Foundation manufactured a theory called *Turk Tarih Texi* (Turkish History Thesis) and presented it officially in July 1932 at the Turkish History Congress.

The idea was based on a simple, radical view: Central Asia, the homeland of the Turks, was the cradle of human civilization, and from there, the Turks had migrated and spread throughout the Ancient World, including into Anatolia, where they had been ancestors of the Hittites. Hittites were, therefore, the forebears of the Turkish people. The theory was outlandish but satisfied Atatürk, and the Turkish population largely embraced it. If France had seen its "Egyptomania" at the beginning of the nineteenth century, during the 1930s Turkey witnessed a "Hittitomania." Hittite-looking motifs were seen in the décor of buildings, Hittite-reminiscent monuments were erected throughout the country, and a state-owned bank was even named the "Hittite Bank" (*Etibank* in Turkish).[1] Ironically, the Hittite Bank was the main bank of the state-owned Turkish mining industry, administering the revenues of metal extraction on Anatolian soil, the same activity the Hittites had been known for.

What could such an appalling theory as the Turkish History Thesis be based on? The entire movement, it turns out, traces its roots to one single source, a publication from 1922 called *Pontus Meselesi* ("The Pontus Question").[2] Pontus Meselesi was an insignificant booklet published by the Ankara Government Information Agency, an information organ "impartial" on paper but, really, one of Atatürk's propaganda machines.

9. Between the Two Wars

It was written to discuss an issue of territoriality in a region called Pontus, located in northeastern Anatolia on the shores of the Black Sea. The area was contended between Greeks and Turks and had been a site of international conflicts. The text aimed at persuading audiences at home and abroad of the legitimacy of the Kemalist movement and the nefarious nature of Greek orthodox claims on Anatolian soil.

The man behind this publication, and author of its lengthy preface, was Ağaoğlu Ahmet Bey (1869–1939), an elegant, well-traveled, and well-educated child of the Azerbaijan bourgeoisie. Ağaoğlu was an intellectual, a journalist, a politician, and a man who strongly believed in the power of culture. Like many others who had grown up in a contended territory, Ağaoğlu lived his life in a perpetual identity crisis. When he was twenty years old and moved to Paris to study, he identified himself as a Persian because Azerbaijan was culturally Persian. Once he finished his studies and returned to Azerbaijan, he became a member of the Russian parliament because, at the time, Azerbaijan was under Czarist rule. Once his homeland gained independence from Russia in 1918, he was happy to represent the newborn nation of Azerbaijan at the Paris Peace Conference, except moving two years later to the other nascent nation of Turkey and starting to identify as Turkish. In Turkey, he collaborated closely with Atatürk, who put him in charge of supervising the publication of the propaganda booklet about the Pontus Question, which contained a brief overview of Turkish history.

It is surprising that a man of culture like Ağaoğlu could preside over such a slapdash text. In his preface, Ağaoğlu based his work on publications about the Hittites which dated to forty years earlier, to the time of Wright (the finder of the Hamah Stones) and, completely unaware of Hrozný's discoveries of almost a decade earlier, he declared that the Hittite language had not yet been deciphered and concluded that the Hittites could likely be the ancestors of the Turks.[3] Despite being arbitrary, these concepts caught on the public, and most Turks believed the story that the Hittites were their ancestors.

The propaganda was not limited to history. Under Atatürk's auspices, other disciplines like linguistics attempted to bring glory to the newborn country of Turkey by glaringly ignoring common scientific knowledge. Some scholars at the Institute for Turkish Linguistics (another of Atatürk's rather partial creatures) started introducing fanciful theories based on adventurous philology to purport the Turks as the ancestors of the most diverse people, from Sumerians to Etruscans.

Some of the most outlandish ideas were heard on October 5, 1932, at the Turkish National Linguistic Congress. Some members of the Institute for Linguistics tried to subvert the notion that Hittite was an

Indo-European language (almost forty years after Knudtzon demonstrated the Indo-European origin of Hittite). Other members went in the exact opposite direction and proposed that Turkish was an Indo-European language or even came as far as attempting an eccentric compromise: they proposed to change the adjective "Indo-European" into "Turco-European." Outside of Turkey, none of these "Turco-centric" theories gained any traction whatsoever, and they were later abandoned.[4]

Attempts to appropriate the Hittite culture for political reasons were not limited to Turkey. Since its inception, the German Nazi party had been fascinated with theories that placed the German people within a made-up ethnic group called the "Aryan Race." The notion that the Aryan race was superior to all other races followed shortly after. The term Aryan was old (it was introduced in the eighteenth century) and outdated, used only to partially describe a sub-branch of the Indo-European language family in linguistics. Still, the Nazis were keen on finding whatever possible historical support for their theory. In particular, they were looking to find the influence of the Aryan Race on the development of the great civilizations of the Ancient Near East.

Assyria, Babylonia, or Egypt were not suitable to fit in this propaganda because of their proven Semitic origin, so the Nazi echelons tried their luck with the Hittites, who were by then accepted to be of Indo-European origin. Among Winckler's findings at Hattusa were a group of tablets that referred to a people called Hurri or Harri (the signs could be read either way), governed by kings with Indo-European-sounding names like Tushratta. Nazi scholars jumped on the opportunity and immediately proposed an association between the name Harri and their misnomer "Aryan," suggesting that the tablets could prove Aryan presence in Bronze Age Anatolia. Soon, they were proved wrong. Further study showed that the Harri were none other than the Hurrians, the habitants of the Kingdom of Mitanni in northern Mesopotamia, whom we have already encountered in one of the Amarna letters, and they were not of Indo-European ethnicity.*

Back in 1930s Turkey, the propaganda machine was unstoppable, influencing all areas of historical research, archaeology included. Atatürk strongly promoted government-driven campaigns of excavation at Hittite archaeological sites. However, notwithstanding his nationalism, it was soon clear to him that his nascent nation was not self-sufficient in the field.

---

* Hurrians is what they are called today. The Hittites called them "People of Harri," the Egyptians "People of Mitanni" or "People of Nahrin" and the Assyrians "People of Hanigalbat," generating some confusion among historians. We actually do not know what the Hurrians called themselves.

9. Between the Two Wars

There simply were no Turkish archaeologists with sufficient experience to re-initiate the excavations at Hattusa, which had been at a standstill since Winckler and Makridi abandoned the site in 1912. The country still needed foreign archaeologists to direct the excavations.

Once again, the choice fell on a German. In 1929, the Weimar Republic finally succeeded at what Kaiser Wilhelm was trying to do when the Great War broke out and disrupted his plans: opening a permanent German archaeological mission in Anatolia. The institution was the prestigious Istanbul branch of the German Archaeological Institute, and the man who would pick up where Winckler left was called Kurt Bittel (1907–1991).

Bittel was born in a small town in the south of Germany, near the Swabian Alps, where, at the age of just thirteen, he pestered the people at the local department of forestry to permit him to dig out a Celtic tumulus near his house; he then unearthed a Celtic urn with human remains.[5]

After this macabre start, Bittel's fascination for archaeology would follow him throughout his life. Bittel studied archaeology and prehistory with some of the leading scholars of the age in Heidelberg, Marburg, Vienna, and Berlin. In 1930 he won a three-year travel scholarship from the German Archaeological Institute and decided to spend it visiting Anatolia. When Bittel arrived in Istanbul on his scholarship, he was received by the Director of the Istanbul branch of the Institute, German archaeologist Martin Schede (1883–1947), a man who bore an uncanny resemblance—mustache included—to his contemporary Adolf Hitler. Schede invited Bittel to join him on a reconnaissance expedition to Boghazkoy. Bittel was just twenty-three, and the moment he set foot in Hattusa, it was love at first sight. In a few years, he would become the site director, then succeed Schede as Director of the Institute in Istanbul. He would dedicate the following forty years of his life, until his retirement, to Hittitology.

When Bittel arrived at Hattusa for his excavation mission, it was like time had not passed. The expedition was financed by a trust fund established in honor of James Simon, the same man who had financed Winckler's expedition twenty-four years earlier. To welcome Bittel to the site was none other than Zia Bey, now in his sixties: a little aged but still the same flamboyant and high-handed character.

Bittel's early days at Hattusa weren't easy. The first morning, when a large crowd of workers gathered ready to start the dig, Bittel realized that he did not speak a word of Turkish and had no idea how to direct them. In the dismay of the moment, an unfamiliar voice from the crowd addressed him in perfect German: "Morgen Herr Hauptmann" ("good morning, Captain"). The man who spoke these words was a Turkish peasant who had fought in the Great War with a German regiment in Romania. He became his interpreter so Bittel could instruct the workers to start excavating. It wasn't long, though, until he encountered more troubles.

Unbeknownst to Bittel, the overbearing Zia Bey, who had imposed himself as the foreman recruiter and manager, started topping his earnings by taking a substantial cut on the worker's payroll. The workers, offended by an extremely meager pay, went on a strike and proceeded to march towards Bittel's room armed with pickaxes and stones. Bittel understood very little of what was going on but realized there was an easy way out of the life threat: he promptly doubled the worker's pay and saved himself from becoming a martyr of Hittitology.[6]

Once the staff issues were solved, his mission picked up speed and went from one success to another. Bittel was a prehistorian and not a philologist, so his career and modus operandi were opposite to his predecessors at Hattusa. Winckler had only one thing in mind: to unearth as many cuneiform tablets as possible. In contrast, Bittel had a more comprehensive approach, did not restrict himself to one field of archaeology, and consulted many experts from all specialties to organically expand historical knowledge about the Hittites. Nevertheless, and by pure luck, his most significant find was a cache of tablets just within days from the beginning of his excavation. It was the first set of Hittite texts unearthed in two decades, so philologists were understandably excited. Their excitement would be rewarded because some of the tablets in the cache finally shed light on a period of Hittite history that was hitherto little known: the emergence of the so-called New Kingdom, the height of Hittite civilization.

After the death of King Telipinu in 1500 BCE, which ended the Old Hittite Kingdom, the Hittite reign had gone through a century-long period of instability and misfortune, a true dark age. The kingdom re-emerged with King Hattusili II, the first ruler of what historians define as the New Kingdom. The kingdom then re-gained lost territories under King Tudhaliya I/II, who extended Hittite dominion over different people and such a vast territory that it came to be defined as an empire. This moment of expansion, however, was not destined to last long. Hittite history is characterized by a series of dramatic ups and downs. When Tudhaliya III succeeded his father Tudhaliya I/II to the throne, the empire was attacked from all sides, an event which some historians have dubbed the "concentric invasion."

The Kaskan, Hittite archenemies from north Anatolia, the Arzawa lands from west Anatolia, and numerous other hostile people from the south and south-east borders of the empire attacked simultaneously. The enemies forced their way into the core of the Hittite territory, and even the capital Hattusa was sacked. The times were dire. In the famous Amarna letter EA31 (one of the two Arzawa letters studied by Knudtzon, see

Chapter 4), Egyptian pharaoh Amenhotep III writes to the king of Arzawa: "I have heard that everything is finished and that the country Ḫattuša is shattered."[7]

The power vacuum which arose from Hittite weakness may have been the cause for the emergence of Hurrians, who organized themselves in the kingdom known as Mitanni. Mitanni seized control of the northeastern part of Mesopotamia along the Euphrates River and extended into northern Syria. The people of Mitanni were acknowledged horsemanship experts and were sometimes hired by the Hittites to train their army in horse-drawn chariot warfare. One of the earliest Hittite texts translated by Hrozný was a perfectly preserved tablet found by Winckler at Hattusa, the *Kikkuli Text*.

The Text starts with the words: "Thus speaks Kikkuli, master horse trainer of the land of Mitanni." Kikkuli describes in detail the training needed to condition war horses over exactly 214 days. Curiously, modern experts of equine sports have assessed the program suggested by Kikkuli and found that his methods were surprisingly efficient. In 1991, Australian equestrian and researcher Ann Nyland replicated the seven-month training regime described in the Kikkuli Text on Arabian horses. According to Dr. Nyland, the methods were, in some ways, superior to their modern counterparts.[8]

The Hittite Empire had suffered its worst blow yet. After the "concentric invasion" left it militarily and politically on its knees, and Mitanni at the southeast border was gaining strength, the future of the Hittites may not have seemed bright. But a new leader would arrive on the scene, and this leader would be second to none for shrewdness at war and a thirst for power. His name was Suppiluliuma. He may have been a son or son-in-law of Tudhaliya I/II and came to the throne in 1344 BCE. He is the ruler who most contributed to the Hittite expansion; under him, the empire reached its apogee.

For decades, Hittitologists had gathered a piecemeal knowledge of Suppiluliuma. He had become known as the author of one of the Amarna letters addressed to the Egyptian Pharaoh. The letter was poorly preserved and did not conclude much about his kingship, but it was proof that he was a powerful ruler, respected and considered of equal rank by the King of Egypt. When Winckler translated the Akkadian documents he found at Hattusa, Suppiluliuma's name was a recurrent one, and it was understood that the Hittites had expanded their dominion under his leadership.

Ten years later, when Forrer went through the entire extant corpus of Hittite tablets, the character of Suppiluliuma started to be delineated. He was a warrior king. He had been a victorious general when he came to the throne by violently overthrowing his older brother Tudhaliya III. He led countless military campaigns and contributed to re-arrange the international hierarchy of the age. Scholars knew him as a powerful, ruthless, and cunning ruler, but the details of his kingdom were obscure. Forrer realized that spread among the material he studied, there were small pieces of a biography of Suppiluliuma written by one of his sons, but the tablets were highly fragmentary and frustrated all attempts at reconstruction.

But one of Bittel's findings would make all historians' dreams come true: buried under the ruins of Hattusa, he found a longer, readable copy of the text the *Deeds of Suppiluliuma* as told by his son Mursili II. The translation took years. The text fragments were scattered and unearthed over the span of three excavation campaigns between 1931 and 1933. They had to be interpreted and re-ordered, and missing parts had to be integrated with earlier texts from different formats buried in Forrer's archive. It was an actual puzzle, and the scholar who managed to solve it[9] was Hans Gustav Güterbock (1908–2000).

Güterbock was a young, gifted Hittitologist who left Nazi Germany in the nineteen-thirties due to his family's Jewish origins. His efforts in painstakingly reconstructing this maddeningly fragmented text were rewarding. The story told in the biography became a central chapter of the Hittite saga. Historians finally reconstructed the life story of the great Suppiluliuma, who immediately became the best-known Hittite king and probably the only Hittite character to gain a place in popular culture. (A few years later, he would even be featured as one of the main characters in the bestseller novel *Sinuhe the Egyptian*, later made into a Hollywood blockbuster movie.) The *Deeds of Suppiluliuma* depict a man of solid character and humane weaknesses, ultimately a victim of his thirst for power.

After stabilizing Hittite dominion over Anatolia with a series of military incursions, about halfway through his twenty-year reign, Suppiluliuma turned his gaze towards the neighboring kingdom of Mitanni in northern Mesopotamia, populated by the horse-rearing Hurrians and on the rise within the Ancient Near East. Rather than facing the Hurrians militarily, Suppiluliuma chose to back an attempt to a coup to overthrow the Hurrian king Tushratta.

Tushratta, however, was under the protective wing of the Egyptian Empire, and the coup failed. Mitanni and Egypt had amicable relationships: Tushratta's daughter was given as wife to Egyptian pharaoh Amenhotep III, and the two called each other "brother" in their correspondence. Rather than ending up at loggerheads with the Egyptians, Suppiluliuma shifted aim and established a military presence in northern Syria, bordering Egyptian colonies in the area. At the time, Egyptians were going through difficult times with the political instability brought by the reign of heretic pharaoh Akhenaten; they took notice of Suppiluliuma's show

9. Between the Two Wars 115

of muscle and let him know they were withdrawing their protection of Mitanni.

Suppiluliuma turned back onto Mitanni, ordered the assassination of Tushratta, and installed what he thought would be his puppet ruler, General Artatama II, on the throne. Within a very short time, Suppiluliuma was disappointed by Artatama's policies and worried he could allow the other superpower of the age, Assyria, to increase their power into Mitanni. So, in a rapid change of sides, he gave away in marriage his daughter to Kili-Tesub, the son of Tushratta, the very king whom he had assassinated; then, he marched over Mitanni conquering its capital Washukanni, overthrew Artatama, and installed his new son-in-law as ruler of Mitanni, which promptly became a Hittite vassal state. As Australian Hittitologist Trevor Bryce commented: "Suppiluliuma was never one to let promises he had made, or indeed any considerations of honor, loyalty, or fair play, stand in the way of the achievement of his objectives."[10]

Suppiluliuma then went on to attack Karkemish in Hurrian territory as well but in a different region called Ashtata. Rather than keeping the conquered land of Mitanni under one vassal ruler, Suppiluliuma split the country in two and put his son Piyassili on the Ashtata throne. "Divide and rule," the strategy attributed to Alexander the Great, became Suppiluliuma's *modus operandi*. Suppiluliuma's ambition knew no boundaries, and he decided to force his hand on Egypt even more by invading one of the vassal kingdoms at the fringe of their empire, Byblos, in modern-day Lebanon.

Had the Egyptian Empire been going through a good phase, such an act of hostility would have resulted in a military retaliation. However, Egypt was undergoing a crisis in leadership. The Egyptians did try a timid resistance in the occupied colony but without the involvement of the central army. The Hittite court must have been on high alert, waiting for a message of reaction from the Egyptian court, a threat, or the request for a meeting, but no such news arrived. Instead, what did arrive from Egypt was one of the most bizarre requests in the history of ancient diplomacy, probably the earliest international scandal of which we have a record. According to the *Deeds*, one day, an Egyptian envoy came to Suppiluliuma as he and his entourage were camped outside Karkemish. He carried a letter written by the queen of Egypt.* The letter bore a concise, unexpected message: "My husband died. I do not have a son. But they say you have

---

* In the account, the name of the queen is Dakhamunzu. Scholars think that the Dakhamunzu of the Hittite account is not the proper name of the queen, but rather a Hittite phonetic rendering of the Egyptian expression *t3 ḥmt nswt* which means "the wife of the King," i.e., the Queen. Historians have tried to identify what queen the account refers to and the most likely hypothesis is Ankhesenamen, Tutankhamun's widow.

many sons. If you would give me one of your sons, he would become my husband. I could never accept to choose a subject of mine and make him my husband. I am afraid."[11]

The Hittites were appalled. There they were, challenging Egyptian dominion with military incursions, showing their muscles, and getting ready for a confrontation, and what they received instead was a proposal of matrimony? Suppiluliuma and his entourage were well-versed in arranging political weddings, but as far as proposals of matrimony went, this was the most unexpected. Hittites were fully aware that it was not the custom of the Egyptians to give away in marriage female members of the royal family. Whoever married into the Egyptian Royal Family became the ruler of the oldest nation on Earth *and* a deity. In one of the Amarna Letters, a member of the "Club of Brothers," Babylon King Kadasman-Enlil famously questioned Pharaoh Amenhotep III's reluctance to give away one of his daughters in marriage to a foreign king:

> My brother, when I wrote to you about marrying your daughter, in accordance with your practice of not giving a daughter, you wrote to me saying, "From time immemorial no daughter of the King of Egypt is ever given to anyone." Why not? You are king, you do as you please! Were you to give a daughter who would say anything? Since I was told of this message I wrote as follows to my brother saying "Someone's beautiful grown daughters must be available! Send me a beautiful woman as if she were your daughter. Who is going to say she is not the daughter of the King?"[12]

But besides going against the custom of a centuries-old tradition, the message sent to Suppiluliuma was a sign of the weakness of the Egyptian court. The Queen made it clear by writing "I am afraid" and revealing that her position was at stake. If one of the sons of Suppiluliuma would travel to Egypt, marry the Queen, and become ruler of the most powerful empire of the age, the only serious obstacle to Hittite supremacy over the whole of the Near East would cease to exist. But the offer seemed too good to be true: Suppiluliuma was skeptical. He summoned his chamberlain Hattusa-ziti and sent him to Egypt with these words: "Go and bring the true word back to me! Maybe they want to deceive me! Maybe, in fact, they do have a son of their lord!" It took months, but Hattusa-ziti eventually returned to Hattusa, accompanied by an Egyptian ambassador with a new message for the king of the Hittites. The new message, if possible, even more appalling than the previous, read:

> Why did you accuse me of deceiving you in that way? Had I a son, would I have written to my own and my country's shame to a foreign land? You did not believe me and even spoke thus to me! He who was my husband has died. I don't have a son! Never shall I take a subject of mine and make him my husband! I have written to no other country; I have written only to you! They say

your sons are many: so, give me one son of yours! To me, he will be husband, but to Egypt, he will be king.

The Egyptian ambassador, a man called Hani, spoke too and reportedly stated the same argument as the Queen. Suppiluliuma was still diffident and angrily replied: "You keep asking me for a son of mine as if it were my duty. He will in some way become a hostage, but king you will not make him!" In the end, reluctantly but pressed by his advisors, Suppiluliuma agreed to send one of his sons. His firstborn, Arnuwanda, was the heir to the throne; he could not risk him, so he chose his middle son Zannanza. Zannanza and his entourage packed their belongings and left for Egypt. Sadly, Suppiluliuma's fears became a reality. Zannanza's traveling party was ambushed on the way to Egypt, and Zannanza was killed.

We will never know who killed Zannanza and why. However, it is reasonable to imagine that the idea of a Hittite prince marrying the Queen of Egypt may have worried many in the Egyptian court. In Egyptian tradition, whoever married the widowed Queen would have become the nation's leader. Many at the court aspired to take that role. The delicate balance of international powers was at stake. Suppiluliuma had made the Hittite the most powerful empire of the age. With one son leading Mitanni and another leading Egypt, Hittite supremacy over the Near East would have no boundaries.

After Zannanza's assassination, the Queen eventually married an Egyptian named Ay. The move was not very successful: Ay reigned for a mere four years, an uncharacteristically

New Kingdom

Hattusili II	1420 – 1400
Tudhaliya I	1400 – 1390
Arnuwanda I	1390 – 1380
Tudhaliya II	1380 – 1370
Tudhaliya III	1370
Suppiluliuma I	1370 – 1330
Arnuwanda II	1330
Mursili II	1330 – 1295
Muwatalli II	1295 – 1282
Mursili III	1282 – 1275
Hattusili III	1275 – 1245
Tudhaliya IV	1245 – 1215
Arnuwanda III	1215 – 1210
Suppiluliuma II	1210 – 1190

List of kings of the New Kingdom. The existence of Hattusili II is disputed. It is still debated whether there were two separate kings, Tudhaliya I and Tudhaliya II, or one single king who lost power and then regained it. For this reason, it is customary to refer to a king "Tudhaliya I/II." All dates are BCE and according to the Middle Chronology.

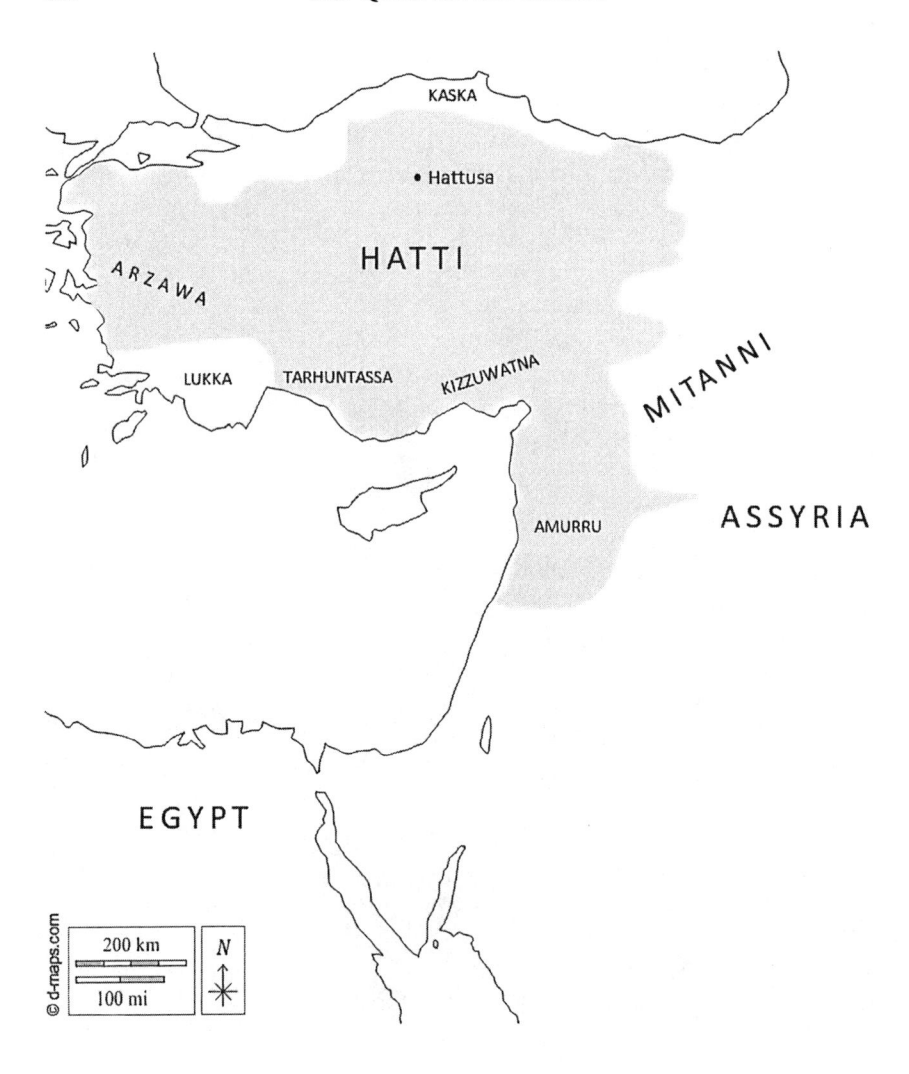

The Ancient Near East around 1300 BCE. In grey, the extension of the Hittite Empire. By the author. www.d-maps.com.

short kingdom in ancient Egypt, and underwent *damnatio memoriae*, the erasing of his name from inscriptions and monuments, at the hands of his successor. At the Hittite court, Suppiluliuma was furious. He was sure that his son had been the victim of a political assassination, a plan of deception by the Egyptians. He addressed the gods, crying: "Oh gods! I did no evil, yet the people of Egypt did this to me, and they also attacked the frontier of my country."

The honor of the Hittite royal house was at stake. Suppiluliuma had to retaliate, and he retaliated the only way he knew, with a severe military offense into Egyptian territory, conquering the Egyptian colony of Amqu in modern-day Lebanon. At the end of this successful campaign Suppiluliuma triumphally returned to his capital, Hattusa, followed by thousands of war prisoners in shackles. The parade was supposed to be a vindication of his son Zannanza. Still, in a twist of destiny, his pride turned back heavily against the Hittite people: the Egyptian prisoners carried with them the plague.

10

From Plague to Family Dramas

In 1300 BCE, the plague became the scourge of the Near East. Modern historians learned about the plague through one of the Amarna Letters. When scholars translated EA96 in 1962, they came across a curious exchange that took place at the beginning of the epidemic. It was a letter written to Rib-Addi, King of Byblos, an Egyptian colony in modern-day Lebanon, by one of his generals. In the letter, the general appears worried, reporting a pestilence affecting Simyra, a coastal city within the kingdom. The general agrees with his King's decision of not letting any man from Simyra within the walls of Byblos to prevent the contagion. However, he cannot understand the King's decision of not letting in the donkeys which carried goods. "What pestilence affects donkeys so they cannot walk?"[1] he asked.

Clearly, the general failed to understand that the donkeys were perfectly able to walk, but the King realized that they could carry the plague and wisely banned them from entering Byblos. Although King Rib-Addi did not know how the donkeys could carry the plague, he would go down in history as the first ruler to enforce a public health policy against an epidemic. It would take medicine another three millennia to figure out how livestock transmitted disease to humans: through the bites of fleas which at that time would commonly infest animals as much as humans. Paleopathologists, scientists who study ancient diseases, wonder which bacteria were responsible for the Near East plague of the Late Bronze Age.

In an article from 2007,[2] it was hypothesized that the germ responsible for the plague was *Francisella tularensis*, a bacteria known to infect animals (mainly rodents) and occasionally infect humans, which could cause pneumonia and would have been highly lethal in the pre-antibiotic age. Somehow the article has become very popular in archaeological circles and was even quoted in monographies on disease in the ancient world.[3] Unfortunately, there is no biological or epidemiological evidence

10. From Plague to Family Dramas

to back this hypothesis, which was the result of pure guesswork. At the time, the journal in which it was published, *Medical Hypotheses*, was not peer-reviewed and was notorious for publishing wildly implausible theories bordering pseudoscience.[4] No further research has proven or corroborated the hypothesis that the Hittite plague was an epidemic of tularemia.

Based on the history of human epidemics, on the other hand, the most likely infectious agent responsible for the disease is *Yersinia pestis*, the same pathogen which caused the Black Death, the epidemic which brought Europe to its knees in the Late Middle Ages, killing a third of its population.

Not all ancient rulers were as cautious as Rib-Addi, enforcing quarantines, so the plague spread relentlessly and was rampaging through Canaan when Suppiluliuma attacked to avenge the assassination of his son Zannanza. It is thought that when Suppiluliuma brought his war prisoners and their livestock back to Hattusa, the epidemic broke out among his people and quickly spread throughout the Hittite territory. Suppiluliuma contracted the plague and died. The reign of the still young warrior-king, the man who single-handedly turned the Hittite Kingdom into an empire, ended abruptly. The throne went to his son Arnuwanda, but his was a very short reign. Within months he fell ill with the plague and died.

Suppiluliuma had five children. With one child assassinated, one dead of plague, one already sitting on the throne of the Hurrians, and one serving as High Priest at the empire's periphery, there was only one natural successor to the throne left: his name was Mursili II. Mursili II was a promising young man who immediately stepped on the throne, but his reign was difficult. Throughout it, he had to deal with the catastrophe of the plague and the problem of being considered too young to be a king.

Historians had just learned about the life and deeds of Suppiluliuma through the translation of his newly recovered biography when in 1933, two years later, another lucky excavation at Hattusa recovered the biography of Suppiluliuma's heir, Mursili II.

The tablets of Mursili II biography were translated and published almost entirely by one of the giants of Hittitology, the man who most advanced cuneiform studies in America. His name was Albrecht Götze (1897–1971), and he was born in Leipzig, Germany, in the early 1930s.[5] He was a brilliant student of linguistics, versed in Indo-European and Semitic languages, who would have made a brilliant career in his own country had it not been for the scourge of Nazism. When the Nazi party started gaining ground, Götze foresaw the dangers and campaigned against it, distributing flyers around town.

The moment the Nazi party took absolute power, Götze was a marked man, dismissed from his university post by the Nazi regime in November 1933 for being deemed "politically unreliable." It didn't matter that he was a war hero (injured three times during the Great War) and an excellent scholar; his only option was to leave the country. He spent some time in Norway and Denmark before relocating to the USA with his family, having been offered a position at Yale. In America, his research skyrocketed, and he became one of the most prominent linguists in the country.

Götze was loved by his students for his gentle disposition, respected by the other academicians for his knowledge, and courted by publishers for his brilliant writing. He became a household name within the circles of American orientalism. This discipline was gaining momentum on that side of the Atlantic (with a delay of several decades compared to European orientalism). But for how gentle and humble he was, Götze was a man with a grudge. The grudge he bore was against his homeland, Germany: a nation that disappointed him and let him down. He swore not to write in German for the rest of his life and even came to the point of speaking English when he went back to visit Germany years later. Götze's most significant contribution to Hittitology was the translation of the *Annals* of Mursili II, a document in several copies of different lengths, an autobiographical record of the first ten years out of the twenty-year kingdom of Mursili II.

The story told in the *Annals* is touching. It is the living parable of a king who came to the throne very fast, young, and unprepared after the death of his father, Suppiluliuma, and his brother Arnuwanda, and immediately found out how hard it was to be a ruler in the Bronze Age. Like a pack of wolves sniffing fear in the weakest pup, the other kings scornfully threatened him. An unnamed enemy king wrote him: "You are a child. You know nothing and instill no fear in me. Your land is now ruins, and your infantry and chariots are few. Against your infantry, I have many infantries; against your chariots, I have many chariots. Your father had many infantries and chariots. But you, who is a child, how can you match him?"[6]

Right from the opening of the *Annals*, a pattern emerges: Mursili II is compelled to justify his acts and decisions in front of the gods and the readers. Of course, he had to attack his neighbors: they had humiliated him, calling him a child. Of course, he had to burn and sack cities, deport prisoners, raid the countryside, and extort taxes: he had to vindicate his people. Despite the dry prose and line after line repetitively listing military campaigns, at a deeper level, the autobiography shows an internal struggle. The struggle of a reluctant warrior, a man who was catapulted too

10. From Plague to Family Dramas

young into the role of successor to the most potent Hittite king ever and felt the weight of this responsibility.

The Hittite population was overwhelmed by the plague. Priests were constantly asked to devise rituals and sacrifices to persuade the gods to relieve the country from it. In 1976, British Hittitologist Oliver Robert Gurney (1911–2001) published the translation of a tablet containing a ritual for sending the plague away from a military camp. The ritual, called *Ritual of Askhella* after the priest who wrote it, gives an interesting insight into the Hittite belief system. According to the Ritual of Askhella, a priest should prepare several rams by adorning them with amulets. Then he should hand them with ritual bread to a woman who should herd them away from the military camp.

> Then they bring the rams and the woman and the bread through the camp and they drive them away onto the steppe. And the rams run away to the enemy border without coming to any place of ours. And they say repeatedly as follows: "Behold! Whatever evil there was in the camp among the men, oxen, sheep, horses, mules, and donkeys, now, behold! These rams and this woman have taken it away from the camp. And the one that finds them may that land take this evil plague."[7]

At first sight, this is a classic "scapegoat" ritual attested in many ancient cultures: the evil which afflicts the community is symbolically transferred to a scapegoat (in this case, "scapesheep" as the subjects of the ritual are rams) and sent away from the community. The twist of this Hittite version is that the ritual not only takes away the disease from the camp but also transfers it to the enemy country. This may not just be a symbolic subtlety: because rams, like other livestock, can be carriers of plague themselves, it is possible that Hittites could have used them to transfer the disease to their enemies, making this history the earliest example of biological warfare.[8]

Priests were busy throughout the country attempting to appease the gods and keep the plague away with all manners of rituals. Mursili II, who as king was the highest priest, was believed to be in direct communication with the gods. Therefore, he, on repeated occasions, officially invoked their intervention on behalf of the entire population to put a stop to the plague. Once again, it was through a translation by Albrecht Götze that historians learned about Mursili II's prayers against the plague.

Mursili II's prayers against the plague form an exceptional document. They show the peculiarities of Hittite religion and the unique relationship of Mursili II with his gods and provide unique insight into the politics of the age. To modern eyes, Mursili II's prayers to relieve the Hittites from the pestilence appear very odd. They do not even appear as prayers. They are more a harangue, a well-articulated speech in which the king-priest tries to persuade the gods of why it would be better for them to stop testing his people with the disease. In religious literature, this style is sometimes defined as *argumenta ad Deum*, which roughly translates as "arguing with God" and is characteristic of Hittite prayers.[9] The style appears even more peculiar compared to Christian prayers written for the same purpose at times of pestilence through the centuries. For example, a ninth century CE Christian Irish monk, Sedulius Scottus, praying for the end of a plague, wrote to his God:

> May you shine upon us your former compassion; we beg you to hear us. Destroy our evil deeds, we pray; save us, blessed Prince. Disperse dark shadows covering our minds, faithful light of the world. Holy of Holies, Lord of kings, may your right hand be with your lowly ones, may your serene face look upon us, or else we perish.[10]

Whereas the Christian monk assumes the sinners have sinned, calling upon themselves a deserved punishment, and begs for mercy, Mursili II's prose could not be more different. Addressing his gods, he opens by making no secret of his disappointment:

> What have you done? You have let loose the plague in the land of Hatti. And the land of Hatti has been sorely, heavily oppressed by it. Under my father and my brother, there was constant dying. And since I became a priest of the gods, there is now constant dying under me. Behold, it is twenty years since people have been continually dying in the land of Hatti. Will the plague never be eliminated from the land of Hatti?[11]

He resentfully reminds the gods how good the Hittites had been at honoring them. He implies that they should not deserve such a punishment:

> Only in Hatti you have lofty temples adorned with silver and gold, and in no other land are there any such for you. Only in Hatti you have cups of silver, gold, and precious stones. Only in Hatti they celebrate festivals for you—the festival of the month, festivals throughout the course of the year, winter, spring and fall, and the festivals of the sacrificial rituals. In no other land do they perform anything for you?

Then he deviously proposes that the gods should punish someone else instead of the Hittites: "The Kaska land ... they discontinued the payment of their tributes and began to attack Hatti. ... Let this become a further reason for vengeance for the Sun-goddess of Arinna. Goddess, do not degrade your own name!"

Then he argues that it is unfair that the whole population should suffer if only some have sinned: "Whoever is a cause of rage and anger to the gods, and whoever is not respectful to the gods, let not the good ones perish with the evil ones. Whether it is a single town, a single house, or a

10. From Plague to Family Dramas

single person, oh gods, destroy only that one! Look upon Hatti with pity and give the evil plague to other lands."

Finally, he makes passive-aggressive threats: "You have allowed a plague into Hatti, and the whole of Hatti is dying.... The grinding women who used to make the offering bread for the gods have died, so they do not make the god's offering bread any longer." Implying that if the gods let this punishment go on, it will be to their detriment.

It is hard to fully appreciate Mursili II's arguments if looking at them with modern eyes. Religion at the time of the Hittites was more utilitarian than in our times. It is a peculiarity of Hittite prayers to include a transaction in which "the supplicant promises something valuable in order to persuade the gods to forgive the sins."[12] In antiquity, it was customary for believers to perform rituals not out of love or devotion but out of fear of repercussion from the disgruntled deities; the cult was based mainly on appeasing supernatural entities rather than their worshipping.

The scholar who most contributed to our understanding of the prayers is Itamar Singer (1946–2012). Born in Romania to Hungarian Jewish parents, he grew up and studied in Israel, where he became a professor and the leading Hittitologist. His studies, which brought him to teach and work at academic institutions on five continents, left a powerful mark in the field.

Mursili II's prayers are hugely helpful also for historical reasons. In one of the prayers from his tenth year of reign, Mursili II refers to the Sun-God as giving "a sign." Researchers have proposed that the sign of the Sun-God could have been an eclipse. There is astronomical evidence for solar eclipses visible from Anatolia in 1312 and 1308 BCE. While historians debate over the former or the latter as the most likely observed by Mursili II, in either case, this would place Mursili II's ascent to the throne between 1322 and 1318 BCE, which would strongly favor the Short Chronology over the Middle Chronology (see Chapter 7 regarding the Ancient Near East Chronology).

The episode of the "sign" from the Sun-God is mentioned in the context of another contentious relationship. Through one of his translations, Singer tells us how Mursili II resented Suppiluliuma's last wife, the reigning queen-mother of Babylonian origin, Tawananna. According to Mursili II, the cause of this resentment was that she had interpreted the Sun-God sign as an omen predicting his death. The relationship between Mursili II and queen-mother Tawananna became so tense that he had her exiled, accusing her of praying to the gods for the death of his wife, Gassulawiya. In a document called *Mursili's Accusations Against Tawananna*, also translated by Singer, Mursili II says that while Gassulawiya was in poor health.

He describes Tawananna as "standing day and night before the gods and cursing my wife before the gods ... and she wishes for her death," saying: "let her die!"[13]

Nor are the contents of Mursili II's prayers less relevant from a political history standpoint. Mursili II's purpose was to prove to the gods that he and his people did not deserve such punishment. Therefore, in the *Plague Prayers*, he reviewed the current political situation, providing precious insight into the history of his reign as he tried to justify the acts of his father. At one point, he explains that it is true that his father Suppiluliuma made an unwarranted military attack on the Egyptian empire, but he writes that the Hittites regret that and hopes that it can be considered "water under the bridge." In another very relevant passage, he refers to how his father came to power: "Now I have confessed it to you, oh gods. Because my father [killed (?)] Tudhaliya, my father, therefore, performed a ritual for the expiation of blood."

The most critical word of the entire text, "killed," is questioned because the text was corrupted and Götze could not confidently read it. However, the context is quite telling. Mursili II is embarrassed by his father's behavior as a sanguinary leader. Once again, the character which transpires through Mursili II's autobiographic writings is that of a man fighting an internal struggle. In the *Annals*, he appears as a reluctant warrior. In the *Plague Prayer*, a man torn by regret for the actions of his family. This was not a unique trait in Hittite history as one of his sons and successors lived through a similar internal struggle: his youngest son Hattusili, initially a minor figure in court but destined to become later central in Hittite history. At the death of Mursili II, the crown went to the oldest son, Muwatalli II.

Muwatalli II inherited a relatively stable empire, which was slowly recovering from twenty years of plague and extended from the Aegean Sea to the Euphrates River and along the coast of the western Mediterranean into modern-day Lebanon. After a few years of reign, Muwatalli II moved the empire's capital from Hattusa to the south-eastern city of Tarhuntassa, in the area the Hittites called the Lower Lands. Historians have not been able to figure out the reason for this move. On the one hand, Hattusa was a complex city to protect as it was dangerously close to territories populated by marauding nomadic tribes, so the decision may have been based on military advice. On the other hand, the reasons may have been based purely on religious choices.[14]

Evidence tells that Muwatalli II elevated his personal deity, the Storm-God Pihassassi, to a leading role in the Hittite pantheon and his seals, which he used for signature, show his name consecrated to this god only. Tarhuntassa was the town where the cult of the Storm-God originated, so the move bears resemblance with Pharaoh Akhenaton's move of the Egyptian capital from Thebes to Akhetaten in honor of Aten. Muwatalli II knew that he could not just abandon Hattusa and the north of the reign, the area the Hittites called the Upper Land, so he appointed his brother Hattusili as its governor by making him king of the city of Hakpis. Hattusili was one of the generals who fought for King Muwatalli II when he led the Hittites against the Egyptians in the famous Battle of Kadesh, of which we read in Chapter 3, he was celebrated and respected for his courage and strength and, as we will see soon, he was destined to become a key figure in Hittite history.

When Muwatalli II died, after a reign of 23 years, the crown passed to one of his sons, Urhi-Tesub, who ascended to the throne with the name of Mursili III in 1282 BCE. Mursili III had an unfortunate reign. It was short—just seven years; it saw the empire being attacked and losing a part of its territory and ended in a family drama created by the jealousy of his uncle Hattusili.

At the time, the main threat to Hittite dominance came from Assyria. The long-reigning King of Assyria, Adad-nirari, was an ambitious warrior who had succeeded in unifying a large portion of Mesopotamia by defeating and subjugating the Kassites, who ruled over Babylonia, the region to the south, and also by conquering minor states east and north of Assyria. Towards the end of his reign, Adad-nirari's appetite for conquest turned towards Mitanni. Mitanni, once an independent and powerful state, had now been a Hittite vassal state for many years and acted as a buffer between Hittite and Assyrian territory. With a bold move, Adad-nirari invaded Mitanni, deposed its king Shattuara and took control of the capital Washukanni. Adad-nirari may have been a victorious warrior, but diplomatic tact, he had not. Shortly after his conquest of Mitanni, he wrote to Mursili III, from whom he had just snatched a vassal state, and in a letter destined to become famous, he took the unilateral decision of greeting him as "brother" and even invited himself to visit Mount Amman (a place of worship) in "his brother's territory."

Mursili III was furious. How dare this lowly Assyrian king address him as a brother right after snatching a territory which had been under the Hittite rule for so long? What impudence. His reply became a classic in the history of ancient diplomacy: "You keep on talking about your conquest … of the land of Hurri … and how you have become a Great King. But why do you keep on calling me brother and asking to visit Mount Amman? What brotherhood? And what visit to Mount Amman? Why should I call you brother? … Were you and I born to the same mother? As my grandfather and my father did not call the King of Assyria 'brother,' you shall not write to me about brotherhood and great kingship. It is not my wish."[15] Truncating any hope of peace between the Hittites and Assyrians.*

If Mursili III's foreign relationships were not easy, the most serious issues were at home within his empire and, ultimately, within his own family. Mursili III recognized that his father's move of the capital to Tarhuntassa did not work. He probably suspected that this could bring to fragmentation of the empire, so he packed up the statues of the gods, which belonged to the state capital and his cult, and moved back the capital to Hattusa. As yet another act to contrast past with decisions, he also reinstated one of Muwatalli II's widows, Danuhepa, in the role of *tawananna* or Great Queen.

But the move back to Hattusa was not free from complications. The old capital was within the sphere of interest of his uncle Hattusili. Hattusili was disappointed, and his displease grew even more, when the king sought to further reduce his power by seizing the cities of Hakpis and Nerik, two of Hattusili's strongholds.

This was more than Hattusili could tolerate. He was consumed by jealousy of his nephew. Hattusili had helped Mursili III rise to the throne, but the king was now stripping him of all his power. Hattusili is one of the most complex characters in Hittite history.

Although growing up as a sickly child, he had become a successful military leader. He had no shortage of allies who would not hesitate to go to battle with him, so he decided to march over Hattusa to attack the legitimate king. For this strike, Hattusili even enlisted mercenaries from the Kaska tribes, Hittite archenemies. Mursili was at a numeric disadvantage and in hostile territory. He retreated to the nearby city of Samuha, which was quickly placed under siege (Hattusili would later write "like a pig in a sty"). Once the city fell, Mursili III was captured and moved to a couple of different locations before finally making an escape and seeking refuge in Egypt under Ramesses II, the pharaoh who had fought against his father Muwatalli II at Kadesh.

In 1275 BCE, Hattusili, now on the throne at Hattusa as Hattusili III, immediately wrote to pharaoh Ramesses II demanding that his nephew

---

* Assyrian kings had a tradition of diplomatic audacity. Years earlier, Adad-nirari's great-grandfather Assur-uballit wrote to the Pharaoh of Egypt announcing that, although his predecessors had never written to the Pharaoh, he was now initiating a correspondence. Basically, he was trying to break into the "Club of Brothers." The Pharaoh graciously accepted to correspond with Assur-uballit and sent a gift of gold as a propitiative gesture. Assur-uballit's appalling reply was: "I am the equal of the king of Hanigalbat, but you sent me an amount of gold which is not even enough to pay my messengers on the journey to and back! If your purpose is to keep our friendship, send me more gold" (EA16, via Moran, W.L.).

10. From Plague to Family Dramas

be extradited to Hattusa. Ramesses II denied knowledge of Mursili III's whereabouts, leading to tense relationships between the two rulers. The fleet to Egypt of ousted king Mursili III is a detail to remember, as it will come back again as a point of contention shortly.

Hattusili III is the Hittite ruler of whom we have the most extensive written record. Archaeologists found hundreds of letters and documents written during his reign at Hattusa. Still, of all of them, none is as striking as the autobiographic account called the *Apology of Hattusili III*.

Like the Annals written by his father, Mursili II, the *Apology* is a long text that provides a double insight. On the one hand, it tells us about the character, allowing the reader to understand the internal struggle Hattusili III, like his father, had to endure. On the other hand, it provides a precious historical record.

> For seven years, I submitted to the king. But at a divine command and with human urging, Urhi-Tesub* sought to destroy me. He took Hakpis and Nerik from me. Now I submitted to him no longer. I made war against him. But I did not do this in a violent way, by rising up against him with chariots or in the palace. No, in civilized manner I told him: "You have begun hostilities with me. Now you are a Great King, but I am king of only one fortress. That is all you have left me. Come! Istar of Samuha and the Storm-God of Nerik shall decide the case for us!"† Since I wrote to Urhi-Tesub in this manner, if anyone now says: "Why after previously making him king do you now write to him about war?" (my reply would be) "If he had not begun fighting with me, would Istar and the Storm-God have now subjected him to a small king?" Because he began fighting with me, the gods have subjected him to me by their judgement.[16]

As in several other Hittite documents, such as the *Annals* and the *Plague Prayers*, "justification" is the central theme of Hattusili III's *Apology*. Already from the first pages, the new king is keen to depict himself as the one who was forced to take action to straighten things up, and, to strengthen his point, he describes the tremendous support he received from the international community after the events: "The kings (who were) my elders (and) who had been on good terms with me, they remained on just those good terms with me, and they began to send envoys to me. They began to send gifts to me, and the gifts they keep sending me, they never sent to any (of my) fathers and grandfathers." Making himself out as a ruler who was liked even more than his predecessors.

---

* When he ascended to the throne, Urhi-Tesub took the regnal name of Mursili (III). The fact that Hattusili III refers to him by his given name may be interpreted as a sign of disrespect for his title.

† This expression meant he was inviting him to a military confrontation, a pitched battle.

Even if his autobiography had clear propagandistic aims, Hattusili III must have been a skilled diplomat. It was he who, in the thirteenth year of his reign, signed the Egyptian-Hittite peace treaty with Ramesses II. The treaty seen in Chapter 1, inscribed in the temple halls of Karnak and translated by Champollion, and of which Winckler found an exact copy in Akkadian in Hattusa. This historical treaty marks the beginning of what Itamar Singer called *Pax Hethitica*, a golden age of stability and prosperity in Hittite history. It wasn't fated to last long, but it was indeed a time of economic and cultural flourishing and good relationships with neighboring countries. That the relationships with Egypt became excellent is well documented. Trade routes were opened, and marriages between royal houses were arranged.

The level of friendliness between the pharaoh and the Hittite king was unprecedented. When his sister Massanauzzi, who had married Masturi, the king of Mira (a small vassal state in west Anatolia), failed to have children, Hattusili III did not hesitate to write to Ramesses II and ask him to send an Egyptian physician to help her: "I would be most grateful if you would send me a man to prepare medicines so that my sister may bear children," although later admitting that the request was quite unusual, as the princess was no longer a young woman[17] (quite an understatement, as the lady was pushing sixty, hence some objection from the pharaoh in his polite reply).

Hattusili even tried to rekindle the relationship which King Adad-nirari of Assyria wanted to begin and which Mursili III rejected with contempt. In a letter to Adad-nirari, Hattusili III wrote: "Did not my father send you fine gifts? When I assumed the kingship, you did not send a messenger to me. It is the custom that when kings assume kingship, the kings, his equals in rank, send him appropriate gifts of greeting, clothing befitting kingship, and fine oil for his anointing. But you did not do this today."[18] This, which may sound like a bitter reprimand, could also be interpreted as an opening to friendship with Assyria. In the letter, Hattusili III invites Adad-nirari to recognize him as king equal in rank and start their relationship afresh. There is evidence that this attempt worked, likely because it spoke the straightforward and cynical language of the Assyrian royals. Later, the two would address each other as brothers.

The *Apology* also introduces another important character of Hittite history: Hattusili III's spouse Queen Puduhepa, a real "Iron Lady" and central character of the Bronze Age. Puduhepa was not Hittite; she came from yet another of the many vassal states of the empire, Kizzuwatna, in the highlands of south-east Anatolia, an area primarily populated by Hurrians. When Hattusili met Puduhepa, he was a respected warrior, a general of the Hittite army coming back victorious from Kadesh, probably in his

10. From Plague to Family Dramas

forties, when he stopped at Lawazantiya, a town in Kizzuwatna (tentatively identified as modern-day Sirkeli). There he met Puduhepa, of priestly lineage, aged just fifteen but the main priestess of the goddess Ishtar, a divinity of Mesopotamian origin. Hattusili III remembers: "At the behest of the goddess, I took Puduhepa, the daughter of Pentisarri, the priest, for my wife: we joined (in matrimony), and the goddess gave us the love of husband and wife. We made ourselves sons and daughters." The marriage of this celebrity couple must have made the news of the age. Puduhepa would remain his loyal wife for the rest of his life, a caring companion who, when Hattusili III became old and suffered from foot or eye ailments, appealed to the gods on his behalf to heal him.

As in many modern-day stories, the ascent to the throne of Hattusili III catapulted his spouse Puduhepa into the limelight. Instead of taking her role passively, like so many other Hittite queens before her, Puduhepa became a strong female leader in her own right. For the first time in Hittite history, a queen was not subject and inferior to her king but they ruled together. She was depicted reigning hand in hand with Hattusili III in official portraits, and she used her seal for signing correspondence and pronouncements. Archaeologists even found evidence of her decisions on how to run the royal palaces and her judging of court cases. Puduhepa was even one of the co-signatories of the Egyptian-Hittite peace treaty.

Among other things, Puduhepa was strong on foreign relationships. Her correspondence with Pharaoh Ramesses II of Egypt, addressing him as a brother, and with Ramesses II's wife, the great Nefertari, addressing her as a sister, represents a historical change: the Bronze Age "Club of Brothers" became a "Club of Brothers and Sisters."

Hittitologists found evidence of Puduhepa's fond relationship with the legendary Nefertari, who would write her:

> The great Queen Naptera* of the land of Egypt speaks thus: tell my sister Puduhepa, the Great Queen of the Land of Hatti: I, your sister, am also well. May your country be well. Now, I have learned that you, my sister, have written to me asking about my health. You have written to me because of the good friendship and brotherly relationship between your husband and my brother, the great pharaoh of Egypt. The Storm-God will bring about peace, and he will make the brotherly relationship between the Great Egyptian Pharaoh and his brother, the Great King of Hatti, last forever. See, I have sent you a gift to greet you, my sister. For your neck, a necklace of pure gold, composed of twelve bands and weighing eighty-eight shekels, coloured linen *muklalu* fabric, for one royal dress for the king. A total of twelve linen garments.[19]

---

* Hittite rendition of the name Nefertari. The Hittites did not have a sign to express the sound of the letter f, hence the alteration.

Puduhepa was also known for international matchmaking skills, organizing diplomatic marriages for her children and other royalties' children. Two of her daughters were sent to Egypt to be married to the pharaoh. Still today, visitors to Abu Simbel temple in Upper Egypt can see a large stele that records the marriage of the pharaoh and the Hittite king's daughter.

The first daughter's marriage was slightly delayed by difficulties in putting together an appropriate dowry. The letter in which Puduhepa explains this to Ramesses II contains an extremely prickly reference to a still contentious matter: "I have indeed withheld my daughter.... At the moment, I am not able to give her to you. As you, my brother, know, the House of Hatti ... is depleted, and Urhi-Tesub (Mursili III) gave what remained to the Great God. Since Urhi-Tesub is there, ask him if this is so or not so."[20] Cheekily implying that she believed the ousted king, Urhi-Tesub, was still a refugee in Egyptian territory and had not been returned yet. However, Ramesses II had repeatedly denied knowledge of his whereabouts.

The destiny of fugitive ex-king Urhi-Tesub must have been an actual irritation for Hattusili III and Puduhepa. The Egyptian-Hittite treaty they signed even included a clause on the mutual rendition of political refugees. This was thought to have been added to obtain closure on the matter; however, no record of what eventually happened to Urhi-Teshup has ever been found. Therefore, it is unclear if the rendition finally happened.

Puduhepa married another of her daughters to King Kadashman-Enlil II of Babylon, and the daughter of another Babylon king called Kudur-Enlil was accepted to marry into the Hittite royal family, paving the way for a friendship and an alliance with the Babylonians. The news of this intermingling with Babylon even reached Pharaoh Ramesses II, who wrote to Queen Puduhepa to criticize it, as he no longer regarded Babylon as politically significant. Puduhepa's replied to Ramesses II's critiques with great confidence: "If you say, 'The king of Babylon is not a Great King,' then you do not know the status of Babylon."[21]

Hattusili III knew that his leadership had a stain: the coup he made to seize power from his nephew, and he knew the rest of the royal family was not entirely happy with what he did. To appease the opposition, he granted his other nephew, Kurunta, brother of the ousted Mursili III, the regency of Tarhuntassa, which was vacant after the restoration of the capital in Hattusa, creating what is usually referred to as an "appanage kingdom." Although Mursili III was his archenemy, Hattusili III bore no hard feelings towards Mursili's brother Kurunta. A bronze tablet found in 1986 states, "When my father, Hattusili, revolted against Urhi-Tesub, son of Muwatalli and deposed him from kingship, no blame whatsoever attached

10. From Plague to Family Dramas

to Kurunta. For however, the people of Hatti had been at fault, Kurunta was in no way whatsoever [involved] in [the wrong side]."[22]

As the history of modern Europe teaches, appanage kingdoms help decrease the risk of internal opposition but, in the long run, bring political fragmentation. Hattusili III was starting a process of disaggregation of the empire, which would eventually contribute to its collapse.

When Hattusili III died, the crown was passed to his son, Tudhaliya (Tudhaliya IV for historians). The great queen Puduhepa survived Hattusili and became active in religious reforms in her new role as queen mother. Being of Hurrian ethnicity and priestly lineage, Puduhepa imported to Hatti the cults and rites of her country of origin. Throughout their history, Hittites were very inclusive of foreign religious beliefs and deities. The main reason is that in the ancient world, deities were often associated with geographic places, be they mountains, cities, rivers, or lands. As the Hittites went on to include more territories in their imperial expansion, it was only natural that the local deities would be included in their pantheons.

In Puduhepa's actions, there was no real objective of substitution of the Hittite cult with the Hurrian cult; it was instead an example of what anthropologists define as "syncretism," i.e., an amalgamation of cultures, in step with a strong influence of Hurrian culture in the arts and literature as well.

Puduhepa explicitly equated the two primary deities of the Hittite pantheon, the male Storm-God and his consort, the female Sun Goddess of Arinna, to the two primary deities of Hurrian tradition: Tesub and Hepat. In one of her prayers, she wrote: "Oh Sun Goddess of Arinna, My Lady, Queen of all countries! You are called Sun Goddess of Arinna in the Land of Hatti, but in the country which you have made the cedar land you are called Hepat." Puduhepa passed her interest in religion on to her son Tudhaliya IV who, as king, conducted a census of all local cults and all cult places within the empire. Scholars have read in this project a double intent of Tudhaliya IV: earning credits towards the gods and winning over the trust of his subjects by showing them that he would be an inclusive and sensible ruler.

It is from this age that it is believed the Hittite sanctuary of Yazilikaya was built. Yazilikaya, located just a short walk from Hattusa, was one of the sites which attracted the attention of the first European visitors to the area, such as the adventurous traveler Texier and the archaeological surveyor Perrot. The site is an impressive example of Hittite architecture. Dug between two imposing rock outcrops, the sanctuary is constituted of two roofless main chambers. The site had an imposing entrance door and some smaller adjacent constructions, but these were not preserved. The walls of the two main chambers are adorned with rock reliefs.

The elements have worn down the reliefs, but still, it is possible to recognize the figures of deities in procession. The gods are divided, male on one wall and female on the other, except for the goddess of love and war, Shaushka (a Hurrian name for the better-known goddess Ishtar of Mesopotamian tradition), who is in procession among the male gods. The processions of gods converge toward the main point of the sanctuary, where there are effigies of the Storm-God Tesub (also of Hurrian origin) and the Sun Goddess Hebat. Hebat was later syncretized in the Sun Goddess Arinna, brought to popularity by Puduhepa. These two supreme deities of the Hittite pantheon dominate the scene together with, in their background, their children and grandchildren.

Unfortunately, despite the many tablets related to religious festivals in the Hittite corpus, no clear description of the sanctuary's use has been found. Not even a single tablet refers to the sanctuary, to the point that its original name is unknown, and scholars refer to it with its modern Turkish name. Careful study of the wall inscriptions has led scholars to hypothesize that the first of the two main chambers, the one adorned with the deities in procession, may have been used in connection with specific festivities, particularly with the new year's / spring festival. In contrast, the second main chamber could have been used primarily for the mortuary cult of Tudhaliya IV.[23]

The fact that the sanctuary was not roofed led some researchers to conclude that it may have been used as a calendar for the cult of the gods, as the sun's rays would have illuminated the rock carvings at different times of the year. Based on this and other observations, Swiss archaeologist Eberhard Zangger of the Luwian Studies Foundation has proposed an interpretation of the reliefs on the wall of the Yazilikaya. According to him, the figures of the gods are arranged in groups to mark the days, the lunar months, and the solar years, helping the Hittite priests to determine when additional months were required to keep lunar and solar years aligned.[24] The hypothesis, it has to be said, is purely speculative; however, it provides a fascinating explanation for the complicated patterns seen on the walls.

The religious cult was a matter of primary importance for Hittite rulers, and religion may have become a means of fostering national unity. Unfortunately, Tudhaliya IV's reign had more severe issues than religious unity. Internally, while he succeeded in maintaining a good relationship with Kurunta, king of the appanage kingdom of Tarhuntassa, Tudhaliya IV had to deal with a severe famine that affected most of his empire. Externally, he conducted a victorious raid on the island of Cyprus (the first significant campaign of the Hittites at sea), then part of a kingdom called Alashiya and a coveted strategic target because it was a site of copper extraction and a pivotal place of maritime commerce.

Regarding the growing Assyrian power pressing at the southeast border of the empire, Tudhaliya IV resorted to using its vassal state to isolate Assyria commercially. He wrote to his brother-in-law Sausgamuwa, King of Amurru, on the coast of what today is Syria and Lebanon, and made the following request: "…Since the King of Assyria is the enemy of My Majesty, he shall likewise be your enemy. Your merchant shall not go to Assyria, and you shall not allow his merchant into your land. He shall not pass through your land. But if he should come into your land, seize him and send him off to My Majesty."[25]

And in the same treaty: "[You shall not allow (?)] any ship (of) Ahhiyawa to go to him."[26] Preventing Greek commerce from benefiting Assyria. Professor Eric Cline, historian at George Washington University in the USA, defined this as "the first embargo in history."[27]

Maritime commerce was at least as important as commerce on land but was underestimated by historians for a long time. Commerce on land had always been documented thanks to the remains of the trade routes. On the other hand, Maritime commerce is not easy to trace. In 1982, a fortuitous discovery provided a novel understanding of the extent of maritime trade in the Late Bronze Age. A Turkish sponge diver emerged from a dive off the coast of Uluburun, in southwest Turkey, and reported to have seen the wreck of an ancient ship with a rich cargo. The wreck was inspected by submarine archaeologists who could hardly believe their eyes. Just fifty meters off the coast, at a depth of no more than sixty meters, was one of the most valuable underwater archaeological findings ever.

The wreck was that of a mercantile ship loaded with its excellently preserved cargo. Specialists in dendrochronology (the discipline which dates wooden remains by studying tree rings) were able to date the sunk wooden ship from the late fourteenth century BCE, approximately the time of the Amarna letters.[28] The recovery of the cargo took as many as ten years but was highly rewarding. We do not know where the ship came from or where it was headed, but what it carried became a matter of study for decades.

The vessel transported all sorts of commodities: ingots of copper, tin, and lead, colored glass, jars full of precious resins, and a vast array of other valuables, from ostrich eggshells to ivory, from precious stones to gold jewelry, weapons, and rare spices. The catalog of goods reveals an intense commercial activity. The items transported were the product of at least nine different cultures, from as far as Northern Europe to Africa, from the islands of the western Mediterranean to Mesopotamia. This intriguing shipwreck is like a window into the Late Bronze Age and changed our understanding of the level of sea-borne connection among different areas of the Ancient World.

The clay tablet with the opening of the *Annals of Mursili II*. The first two lines transliterate as: "[UMMA^dUTU]ŠI^mMuršili LUGAL.GAL LUGAL KUR Ḫatti UR.SAG [DUMU^mŠup]piluliuma LUGAL.GAL UR.SAG" and translate as: "Thus speaks Mursili, great king, king of the land of Hatti, hero, son of Suppiluliuma, great king, hero." Credit: hethiter.net/: fotarch BoFN05136

With his land and sea embargo, Tudhaliya IV may have impacted the economy of his Assyrian enemy, but not for long. King Tukulti-Nimurta had started his kingdom with (at least purportedly) conciliating intent and had written to Tudhaliya IV, "My father was your enemy ... but I am the friend of my brother."[29] Later, though, he grew tired and moved to invade the land of Nairi (in Hittite "Nihriya"), a land under Hittite control, in what today is called the Armenian Highlands. The military confrontation which followed ended with a disastrous defeat for the army of Tudhaliya IV.

The reign of Tudhaliya IV was long but largely unhappy, with a constant struggle on both internal and foreign relationships. It resulted in yet another contraction of the area under Hittite rule. At his death in 1215 BCE, his son Arnuwanda (III) took the crown for only five years, succeeded in 1210 BCE by his younger brother Suppiluliuma (II). Despite the name inspired by his victorious ancestor, Suppiluliuma II has the dubious honor of being the last recorded Hittite king and presiding over the demise of a 500-year-old kingdom. Suppiluliuma II reigned for almost thirty years, but records of his reign are scant. We know that he conducted another campaign against the island of Cyprus. His father's raid on Cyprus was probably more an act of sacking than an invasion, so Suppiluliuma II carried out a complete military campaign and subjected Cyprus to his rule.

The expansion towards the Mediterranean Sea could have been the empire's ticket for rebirth, but, unfortunately for Suppiluliuma II, things did not go this way. Instead of a resurgence, the Hittite Empire suddenly, abruptly, and mysteriously collapsed, vanishing from human memory for thirty centuries.

11

Luwian

In the 1930s, the study of the Hittites was living its moment of fastest development. A month would not go without new translations of tablets, revealing more about this elusive people; the permanent archaeological mission at Hattusa, led by Kurt Bittel, kept on delivering materials of Hittite culture, helping in completing the picture.

Through years of research, scholars worldwide gathered extensive knowledge about the Hittites. Their history had been charted, their art and literature, their laws and customs, and the most diverse aspects of their culture and religion were now known in detail.

One aspect, however, remained a mystery: what were Hittitologists to make of the hieroglyphs carved on Hittite monuments in Anatolia and Syria? No one had yet been able to decipher them. Almost a hundred years earlier, the hieroglyphs had been the entry point into the forgotten kingdom of the Hittites.

Hieroglyphs were carved on the Hamah stones recovered by Wright in 1848. More hieroglyphs were found by Smith when he discovered Karkemish in 1876. Sayce had shown the hieroglyphs on the Tarkondemos Seal in 1888. More hieroglyphs were seen on the Mar'asch Lion found by Humann and Puchstein in Anatolia in 1882. At Hattusa, hieroglyphs adorned the walls of the nearby sanctuary of Yazilikaya. Indeed, until the German excavation of Hattusa at the beginning of the twentieth century and the discovery of the tablets, hieroglyphs were thought to be *the* Hittite writing system. When Winckler realized that the cuneiform tablets found at Hattusa were written in Hittite, the theory which immediately gained ground was that hieroglyphs were an earlier writing system of the Hittites, which was later replaced by cuneiform, borrowed from Akkadian. Unfortunately, this simplistic idea, which would remain the paradigm for another two decades, was fallacious.

Attempts at decoding the Hittite hieroglyphs had been made since the time of Sayce, but no scholar had ever gone further than suggesting the interpretation of some scattered signs. Few scholars dedicated themselves to this highly specialized area of Hittitology. The corpus of the hieroglyphs was extremely limited, amounting to just a few dozen poorly preserved inscriptions and few engravings organized by Leopold Messerschmidt (1870–1911) in a book published in 1900 called *Corpus Inscriptionum Hettiticorum*.

Why did Hittite hieroglyphs escape decipherment for such a long time? Historically, decipherment of ancient writing systems hinged on the use of bilinguals. A hundred years earlier, the Rosetta Stone had been the key to the decipherment of Egyptian hieroglyphs by Champollion. Later, the Behistun Inscription was the key to the decipherment of cuneiform by Rawlinson. Hrozný's decipherment of Hittite in 1917 was an exception because it happened in the absence of a bilingual text; however, in his case, the writing system (cuneiform) was known to him from other languages.

The challenge of Hittite hieroglyphs was that the writing system was unique, and no substantial bilingual text was ever found. Scholars were at a loss. The few who dedicated themselves to this field of study had to do a lot of guesswork in the absence of comprehensive sources. Some scholars who approached the hieroglyphs at the end of the nineteenth century had come up with the most outlandish ideas. Based on supposed similarities, the hieroglyphs were related to the Caucasian, Semitic, or Finno-Ugric language families, all hypotheses which turned out to be wrong. Translation attempts were made, later demonstrated to be entirely fanciful,[1] including at least one case in which the translator had based his interpretation of the script by reading its lines in the wrong order.[2]

The quest to understand Hittite hieroglyphs appeared like a hopeless endeavor even to the most motivated scholars. Before dying in 1933, the father of Hittitology himself, Archibald Sayce, otherwise always enthusiastic and positive on scientific matters, weighed in and declared himself pessimistic about the possibility that Hittite hieroglyphs could ever be deciphered.

The few scholars interested in Hittite hieroglyphs held their breath in 1934 when Bittel, digging in Hattusa Royal Palace, discovered a cache of one hundred clay seals. About a third of the seals were bilingual, with cuneiform Hittite and Hittite hieroglyphs inscriptions side-by-side. This could have been the "Rosetta Stone" of Hittite hieroglyphs that everyone was waiting for. However, the texts were all extremely short and were largely names. Some scattered words were obtained, but scholars were far from a complete understanding of the writing system or the vocabulary.

Another German archaeologist, Helmuth Theodor Bossert (1889–1961), made the archaeological discovery that would finally solve the 100-year-old riddle of Hittite hieroglyphs. Bossert was born in Freiburg in 1889.[3] He was a very versatile man with a creative spirit and a distinct sense of aesthetics. The main passion of Bossert's life was art. In his youth, when he studied history and archaeology, it wasn't so much the dates or facts which caught his interest but the beauty of ancient artworks. He was just in his mid-thirties when he published an extensive work on the history of handicrafts.[4] Similarly, when he studied ancient languages, he would inevitably be captured by their visual aspect. More than philology, he would excel in paleography, attracted by the aesthetics of the written word even more than by its morphology.

With a disposition of this kind, it is no surprise that Bossert would be more attracted by the beautifully ornate shapes of hieroglyphs than by the austere and monotonous lines of cuneiform. While he was in his early forties, he expressed his inspiration in writing. He collaborated with the *Frankfurter Zeitung*, one of the most popular German newspapers of the age. He alternated scientific research with creative writing, publishing between 1930 and 1931, two novels that became quite popular: *Kamerad im Westen* (*Comrades in the West*) and *Wehrlos hinter den Front* (*Defenseless Behind the Front*). His works of fiction were heavily influenced by his experience as a soldier in the Great War and were a firm condemnation of the brutality of war.

Unfortunately, the books were not appreciated by members of the Nazi party, which took power in Germany just two years later. For the Nazis, war was not to be criticized: it was sacred. By the mid–1930s, all across Germany, Nazi extremists were lighting bonfires to burn books that were not accepted by the regime because of controversial opinions or simply because they did not celebrate a masculine or heroic outlook on life. Bossert's books ended up in the pyres. But Bossert was no longer in Germany to witness this. In 1933 he had won a scholarship to do archaeological research in the field for one year and had chosen to join the Hattusa's excavation campaign under Bittel.

When Bossert arrived at Boğazköy, he made a good impression on Bittel, who described him as "decisive and dynamic." Unfortunately, despite the good start, the two would not develop a good relationship. Within months of being in Turkey, Bossert was offered a post as professor at the newly founded Faculty of Letters of the University of Istanbul. The circumstances under which he obtained this post were almost whimsical: Bossert was participating in a scientific meeting in Ankara when he had a conversation with a Turkish gentleman. The man, who was very impressed by Bossert's knowledge, revealed himself as Reşit Galip Bey, Turkish Minister of Education, and offered him the post on the spot.

Bossert accepted gladly and was very happy with his new position at Istanbul University, became more and more integrated into the Turkish society, and would later even become the head of the Turkish

Archaeological Institute, marry a Turkish woman, and become a Turkish citizen. His research focused exclusively on Hittite, and he excelled in philological research. Meanwhile, at Hattusa, Bittel, who was not trained in ancient languages and could not translate cuneiform texts, needed the help of a language expert in his excavation campaigns but would refuse to invite Bossert, preferring to him another countryman: Hans Güterbock, the talented philologist who had translated the *Deeds of Suppiluliuma* (Chapter 9). Bittel immediately liked him, and the two developed a friendship that would last throughout their lives.

Only many years later, the light was shed on the circumstances which drew Bittel away from Bossert and towards Güterbock. According to Bittel, Bossert was a Nazi sympathizer, even though his books had been burned in Nazi bonfires. In his autobiography, Bittel describes how Bossert would insist on using the Nazi salute with him. Bittel even says that when the visit of the French Minister of State Édouard Herriot was announced, Bossert took the autonomous decision of flying the swastika flag over the Hattusa excavation site.[5] The visit was eventually canceled, but Bossert's behavior aggravated Bittel, who despised Nazism and did not tolerate unnecessary nationalism.

Even more serious accusations came from Güterbock. After Güterbock's death, some of his correspondence with his good friend Albrecht Götze was found. The two Germans had met in the USA when, after 1948, Güterbock relocated to Chicago and partnered with Professor Harry Hoffner (1934–2015) to create the Chicago Hittite Dictionary, while Götze was a professor at Yale University. In the letters, Güterbock writes to Götze that Bossert was not only a Nazi sympathizer but a true informer of the regime, who would report to Berlin badmouthing Bittel for "Not being German enough."[6]

After the end of the Second World War, when the Nazi regime was finally ousted and universally denounced for its brutality, Bossert denied ever being associated with it. To reinforce this, he added that the Nazis had considered him *persona non grata* many years back because he had abandoned Germany to relocate to Turkey. His student Muhibbe Darga, who worked with him from 1940 on, rigorously rejected the idea that Bossert had ever been associated with Nazism.[7]

However, Güterbock's letters tell a different story. According to him, it is true that Bossert had a breakup with the Nazis, but this was more because he had not been enough of a good informer: "As it is well known"— writes Güterbock—"bad informers are of no use." Güterbock added that the fallout between Bossert and the Nazi party was due to the fact that when the party recalled Bossert to Germany in 1944 (likely to help in the war), he had declined. Güterbock defined Bossert's taking distance from the Nazi party as "jumping from a sinking ship" which "wouldn't fool anyone." He added: "Now he goes around telling people that he was never a Nazi and that he even had to leave the country in 1933 because he had published pacifist brochures—but anonymously (so no one can corroborate this)."[8]

We will probably never know where the truth is, whether Bossert did or did not help the Nazi party. What we are confident of is that the story of these three emigrants from Germany to Turkey, Bittel, Bossert, and Güterbock, is a metaphor for the turmoil the world went through between the two wars, when totalitarian regimes emerged, and the threat of Nazism shook the Old Continent. It is an excellent example of how Nazism upset the conscience and lives of people not just in Germany but worldwide. The life and work of researchers in Turkey were deeply influenced by what was happening in Berlin. Just like the Great War had ruined the dreams and careers of many archaeologists in the Near East, the Second World War caused an abrupt stop to Hittitological research.

The difficulties arose in Europe because of the conflict and in Turkey because of the political repercussions. It seems odd to have to discuss archaeology and politics in the same breath, but this was the reality of German archaeologists in Turkey: it was a "we against them" game. In this game, everyone lost. All three of them—Bittel, Güterbock, and Bossert—had to suspend their activities. Bossert, who had been a tireless writer throughout his life, publishing more than thirty books and hundreds of articles, through four long years during the Second World War, drew his production to an almost complete stop, writing a total of just four publications.

When the Second World War ended in the summer of 1945, it was time for a restart. Bossert was eager to get on the field and get his hands dirty to recover new material for his research on Hittite hieroglyphs. Hattusa was still Bittel's territory. All the digging and research had to go through him, and their relationship had deteriorated. Bossert grew so tired he chose to seek traces of the Hittites elsewhere. He formed a team with three ladies who were his students and assistants and went on a field trip in a remote area of south Turkey in search of any Hittite ruins. For weeks, the party traveled through impervious terrain and in very uncomfortable conditions but covered a lot of ground. As often happens in archaeology, they found fortuitously the clue they sought. Their find would change Bossert's life and the understanding of Hittite hieroglyphs, consigning Bossert to the very selected rank of archaeologists who have significantly contributed to deciphering a language.

The party was tired of days of hard traveling when they came to a nomadic village called Feke, in the heart of southern Turkish countryside and, blocked by the snowfall, spent some time in the local tea houses, in the company of local Yuruk nomads. In a casual conversation, the nomads told them about an unusual artifact they had seen. They described it as the large statue of a lion, a sculpture of ancient appearance lying on a remote hilltop not far east of the small, isolated village of Kadirli, more than fifty kilometers away. It was late in the season, and a detour to reach this site, on the slim hope that the lion statue would be there and would be ancient, did not feel opportune. Bossert and his team renounced pursuing this lead and headed north.

The rumor of this ancient statue lying about in the countryside, waiting to be found by an archaeologist, intrigued Bossert however. He noted its supposed location and promised to investigate it later. As soon as the rainy season ended in February 1946, he organized a new expedition and, this time in the company of his student Alet Çambel only, decided to reach Kadirli. This attempt would finally reward him with splendid findings and bring him to make the history of Hittitology, but it certainly was not obtained easily. It was an arduous trip that proved Bossert's commitment and passion for archaeology. Kadirli was extremely difficult to reach.

The archaeologists, later joined by the director of the Museum of Adana, had to endure enormous unease, riding on hard, horse-drawn wooden carriages through very rough roads. The more they traveled away from the main road towards the open countryside, the more taxing the journey. The wheels of the carriage, as well as the hooves of the horses, sunk in mud, requiring the passengers to disembark the carriage and carry on walking in the rain. The horses collapsed in exhaustion, and the carriage driver gave up. New transport had to be organized on the spot, and the journey got further delayed.

It was dark when, tired and dirty, Bossert and his student finally arrived at Kadirli, where they were welcomed by the warm hospitality of the village chief. Bossert was treated with great respect, and dinner was offered in his honor, with the participation of the elders of the village. In the comfort of the banquet, Bossert started to make polite inquiries about the object of his visit, the lion statue, but grew disappointed by the minute when he learned that none of the locals had seen or heard about this statue. After the lengthy journey and all the discomfort suffered to get there, Bossert was dismayed. Finally, the local schoolteacher, Mister Ekrem Kuscu, was summoned. When the teacher was asked, he revealed that he knew about the lion statue. He had seen it lying on the ground, as described, in a remote area located about fifteen kilometers away, on a hill called Karatepe (Turkish for "Black Mountain").[9]

11. Luwian

Bossert was overjoyed and pleaded with Ekrem Kuscu to guide them on a horseback journey to the site.* The schoolteacher agreed but gave them a stern warning: the ride would be very hard, especially the last bit, before ascending the hill through the swamp. It took all of Bossert's determination to get to the Black Mountain through mud and indiscernible paths, but after a good five hours on horseback, they finally arrived where the teacher had seen the statue.[10] There it was, in the shape of a lion (later research would demonstrate the statue was actually of a bull), lying on the ground, about one meter long, roughly sculpted in sandstone, almost entirely covered in weeds and badly damaged by centuries of exposure to the elements.[11]

Not far away, Bossert found the statue of a man, headless and armless but covered in inscriptions. The inscriptions immediately attracted his attention: they were neither in cuneiform nor hieroglyphs. An alphabetic writing system of some sort, but nothing he could immediately recognize. He hypothesized it could be Aramaic but wasn't sure. The fine sculptures could not be lying about by themselves in the open countryside—reasoned Bossert. The site must have been a sizeable settlement; its potential would be enormous. He thought about his options and realized that he could not do much without equipment or more workers, so he took casts of the inscriptions on the statue and returned to Kadirli. He had to return to Istanbul, organize an expedition, bring men and tools, and start excavating. Who knew how many other invaluable artifacts would be hidden under the dirt, he thought.

However, the opportunity to excavate at Karatepe would not soon present itself. It took Bossert an entire year to obtain the necessary funding to organize the expedition. During this year, he dedicated himself to the inscription he had found. Pretty soon, he realized the alphabet was not Aramaic but Phoenician. Phoenicians were people of Semitic origin who inhabited the coasts of the Levant since the beginning of the Bronze Age. The Phoenicians never united into a unitary kingdom but instead lived in separated city-states and were strong at seafaring and commerce. They exported their culture through most of the coast of the eastern and southern Mediterranean, founding colonies and commercial outposts as far as modern-day Tunisia and Spain.

The area of south Turkey where Karatepe lay would have been within the Phoenician area of commerce, and Phoenicians and Hittites likely cohabited the area. Phoenicians were the first people of the Near East to use a writing system based on an alphabet—as opposed to the syllabaries

---

* Years later, following Bossert's recommendation, Ekrem Kuscu received a civil medal of honour in recognition of his help.

used until then—passing it on to Greeks (who developed it by adding vowels, as the Phoenician alphabet included only consonants).

Bossert was excited: this opened huge possibilities. The inscription could help him trace the history of the site. What was needed was a translation of the Phoenician inscription. Now, that was quite the challenge. The Phoenician language is not well attested (the inscription found by Bossert is, to date, the longest Phoenician text ever found, and true experts were very few throughout the world). For this translation, Bossert put together a posse of highly specialized scholars from the four corners of Europe.

He sent one copy of the text to the British Museum, to the attention of Richard Barnett (1909–1986), a man who was literally born into Oriental studies, the son of the keeper of Oriental books and manuscripts at the British Museum. Barnett was a Cambridge-educated philologist considered one of England's most well-versed in Semitic languages. A second copy was sent to Leipzig, in Bossert's home country of Germany, to Johannes Friedrich, the same scholar who in the 1920s strongly opposed Forrer's Ahhiyawa hypothesis. Friedrich was just about to be nominated University Rector; he held the professorship of Oriental philology and was known for his encyclopedic knowledge of the most diverse ancient languages, Semitic and Indo-European alike. The third envelope reached André Dupont-Sommer (1900–1983) in Paris. Dupont-Sommer was the main Semitologist in France and would later become the world leading authority on the Dead Sea Scrolls.

For the fourth and final copy, the choice was inevitable. The envelope was sent to the library with the most important collection of ancient texts in the world, the Vatican Apostolic Library in Rome, to the attention of the American Jesuit priest Father Roger O'Callaghan (1912–1954). Father O'Callaghan was considered one of the world's leading researchers on comparative Semitology. He could converse in a dozen languages and was described as of "effervescent charm."[12] He later became Bossert's good friend and collaborated with him on the field at Karatepe before prematurely dying at just forty-two.

The first translation came back from Leipzig. Friedrich translated most of the text and concluded the inscription was about the deeds of a local ruler, whose name, in the Phoenician alphabet, was spelled *Ztwd* (the vowels are not spelled). Bossert thought that the name could be Hittite in origin, and being well versed in Anatolian phonology, he worked out that, in Hittite, the corresponding name would have sounded *Asitawanda*. Shortly after, the translations from Paris and the Vatican arrived and were almost identical. Barnett's translation from England was the last to come in and showed some differences, which were later reconciled.

Now Bossert knew more: the ruler must have been reasonably

important if his deeds were immortalized in an inscribed statue. Indeed, the fact that the inscription on the statue was in the Phoenician language meant that the village was sizeable enough to have entertained commercial relationships with neighboring cultures. But, for however good commercial relationships there could be, why would a statue in a Hittite village carry an inscription in a foreign language? Unless ... the inscription in the foreign language was a translation of a Hittite text. Unless it was a part of a bilingual inscription. Could it be? Could he have found one-half of what the world of archaeology was waiting for: a bilingual to decipher Hittite hieroglyphs?

In March 1947, when the mission to Karatepe was finally underway, it wasn't even a full-fledged expedition. With a scarcity of funds, Bossert could depart Istanbul accompanied only by his assistant Bahadir Alkim. For the second time, Bossert traveled the difficult terrain between Kadirli and Karatepe—if possible, under even more dismaying conditions. Drinking water was scarce, and there was mud everywhere. Still, once they came to the site, the duo was rewarded by an astounding find: buried under vegetation and a thin layer of dirt were the fragments of a monumental inscription. On it, Bossert immediately recognized his beloved Hittite hieroglyphs and more Phoenician.[13] He started fantasizing but almost would not dare to imagine it: generations of Hittitologists had looked for a bilingual to interpret the hieroglyphs, and this could finally be it.

He had to remain cautious. There were inscriptions in two languages, but no one could yet tell whether one was the translation of the other. After all, the texts were fragmented, and in no place were the two languages side-by-side. Also, there appeared to be more text in hieroglyphs than in Phoenician. The monumental inscriptions lay next to a wall. It wasn't a small wall. A preliminary survey revealed that it stretched for hundreds of meters. There was also evidence of a fortification and a settlement of a size that Bossert had not dared to imagine. This was a major site. Now he had the evidence, so he called for a large-scale excavation campaign. When he returned to Istanbul, he was received with honors due a man who had single-handedly discovered a Bronze Age village.

In a matter of six months, by September 1947, once the unbearably hot Turkish summer was over, a large expedition, sanctioned by the Turkish Archaeological Institute, was underway. This time, horses were replaced by motorized vehicles (albeit with great difficulties and improvised works of "countryside engineering" to allow the passage of the trucks on the nearly impervious terrain), and a few local workers were recruited. Bossert could also count on the help of some of his closest collaborators and, among them, a student named Franz Steinherr (1902–1974). Steinherr appeared oddly out of place because, at forty-five, he was much older than the other students due to the unusual circumstances which led him to his place by Bossert's side. Unbeknownst to both, this late starter would become a key person in the decipherment of the hieroglyphs.

Born in Landshut, Germany, Steinherr was an ordinary young man who had gone from one ordinary job to another, such as bookkeeper apprentice, rayon manufacturer, bank clerk, and construction company clerk, but he had a hidden, extraordinary gift: his mind was a sponge for languages. He had taught himself Turkish at fifteen, Arabic at seventeen, Japanese at eighteen, and Russian at nineteen without ever leaving his hometown. He also spoke French, English, and native German. When his employer at the construction company realized Steinherr's talent for languages, they proposed that he relocate to Istanbul as a sales representative.

Steinherr accepted the offer and moved to Turkey but soon found himself restless. His work did not satisfy him, and he would dedicate himself to his passion for languages whenever he had the time. During breaks at work, he would walk the streets of Istanbul, befriending locals and expanding his knowledge of Turkish. Reminiscent of those nineteenth-century orientalists, the likes of Burton or Burckhardt, he infiltrated the local circles so well that he gathered a wide-ranging knowledge of local customs (to the point that he published a treatise on the "Colloquial language of the thieves in Istanbul"). In 1939, he met Bossert at a party. Bossert was so impressed by his talent for languages that he suggested Steinherr dedicate himself to archaeology, where he could find the linguistic challenges that would suit his inquisitive mind. Steinherr wanted to follow Bossert's advice, but this called for a courageous move. He would have to ditch everything he was doing and start a career in academia from scratch. Moreover, he did not have the correct educational curriculum to be accepted to study under Bossert at the Faculty of Literature of Istanbul University, so the only way to do this would be to return to study basic subjects such as mathematics and pass the qualification exams.

He considered his choices. At thirty-seven, he could choose to stay in his current job, unsatisfied and bored, or follow his dream of studying ancient languages. It may not have been an easy decision, but he took the plunge, and it is also thanks to this bold move that Hittite hieroglyphs would be finally deciphered. Steinherr left his job and took a part-time position as a bookkeeper of a local hospital to finance his studies, retraced an entire academic career from scratch, joined Bossert's research group, obtained a doctorate, and was invited to join the expedition to Karatepe in 1947.[14]

At Karatepe, Steinherr was tireless. He did all sorts of works, always helpful, digging, cleaning, cooking, driving, and even singlehandedly unearthing a fine artifact, a sphinx covered in hieroglyphs. Steinherr had learned the basics of Hittite hieroglyphs under Bossert, but it was still a great surprise for everyone, including Bossert, when Steinherr looked at the hieroglyphs and, without hesitation, made out a series of signs which spelled out "Azitawanda" (although later research showed the correct spelling was "Azatiwata").

The excitement was enormous. Bossert immediately confirmed Steinherr's interpretation: the name of the king mentioned in the Phoenician inscriptions was found in the hieroglyphic inscriptions, suggesting what everyone was hoping for: that the two texts were each a translation of the other.[15]

Through several months of digging, the Karatepe site gave the archaeologists an enormous number of valuable finds. The archaeologists brought the entire wall system to the surface, identifying two monumental doors adorned by sculptures. The inscriptions, though, remained the most intriguing find. By the end of the campaign, Bossert and his team had discovered two inscriptions very similar to the one written on the royal statue: one at the northern gate of the village, the other at the southern gate. The content of each inscription was essentially identical, which helped the philologists reconstruct the missing bits erased by the centuries. The rich and meaningful text celebrated the deeds of Azitawanda, who spoke about his achievements. The team also found two large hieroglyphic inscriptions, among them the ones in which Steinherr had identified the name Azitawanda. There were all the circumstances to assume the hieroglyph text was a translation of the Phoenician text. However, this had to be proven.

It was Bossert who knew most about Hittite hieroglyphs, probably in the entire world. Yet, with all his knowledge, the work was painstakingly difficult, mainly because the hieroglyphics were found in scattered order. He struggled to find a point-by-point correlation between the two texts, unable to tell exactly where the hieroglyphic text started. But, deep inside, Bossert wanted and hoped that the texts could be correlated.

One day Steinherr listened to Bossert's lecture on the Phoenician text and saw the translation of the sentence "I made horse go with horse, shield with shield, army with army." This sentence caught Steinherr's mind. It reminded him of something, something he could not exactly put his finger on. The story goes that at night, Steinherr had a dream and woke up in haste, suddenly able to focus on the detail. "Horse go with horse." He remembered that he had seen the signs of two horse heads in succession in the hieroglyphic text. Could that be the translation of "Horse go with horse"? Could it be the matching point of the two inscriptions?

The next day, he and Bossert started from that precise passage and were finally able to make out the adjacent sentences. The point of correspondence between Phoenician and hieroglyphic text was finally found.[16] It took Bossert over one year to translate most of the text and another four years to complete it, but he was successful; Hittite hieroglyphs were finally decoded.[17] The door to this elusive script was unlocked, and philologists worldwide began to pore over them. Soon, a surprising truth started to emerge: the language of the hieroglyphs was not Hittite. It was similar: definitely Indo-European and very similar to Hittite, but Hittite it was not.

The thesis that Hittite hieroglyphs were just an earlier way of writing Hittite started to falter. In 1957 Güterbock, who had been in open rivalry with Bossert for years, belonged to a group of linguists who considered the hieroglyphs to be Luwian, one of the languages that Forrer demonstrated were spoken at Hattusa. This hypothesis was not entirely new: it had already been postulated by the Italian Piero Meriggi (1899–1982) as early as 1932,[18] however, it had never gained much traction. Luwians were a people of Indo-European origin, related to the Hittites and who probably migrated into Anatolia at the same time as the Hittites, but over which the Hittites prevailed during their early period of expansion in Anatolia, starting in the Old Kingdom in the seventeenth century BCE.

The similarity between Luwian and Hittite has been compared to the closeness between the Italian and Spanish languages. As will be seen in the next chapter, pockets of Luwian-speaking people survived the collapse of the Hittite Empire by centuries; this explains why hieroglyph inscriptions were more numerous at the periphery of the empire rather than in the capital Hattusa. Scholars are still arguing about how much bilingualism existed in the Hittite Kingdom, which percentage of the people of Hatti spoke Hittite, and which portion spoke Luwian in their everyday life.

According to Dr. Billie Jean Collins of Emory University, Luwians speakers may have been the dominant population group in Anatolia in the latter half of the second millennium BCE.[19] Unfortunately, the study of the tablets does not help determine if this is correct because, as we have seen, the extant written Hittite corpus was almost entirely produced by Hattusa's governmental and clerical elite. It is possible that the balance between spoken Luwian and spoken Hittite was different in different parts of the reign; for example, Luwian appears to have been spoken more in west Anatolia, south-east Anatolia, and Syria, as we will see in Chapter 13.

Sporadically, Luwian had also been written using the cuneiform writing system. Examples of this were known already to Forrer in his translations in the early 1920s. It is still unclear why the Hittite people resorted to writing Luwian in hieroglyphs on their monuments, even in their capital city. Notwithstanding bilingualism, if, as seems likely, Luwian could be written in cuneiform, why would Hittites bother to carve hieroglyphs on

The Phoenician portion of the Karatepe bilingual inscription, discovered in Cilicia by Helmuth Bossert in 1946. This text allowed a better understanding of the hieroglyphs which were earlier believed to be used to write the Hittite language, but were later proven to be Luwian language. Dosseman, CC BY-SA 4.0, via Wikimedia Commons

their monuments instead of cuneiform? One intriguing hypothesis is that hieroglyphs could have been used out of nationalistic pride; after all, the cuneiform script was borrowed from foreign nations, while the Luwian hieroglyphs were autochthonous.[20]

In 1957 Güterbock wrote a seminal article in which he proposed the hieroglyphs should be called Luwian hieroglyphs rather than Hittite hieroglyphs.[21] Many other scholars, though, were resistant to accepting his thesis. The expression "Hittite hieroglyph" had been deeply rooted in archaeological literature for a century. Therefore, it took a long time for scholars to gradually move away from this incorrect term and speak of "Anatolian hieroglyphs" instead. Unfortunately, "Anatolian hieroglyphs" wasn't much more correct either, because Luwians also lived in areas outside of Anatolia, for example, Hamah or Karkemish in Syria, where they left the famous hieroglyph inscriptions covered in Chapter 2. It took a twenty-year-long transition, all the way into the mid-seventies, to finally accept that the correct expression should be "Luwian hieroglyphs," as they are currently known.

The discovery of the Hittites is a century-long adventure of twists, turns, and even blind ends. It was finally demonstrated that the hieroglyphs which sparked the earliest interest in the Hittites, ironically, although they belonged to the culture of the Hittite kingdom, weren't strictly speaking the Hittite language after all. Still, if it hadn't been for these mysterious rock carvings, Hittitology may have never been born.

The journey of Hittitology was not complete. One final question remained to be answered, and it was perhaps the most crucial question of all: how and why did the Hittite Empire end so abruptly and without leaving any account of itself? For decades, archaeologists had tried to reconstruct the final moments of the empire: what caused its collapse? Once again, the possible answer to another one of the Hittite mysteries, probably the most elusive, did not come from the Hittite territory but from Egypt.

12

The Late Bronze Age Collapse

For Ancient Egyptians, the belief that life continued after death was central to their existence. Since the earliest days of their civilization, Egyptians invested considerable resources to ensure their road to the afterlife was appropriately paved. People of importance would use all their power to build tombs worth of their social status because they understood them as their residence in the afterlife. Naturally, the most majestic of all were the pharaohs' tombs. Apart from the great pyramids, most of the funerary monuments of the pharaohs have disappeared in the sands of time or have been destroyed after being sacked by graverobbers.

The funerary monument of Pharaoh Ramesses III (who reigned from 1188 to 1155 BCE), however, had a different destiny. Ramesses III did not mind expenses for his memorial. Built early during his thirty-year reign at a site called Medinet Habu, it consisted of the main temple measuring 141 × 50 meters, surrounded by a series of minor buildings to house the sacred mummy of the Pharaoh and those of his closest officials and priests. The walls of the main temple were covered in paintings and texts which depicted the acts of bravery in the life of the Pharaoh to endear him to the god Amon who was believed to receive him on the other side.

A massive wall eighteen meters high surrounded Ramesses III's funerary complex. With the emergence of Christianity in Egypt fifteen centuries later, most buildings of this type were destroyed because they were deemed impious. Medinet Habu was spared because it was so large and well-built that it became a suitable monastery for Coptic monks, who occupied it for centuries. The monks plastered over the pagan paintings and inscriptions which they found offensive, unwittingly protecting them for posterity. When, in 1850, an American archaeological mission began the systematic restoration of the complex, as they lifted the plaster off the wall, much to their surprise, the work of the Ancient Egyptian artists was perfectly preserved. The Egyptologists of the age translated parts of the inscriptions. Still, it wasn't until another eighty years later, in 1936, that the complete translation was published by two brilliant American epigraphists, Edgerton and Wilson.[1]

The texts on the tomb walls were very useful to historians as they were packed with information on military campaigns and helped trace the history of the reign of Ramesses III during the twentieth dynasty of the Egyptian New Kingdom. His was a tumultuous reign in which he had to defend his country from the attack of people from the west (the Lybians) and people who descended from the Mediterranean Sea into the Nile delta. Ramesses' inscriptions gave scattered descriptions of these people, but ironically, they became more of a key to understanding Hittite history than Egyptian history. The now famous panel XV, a fifteen-meter-long inscription detailing the activities of the eighth year of the reign of Ramesses III (1177 BCE), contains a single, essential line.

The line reports how the attacks on Egypt started, a rather dramatic state of affairs: "As for the foreign countries, they made a conspiracy in their isles, and scattered in the fray were the lands at once. No land could stand before their arms: from Hatti, Kode, Karkemish, Yereth, and Yeres on, they were destroyed at once."[2]

Hatti was the land of the Hittites. Kode was Egyptian for Kizzuwatna, the Hurrian Kingdom under Hittite dominion, the one from where Queen Puduhepa came. Karkemish, a city-state in Syria, had been a vassal to the Hittite Kingdom for centuries. Yereth was later identified as Arzawa in western Anatolia, also an area under Hittite dominion. Yeres was the island of Cyprus, which the Hittites had more recently conquered.

The text left no doubt. The attack of these peoples had wiped out the Hittites and all their major strongholds, bringing six hundred years of Anatolian leadership in the Ancient Near East to an abrupt end.

Who were these people? Most historians call them the "Sea Peoples"; however, this is a somewhat misleading name. The expression "Sea Peoples" was introduced by French archaeologist Emmanuel de Rouge (1811–1872) based on limited Egyptian sources, including the texts on the walls of Medinet Habu. The father of Hittitology, Archibald Sayce, had already embraced de Rouge's theory of the Sea Peoples as the cause of the end of the Hittite Empire long before the complete translation of the Medinet Habu inscriptions confirmed their role in the demise.

The name Sea Peoples, however, is in part a misnomer. In the Egyptian texts, these tribes were referred to with a word French philologists translated as people coming from "the isles." However, the Ancient Egyptian language did not have a word for "isle"; the word used would more correctly be translated as "sea country" or "land with a coastline," which does not necessarily mean an island, but simply a country with a shore,[3]

12. The Late Bronze Age Collapse 153

therefore, since there is very little mention of them outside of Egyptian sources, the naming is quite controversial. However, the fact that they came from the sea or moved by sea is established, not just in Egyptian sources but in a few scattered Hittite references as well. For example, Suppiluliuma II wrote a letter to an officer in the coastal state of Ugarit. In the letter, Suppiluliuma II, to gather information, requests he be allowed to interrogate a man who had been kidnapped by the Shekelesh (one of the Sea Peoples) "who live on boats."[4]

Characterizing the Sea Peoples is difficult because they weren't a unitarian population but rather a collection of diverse populations: the Ancient Egyptians depicted them as a confederation. They represented them with different hairstyles and clothing in their art, which in Egyptian symbolism signified different ethnicities. Between the Ramesses III narrative and some scant accounts of a previous pharaoh called Merneptah, nine different peoples are listed as belonging to this "confederation." Most, but not all, are referred to as coming from the sea.

The hypothesis of a confederation of marauding people coming from the far shores of the Mediterranean and bringing down the military powers of the Ancient Near East gained ground among historians and, for decades, determining the identity of these people and whence they came became a popular field of investigation.

Scholars have suggested a rather convincing origin for some people based on their names' sounds. This is the case of the "Sherden" who are thought to come from Sardinia, and the "Shekelesh" who are thought to come from Sicily. The "Lukka" are proven to be the inhabitants of Lycia in western Anatolia, as this name is also known from non–Egyptian sources. The "Peleset" are believed to be the Philistines, mainly because of a single biblical reference (and thus always of doubtful reliability). For the remaining ones, there is no agreement. Half a dozen hypotheses exist about where they came from and why they united in a confederation, but no theory has been convincingly proven.

Perhaps, rather than figuring out where the Sea Peoples came from and why they united to attack the Hittite Empire and later Egypt, it is more relevant to ask if this group of marauding peoples by themselves may be responsible for taking down an entire empire? The current general opinion among scholars is that the attack of the Sea Peoples is a simplistic scapegoat to explain a period of overarching crisis which invested the entire ancient Near East. It was a series of events so disaggregating and disruptive that it has been dubbed the "Late Bronze Age Collapse."

For its magnitude and its importance, and for the relatively short time it took, the Late Bronze Age Collapse is one of the most significant moments in the history of human civilizations, a pivotal event that reshaped history and changed the world order forever. During a mere fifty years between 1200 and 1150 BCE, the Hittite, Minoan, and Mycenaean civilizations collapsed and virtually disappeared; Kassite Babylonia dissolved; organized societies like Arzawa in west Anatolia and Canaan in the Levant slid into chaos and the Egyptian Empire into an age of hardship which it took over a century to recover from.

Today, scholars believe that more than a military attack, the arrival of the Sea Peoples should be seen as mass migration. While outside pressure from groups of migrants may have led to social disruption and maybe even to violence, it could not have been the only cause of the collapse of several advanced civilizations.

Indeed, large-scale destruction happened: archaeologists have been able to prove the nearly simultaneous collapse of major centers in western and central Anatolia (including the Hittite capital Hattusa), the Levant, Mesopotamia, mainland and insular Greece, and Cyprus; however, it is not the catastrophe which comes from a single war, but more a series of damages which took place over several decades.

In particular for Hattusa, since the earliest of Kurt Bittel's excavations, there has been evidence that a catastrophic fire destroyed the city. The excavators found "ash, charred wood, mudbricks and slag formed when mudbricks melted from the intense heat of the conflagration"[5] consistent with its end in the early twelfth century BCE.

Have entire empires collapsed because the Sea People were attacking, or have the Sea People attacked because the empires were collapsing, and they took advantage of their weakness? Archaeological evidence suggests that the major Hittite centers were already abandoned when the Sea People invaded the Hittite territory.

Scholars speculate that changes in warfare may have played in favor of the attackers. If, for example, the attackers had better access to metallurgy and less access to horse rearing, that may have resulted in their attacking with handheld weapons, while the established kingdoms were defending themselves with horse-drawn chariots. Chariot-based warfare is suitable for open battlefield warfare between two large armies but not as effective against small troops armed with swords and ready for close-quarter combat. Therefore, this warfare asymmetry would have favored the attacking Sea People and punished the defending local armies.

More recently, with the advancement of disciplines such as paleoclimatology (the science which studies climate changes in the remote past), the attention of researchers has shifted towards the impact of environmental changes on the disruption of Hittite society. These changes may have led to impoverishment and vulnerability to outside attacks. By observing the patterns of tree remains and studying pollen from alluvial deposits, scientists have proven that during the Late Bronze Age collapse, the Near East was undergoing one of the most severe droughts in history. The societies of the time were strongly dependent on agriculture, and several years of bad crops could easily lead to a social crisis. The findings of the climatologists are consistent with documents from the age. These documents show that rulers were dealing with agricultural hardship. Scattered sources in Hittite literature of the time of King Suppiluliuma II refer to "years of hardship" and "famine."[6]

One diplomatic letter, in particular, gives a brief but poignant account of the difficulties. French archaeologist Claude Schaeffer (1898-1982) discovered the letter at Ras Shamra in coastal Syria. Ras Shamra is where the ruins of the city-state of Ugarit lay. Ugarit, a client state of the Hittite Empire, was once a rich harbor that entertained commercial relationships with Egypt and Anatolia. The city was discovered in 1928 when a Syrian peasant plowed a field and accidentally opened an ancient tomb. French archaeologists immediately started digging and uncovered a well-preserved urban center which also returned large quantities of artifacts and tablets inscribed with diplomatic correspondence. Ugarit had its language, a Semitic language related to Phoenician and written in cuneiform. However, diplomatic correspondence was in Akkadian. One of these diplomatic letters, written by the scribes of King Suppiluliuma II, requests the Ugarit King Ammurapi to send Hatti a shipment of grain. The letter is short and does not explain the context of this request, but the gravity of the situation is condensed in its ominous closing words: "It is a matter of life or death."[7]

The famine brought the Hittite Empire to desperation. This narrative is corroborated by a poorly preserved inscription found at Karnak. In the inscription, Pharaoh Merneptah, another contemporary ruler of Suppiluliuma II, in pure Egyptian style, tells of his accomplishments. Among other deeds, he declares having sent several ships full of grain to the king of the Hittites, adding that it was "to keep alive the land of Hatti."[8] Egyptian Pharaohs were known for sending rich gifts to their Hittite allies, but this is the only evidence of a shipment of foodstuff necessary for sustenance, an extraordinary event in the history of the diplomatic relationships between the two empires.

Invaders backed by changes in warfare on one side and famine on the other can be considered "external causes" of the Late Bronze Age Collapse. Other scholars seek the explanation of the collapse among "internal causes," mainly the relatively fast transformation of society.

British archaeologist Nancy Sandars (1914-2015) was an independent researcher who never joined academia, but this didn't prevent her from publishing several hugely popular history books during her 101-year life.

In her very respected book on the Sea People,[9] she commented that natural disasters, famines, and other catastrophes have always been there in the Ancient Near East, but people just would go through a "dark age," then recover and move on. If this didn't happen, it means the collapse must have been more rooted, a collapse that involved a "system" collapse.

According to the theory of system collapse, the growing complexity and specialization of the Late Bronze Age political, economic, and social organization made civilization too intricate to establish piecewise when disrupted by war or famine.

The internal failure of the fabric of the society would better explain why the collapse was so widespread to such a vast territory and not limited to an area, something invasions are harder to reconcile with. It would also explain why the reigns, reconstituted or created in the aftermath of the Late Bronze Age Collapse, were substantially different. Itamar Singer commented: "Without diminishing the role of the outside enemies in the fall of the Hittite Empire, I feel that more weight should be given to the symptoms of inner decline and disintegration."[10]

There is mounting evidence that the town of Hattusa was already abandoned when it was destroyed, corroborating the hypothesis that external invasions may have been a consequence rather than a cause of the empire's demise. German Jürgen Seeher, historian of the German Orient Society and director of excavations at Hattusa from 1994 to 2005, hypothesizes that the Hittite capital was abandoned gradually. "While there are unmistakable signs of destruction all over the city, the scarcity of valuables among the ruins suggests the richer layer of the society had already moved away when the invasion arrived. While it is possible that valuables would have disappeared at the hands of the invaders, the striking scarcity of official royal records suggests these may have been moved by the king's entourage before the attack."[11]

It is possible that the Late Bronze Age Collapse was a multifactorial event. A set of circumstances, including droughts and unfortunately timed external attacks, combined with the suboptimal organization of the structure of empires that had grown too fast, brought about the collapse of one kingdom, which disrupted commercial routes and created a catastrophic domino effect.

Whatever the cause, the Hittite Empire ceased to exist. The scant historical records of Suppiluliuma II's reign end abruptly, to the point that we don't even know how long he reigned. After him, there is no record of any central Hittite ruler. Since, as we have seen, the entire corpus of Hittite texts were produced by the central government only, the consequence of this political demise is that the Hittite language simply ceased to be written down the moment the centralized Hittite government fell.

12. The Late Bronze Age Collapse

Thus, the end of the reign of Suppiluliuma II, presumed to have taken place around 1778 BCE, marks the collapse of a central Hittite government, national identity, and a unitary Hittite society all at the same time. The Hittite people who formed that society did not simply cease to exist, so what happened to them and their culture? Their destiny is still shrouded in mystery; however, some ancient sources give us clues about what may have happened.

The end of the organized Hittite society came abruptly because the empire was hit at its heart. Whether under the effects of foreign invasions, natural catastrophe, anarchy following political turmoil, or of all three things together, and whether it had already been partially abandoned when the destruction came, there is evidence to affirm that Hattusa, as a city, suffered a brutal end and that its buildings were laid in ruins. However, the same is not valid for Hittite territory outside the capital. When archaeologists consider the entirety of the currently known Hittite sites, the impression is that more centers have been deserted than destroyed.[12] According to history professor Trevor Bryce of Queensland University, Australia: "the collapse of the Hittite Kingdom is not one of widespread destruction and massacre, but of large-scale movements of peoples—abandoning their homelands, grouping and regrouping with other people on the move, then finally dispersing, sometimes to lands far from their places of origin"[13] or, to Professor Kenneth Harl of Tulane University, the Hittite Empire "not so much fell as it fragmented."[14]

So, where are the fragments of this broken empire, and what happened to them? Where did Hittite people move to, and where did they survive the crisis and keep their Hittite traditions and language alive?

Textual and archaeological sources from the period immediately following the Late Bronze Age collapse, eleventh and tenth century BCE, are very poor.[15] However, later sources allow us to identify pockets of Hittite culture surviving in several small kingdoms in Anatolia and Syria. These kingdoms, attested well into the Iron Age, are collectively known as "Neo-Hittite kingdoms." The best way to have an overview of the Neo-Hittite kingdoms is to proceed by geographical areas.

After the collapse of the Hittite empire, central Anatolia was primarily occupied by two non–Hittite peoples. One was the Kaskians, a tribal people coming from the north and called Kaska (also spelled Gasga) in the Hittite sources. They were the archenemies of the Hittites, a real thorn in the side for them since the fifteenth century BCE. The others were the Mushki, probably identifiable as the same people called later Phrygians by the Greeks. With central Anatolia occupied, it is natural that Neo-Hittite kingdoms managed to survive only at the empire's periphery.

In south Anatolia lay the Neo-Hittite kingdom of Tabal. More than one single kingdom was a collection of city-states. Its central ruler lived in the city-state of Tuwana, and the kingdom extended over a territory that included parts of the former kingdom of Tarhuntassa. By the eighth century BCE, the Neo-Assyrian Empire was rising, and Tabal was subjected to their power. Citizens of Tabal had to pay tributes to the Assyrians, as demonstrated in documents from the reign of Assyrian kings Tiglath-Pileser III and Sargon II.[16] The natural question is: how could scholars establish that the Kingdom of Tabal was Neo-Hittite?

Both internal and external sources confirm this. Externally, we know from Assyrian documents that the inhabitants of Tabal were referred to as the "People of Hatti." Internally, because the archaeological remains from Tabal are typically Hittite. The main example of this would be a rock relief (see Chapter 3) in exquisitely Hittite style near the Turkish town of İvriz, depicting King Warpalawa of Tuwana, dressed in unmistakably Hittite clothes, venerating the very Hittite Storm-God.

Sayce was exploring Anatolia for the first time and admired it; the relief was indeed one of the clues which convinced Sayce of Hittite presence in Anatolia. Sayce could not read the Luwian hieroglyphic inscription on the monument—as we have seen, Luwian hieroglyphs were first deciphered after Bossert's discoveries in the 1950s. The inscription on the İvriz relief was only recently translated by an expert of Luwian hieroglyphs, Professor John David Hawkins of Oxford University. It was published in the year 2000 in the most comprehensive collection of extant Luwian texts to date.[17] Tabal is a legacy of Hittite culture, surviving the empire's collapse by at least four hundred years.

In western Anatolia lay a kingdom that the Greek neighbors called Lycia. Lycia is another of the Neo-Hittite kingdoms. The area corresponds geographically to what the Hittites called Lukka. It is unequivocal that the Greeks based their naming of the kingdom on its original Hittite name, which witnesses a cultural and ethnic continuity in the area, past the Late Bronze Age collapse and well into the Iron Age. Even the capital of Lycia, although it is better known to us through its Greek name Xanthos, was called Arinna by its population, a name which derives from the Luwian-Hittite name Arinna.[18] There is no doubt that the language spoken in the region in the Iron Age, called Lycian, is derived from Luwian.

Besides this continuity in the language spoken by the inhabitants and in their toponyms (names of places), archaeologists have found several cultural references to the Hittite past of Lycia. For example, in the local art and architecture and the name of the deities venerated. Therefore, Lycia represents a direct continuation of Hittite culture past the empire's fall.

In south Anatolia, in the region called Cilicia, lay the Kingdom of Tarhuntassa. In Chapter 10, we saw how, for a brief period between the

12. The Late Bronze Age Collapse 159

fourteenth and thirteenth century BCE, Tarhuntassa was the Hittite capital. Later, Hattusili III assigned Tarhuntassa as an appanage kingdom to Mursili III's brother Kurunta. Although the sources are scarce, we can affirm that Kurunta's cadet branch of the Hittite royal family continued to reign in the area until the fall of the Hittite Empire. But what happened after that?

Some Luwian hieroglyphic inscriptions found at Kizildağ, an archaeological site on a mountain top, and other nearby locations within the territory of Tarhuntassa, describe a Great King Hartapu (a name of Hittite origin), "son of the Great King Mursili." It is reasonable to assume that Mursili is the Mursili III ousted by Hattusili III, i.e., a brother of the previously appointed king Kurunta. The most intriguing aspect of this inscription is that Hartapu styled himself as the "Great King." This would have put him in open conflict with the rulers at Hattusa, who claimed to be the only Great Kings of the Hittites. This conflict is probably confirmed by a military campaign of Suppiluliuma II towards the end of his reign to conquer Tarhuntassa.[19]

However, another Luwian hieroglyphic inscription on a stele found at the considerably distant site of Karahöyük in the mountains of south-east Anatolia celebrates the visit of another Great King, called Ir-Tesub. Based on epigraphic similarities with the inscriptions of Hartapu, it appears that Ir-Tessub would have been a successor to the throne of Tarhuntassa. If this is true, the Tarhuntassa branch would have continued ruling over southern and southeastern Anatolia well into the Iron Age.[20] Thus, Tarhuntassa is another one of the Neo-Hittite states, for which we have evidence of rulership of Hittite descent.

Outside of Anatolia, in north Syria, lay the city-state of Karkemish. During the last two centuries of the Hittite Empire, Karkemish was, together with Aleppo, one of the two viceregal seats in Syria. We have historical evidence to affirm that Kunzi-Tesub, who reigned over Karkemish at least one generation after the Late Bronze Age collapse, was a direct descendant of Suppiluliuma I, which means the very bloodline of Hattusa survived the fall of the empire in north Syria. When Assyrian King Tiglath Pileser I conquered Karkemish in the second half of the 1200s BCE, he reported this conquest in the famous prism, retelling the story of his kingship. As we saw in Chapter 1, Rawlinson translated the prism from Akkadian. Its text referred to Karkemish being "in the land of Hatti." Also, in Chapter 1, we saw how George Smith discovered a stele in Karkemish, demonstrating Hittite presence in this city. The stele, inscribed in Luwian hieroglyphs, was later identified as a devotional item dedicated by King Kamani (a Hittite name) to the goddess Kubaba (a Hittite deity) and dated from the eighth century BCE.[21] Taken altogether, the evidence is enough to count Karkemish among the Neo-Hittite kingdoms.

Thus, Tabal, Lycia, Tarhuntassa, and Karkemish, are all Neo-Hittite kingdoms, for which historical and archaeological evidence shows that Hittite culture, tradition, and perhaps even royal bloodline were preserved for many generations after the fall.

Assyrians referred to these territories as the "Land of Hatti" as late as the ninth century CE. This is seen, for example, in an inscription by King Adad-nirari III, "I subdued ... the land of Hatti."[22]

Moreover, if we consider the Luwian language an expression of Hittite culture, then we have evidence of this culture well into the eighth century BCE, four hundred years after the fall.

This begs the question: if the Neo-Hittite kingdoms represent the natural continuation of the Hittite civilization, why was the language spoken in the kingdoms Luwian rather than Hittite?

There is evidence of Hittite-Luwian bilingualism throughout the history of the Hittite civilization (see Chapter 11). Moreover, we have evidence that, by the time the empire collapsed, Luwian had become the main vernacular of Anatolia.[23] How and why this happened, however, is not clear. Theories include an imbalance within the empire, centrally-spoken Hittite versus periphery-spoken Luwian. This balance may have been tipped towards Luwian by destructive events in the capital, like the plague.[24] Some have even argued that finding Luwian inscriptions on monuments in the Neo-Hittite kingdom is not enough to conclude a widespread use of Luwian over Hittite. After all, the Neo-Hittites could have used Luwian for inscriptions but Hittite for all other uses. Recent discoveries, however, have disproven this.

Luwian was not just a language for inscriptions; it was used in everyday writing in the Neo-Hittite kingdoms. Evidence of this comes from some strips of lead inscribed with administrative texts found in the Kingdom of Tabal and six letters found in Assur, Assyrian territory, both from the eighth century.[25] Conversely, the absence of any Hittite text past the reign of Suppiluliuma II is evidence that Luwian must have been the main or only language committed to writing within the Neo-Hittite kingdoms.

Thus, the Hittites lived on. They were severely diminished in numbers by invasions, lacked a unitary identity as their central government collapsed, and spoke Luwian rather than Hittite, but they lived on. They lived on for centuries until their Neo-Hittite kingdoms were successively absorbed by the expansion of other civilizations, like Assyria.

The Neo-Hittite kingdoms existed from the fall of the Hittite empire in the twelfth century BCE until well into the eighth century. This was when the books of the Old Testament were written. It is, therefore, logical to turn to the Old Testament for mentions of the Hittites. Circling back to Chapter 1 when we saw that for early 1800s historians, the only source

12. The Late Bronze Age Collapse

which mentioned the Hittites was the Bible. As we have seen, the Bible makes numerous references to the Hittites. However, instead of shedding light on the Hittites, these references make for a somewhat problematic reading and raise further questions.

There are 48 references to the Hittites in the Old Testament. Hittitologist Itamar Singer divided them into "outland references" and "inland references." There are just six outland references; they mention the "land of the Hittites" and the "kings (notice the plural) of the Hittites." Singer called these outland references because, he argued, they referred to Hittite lands and Hittite people outside of Palestine.

For example, in the book of *Josh*, "all of the lands of the Hittites" are described to stretch "between Lebanon and the Euphrates" and from there "toward the setting sun" (i.e., to the west). In the book of *Judges*, an unnamed man from Bethel is described as fleeing to the "lands of the Hittites." Later in the same book, we read: "And they said one to another: 'lo, the king of Israel hath hired against us the kings of the Hittites, and the kings of the Egyptians, to come upon us,'" and in the book of *Chronicles*: "And so brought they out horses for all the kings of the Hittites, and for the kings of Syria, by their means."

The common trait of these passages is that they all convey the impression of several more or less powerful, independent Hittite kingdoms outside of Palestine. It is reasonable to conclude that these references describe the Neo-Hittite kingdoms of South Anatolia and Syria, which, as we have seen earlier, were called "Lands of the Hatti" by Assyrians into the eighth century BCE.

The inland references are more numerous; they are forty-two and mention either single individuals who are referred to with the appellative "the Hittite," or cite the Hittites as an ethnic group settled in Canaan rather than the inhabitants of a foreign kingdom. Singer called them inland references because, he argued, they referred to people who lived within Palestine.

For example, in the book of *Genesis*, Abraham is said to have bought a sepulcher from a Hittite. In the book of *Kings*, Solomon conscripts Hittite men to carry out his building projects. In many references, the Hittites are depicted as epitomizing the sinful idolaters, in contrast to the God-devoted Israelites. So, when God speaks to the prophet Ezekiel and chastises the habitants of Jerusalem for their sins, he calls Jerusalem the "daughter of Amorites and Hittites" and in the book of *Judges*, it is written that Israelites who dwelt among the Hittites ended up being idolatrous.

Furthermore, when the Priest Ezra led the Judeans back to Israel at the end of the Babylonian exile, on his arrival in Jerusalem, he learns that the leaders who had remained in Israel had been "polluted" by mixing with the Hittites. The same disparaging undertone, but aimed at Hittite women, is seen in the book of Genesis when Rebekah is worried that Jacob may take a Hittite wife: "And Rebekah said to Isaac: 'I am weary of my life because of the Hittite women; if Jacob takes a wife of the Hittite women ... what good shall my life do me?'"

The common trait of these passages is that they all describe Hittite men and women as individuals who carry Jewish names and are integrated into the Palestinian society or, collectively, as an ethnic group that inhabited Palestine, and even more specifically, Jerusalem. And this is where the historical problem of the inland references arises, an issue that has puzzled historians for decades: no historical or archaeological record of Hittites ever inhabiting Palestine exists.[26]

Regarding this problematic reading, called "the question of biblical Hittites," scholars are divided into two schools of thought.

One school of thought is that the outland and inland references are not about the same people. According to this theory, while the outland references refer to the Neo-Hittite kingdoms and their inhabitants, the inland references refer to a minor ethnic group that inhabited Palestine at the time of the arrival of the Israelites and which only by coincidence had a name phonetically similar to the Hittites.[27] Some propose that evidence for this can be found in the original Hebrew texts, in which slight linguistic differences in the wording used in the references appear to discriminate between these two different entities. According to this theory, early translators of the Bible did not pick up on this linguistic nuance and clumped both peoples under the same name.[28]

The other school of thought is that the outland and inland references refer both to the Neo-Hittites. For this to be true, however, either Neo-Hittite people migrated to Palestine (against what archaeological records show), or the reference to the Hittites is figurative, symbolic, and the Hittites are only a name to represent the foreigner, the "other." Those who defend a possible migration of Neo-Hittite people into Palestine argue that other "nations" repeatedly mentioned alongside the Hittites in the Old Testament were of foreign origin too. For example, the Hivites are believed to be inhabitants of Cilicia, and the Jebusites are of Hurrian origin. Some have even hypothesized that the names of the Hittite characters in the Old Testament are not necessarily Semitic and could be interpreted as foreign.[29] Were these theories correct, the Bible could be the only evidence in our hands to trace a movement of Hittite people from Syria to Palestine in the Iron Age.

On the other hand, those who maintain that the biblical references to the Hittites in Palestine are figurative and symbolic argue that the Old Testament makes extensive use of symbolism, sometimes at the cost of

12. The Late Bronze Age Collapse

historical accuracy. Assyrians used the expression "land of Hatti" quite loosely. They generically applied it disparagingly to various territories that rebelled against their power throughout Syria and even north Palestine.[30] This use could have leached onto the oral tradition from which the Old Testament originated to the point that the name Hittite lost its historical meaning and came to signify the "other," the foreigner, the sinner dedicated to idolatry. This would even be consistent with the appellative "Hittite" used to characterize particular individuals who invariably played the role of the "other" in opposition to the Israelites in the tales of the Old Testament.

Unfortunately, the question of the historicity of biblical Hittites is far from being solved. The history of archaeology teaches us that historical evidence can come from the most diverse sources. Indeed, Hittitology started from Archibald Sayce's interest in biblical archaeology. On the other hand caution must be used in reading a religious text as a history book.

In conclusion, the Hittites lived past the Bronze Age, but not long. The sources reviewed herein provide a confusing and somewhat contradicting image of Neo-Hittite presence in the Ancient Near East up to the eighth century BCE. Looking further later, no concrete trace of this people can be found.

After this time, the Hittites disappeared from the map and historical memory for many, many centuries until modern historians like Archibald Sayce brought them back to life.

Epilogue

This book tells how, starting from a few scattered hints, some brilliant scholars have lifted the veil off an ancient civilization that had been lying forgotten for almost thirty centuries. The journey of discovering the Hittite civilization has been long and full of surprises, some genial intuitions, some moments of bravery, some wrong turns, and even some missed opportunities. This journey is far from being concluded: many aspects of Hittite history and culture remain unclear. The future of Hittitology is likely to reserve some intriguing surprises.

Most of the knowledge on the Hittites comes from relatively limited material remains.

Although excavations have been going on in Hattusa for over a hundred years, the search is far from over. For example, the residential quarters of Hattusan nobility have eluded researchers and all evidence points in the direction that monumental burying of the kings existed but has not been found yet.

Findings of tablets have been plentiful in Hattusa, and their complete translation is just recent, but the other Hittite towns have yielded very little so far. Indeed the main issue is that most Hittite towns we know about from ancient texts have not yet been geographically located. It is possible that digging at new sites may bring new findings of tablets. The tablets may shed some light on open questions such as the "Ahhiyawa question," or even allow a fuller understanding of the Hittite language and its vocabulary, filling the gap in the corpus discussed in Chapter 6.

Languages other than Hittite were spoken in many parts of the Hittite empire. The study of these languages, which is increasing in recent times, represents a new avenue for gathering knowledge on the Hittites, particularly in the late phase of their civilization. As shown, Luwian gathered momentum and became the most widely spoken language in Hittite territory towards the end of the empire.

Even with the available sources, determining a Hittite chronology has been an enormous challenge, as seen in Chapter 7. Modern techniques may allow us the direct dating that textual sources have not provided; The involvement of other disciplines, for example, chemical dating, paleoanthropology, or linguistics, may be vital to obtain new results.

The future looks encouraging because the number of scholars in the field worldwide is constantly growing. More departments of Hittitology exist in universities, more meetings are held, and more research is funded than ever before.

But the study of the past is not always pleasant and smooth. Every story has its villains, and if we look back at the history of Hittitology, the "villain," the most significant obstacle to its progress, has been the many conflicts that have hampered or marred the quest. Conflicts between nations, like the First and Second World Wars, conflicts between ethnic groups, like within the Ottoman Empire, or disputes between people, like the jealousies of some individual scholars.

In particular, we have seen how, too often, the interests of the territory and people where the archaeological site lay were put in second place. Lands have been divested of their treasures, local populations have been disrespected, and cultural heritages have been ignored. If the history of Hittitology teaches us a lesson, it is that the advancement of knowledge depends on favoring human collaboration over conflict and division. Hopefully, the level of human connection provided by modern-day technology will help the community of Hittitologists to avoid these stumbling blocks.

Finally, history and archaeology are noble endeavors because they nourish the need of human beings to know their past to better understand the present. Throughout the writing of this book are glimpses of the lives of those who have contributed to this advancement. This book seeks to celebrate the braveness of the researchers who followed this dream and inspired all of us.

Chapter Notes

Introduction

1. War, T. 1926. *History of the Athenæum 1824–1925*. London: Athenæum Club, §II–IV
2. Sayce, A, 1923. *Reminiscences*. London: Macmillan and Co., 123–124.

Chapter 1

1. Robinson, A. (2012). *Cracking the Egyptian Code: The Revolutionary Life of Jean-Francois Champollion*. Oxford: Oxford University Press, §10.
2. Langdon, S., & Gardiner, A. H. (1920). The Treaty of Alliance between Ḫattušili, King of the Hittites, and the Pharaoh Ramesses II of Egypt. *The Journal of Egyptian Archaeology*, 6(3), 179–205, 179–180.
3. Brugsch, K. H. (1860). *Geographische Inschriften altägyptischer Denkmäler Band II*. Leipzig, 24–26.
4. Sayce, A. (1907). *The Archaeology of the Cuneiform Inscriptions*. London: Society for Promoting Christian Knowledge, 13.
5. Grotefend, G. F. (1805). Über die Erklärung der Keilschriften, und besonders der Inschriften von Persepolis. In *Ideen über die Politik den Verkehr und den Handel der vornehmsten Völker der alten Welt* (pp. 931–960). Gottingen: Vandenhoek und Ruprecht.
6. Saint-Martin, A.-J. (1823). Extrait d'un mémoire relatif aux antiques inscriptions de Persépolis lu à l'Académie des Inscriptions et Belles Lettres. *Journal Asiatique*, 65–90.
7. Adkins, L. (2003). *Empires of the Plain: Henry Rawlinson and the Lost Languages of Babylon*. New York: Thomas Dunne Books, §11.
8. Luckenbill, D. D. (1926). *Ancient Records of Assyria and Babylonia*. Chicago, Illinois: The University of Chicago Press, 83.

Chapter 2

1. Burckhardt, J. L. (1822). *Travels in Syria and the Holy Land*. London: Association for Promoting the Discovery of the Interior Parts of Africa, 146–147.
2. Johnson, A. J. (1871). *Inscriptions Discovered at Hamath in Northern Syria*. New York: Pelstine Exploration Society, 174.
3. Burton, R. F. (1873). Notes on the Hamah Stones, with Reduced Transcripts. *The Journal of the Anthropological Institute of Great Britain and Ireland*, 2, 41–52.
4. Ginsburg, C. D. (1871). *The Moabite Stone; A Fac-Simile of the Original Inscription, with an English Translation, and a Historical and Critical Commentary*. London: Reeves and Turner, 10.
5. Alaura, S. (2017). Setting the stage for Hittite studies in Victorian England: practices and methods of the 1870s. *Anabases*(26), 34.
6. Wright, W. (1874). The Hamah Inscriptions: Hittite Remains. *British and Foreign Evangelical Review*, 23, 90–99.
7. Panayotov, S. (2014). George Smith's Identification of Karkemish: From the Account of his Assistant Mathewson. In *Karkemish: An Ancient Capital on the Euphrates* (pp. 44–51). Bologna: Ante Quem, 47.
8. Smith, G. (1876). Letter from George Smith to Samuel Birch, Department of Oriental Antiquities at British Musem, Aleppo April 5th. London: British

Museum Original Papers 51 May-July 1876, c5 Aug. 76 Stamp: BM 14 Jun 1876 No. 3024.

9. Colebrooke, T. E. (1877). Royal Asiatic Society. Proceedings of the Fifty-Third Anniversary Meeting of the Society. Held on the 29th of May, 1876. *Journal of the Royal Asiatic Society, 9*(2), 1-63, XLVIII.

10. Marchetti, N. (2014). *Karkemish: An Ancient Capital on the Euphrates (OrientLab 2)*. Bologna: AnteQuem.

11. Sayce, A. (1876). George Smith. *Nature, 14*, 421-422

12. Sayce, A. (1923). *Reminiscences*. London: Macmillan and Co.

13. Sayce, A. (1890). *The Hittites, the Story of a Forgotten Empire*. Oxford: The Religious Tract Society, 73-77.

14. Davis, E. J. (1879). *Life in Asiatic Turkey: a Journal of Travel in Cilicia (Pedias and Trachoea), Isauria, and Parts of Lycaonia and Cappadocia*. London: Stanford, 252-256.

15. Herodotus, *Historiae*, Book 2, § 106 as translated by Rawlinson, G.

16. Texier, C. (1839). *Description de l'Aise Mineure: faite par ordre du gouvernement francais de 1833 á 1837*. Paris: Didot Frères, 607-616.

17. Perrot, G. (1872). *Exploration archéologique de la Galatie et de la Bithynie d'une partie de la Mysie de la Cappadoce et du Pont exécutée en 1861, avec Edmond Guillaume et Jules Delbet*. Paris: Firmin Didot.

Chapter 3

1. Alaura 2018. "Austen Henry Layard and Archibald Henry Sayce. An Anatolian Perspective." *Rethinking Layard 1817-2017*. Venice: Istituto Veneto di Scienze, Lettere ed Arti, 25-62.

2. Sayce, A. (1880, NS 22). A Forgotten Empire in Asia Minor. *Fraser's Magazine*, 223-233.

3. Flinders Petrie, W. M. (1914). The Poem of Pentaur—Battle of Kadesh. In *The World's Story: A History of the World in Story, Song and Art* (pp. 154-162). Boston: Houghton Mifflin, 154-162.

4. Collins, B. J. 2007. *The Hittites and Their World*. Atlanta: Society of Biblical Literature, 55.

5. Alaura, S. (2015). "Little by little the obscurity is being cleared away from the earlier history of Asia Minor." Searching for the Hittites, from Sayce to Winckler. *The Discovery of an Anatolian Empire. A Colloquium to Commemorate the 100th Anniversary of the Decipherment of the Hittite Language* (pp. 13-27). Istanbul, 13.

6. D'Alviella, G. (1894). *The Migration of Symbols*. Westminster: Archibald Constable and Co., 21-22.

7. Alaura, S. (2015). Lost, Denied (Re)Constructed: The Identity of the Hittites and Luwians in the Historiographical Debate of the Late 19th and Early 20th Centuries. *Transformations and Crisis in the Mediterranean. "Identity" and Interculturality in the Levant and Phoenician West during the 12th-8th Centuries BCE*. Pisa—Rome, 23.

8. Ronder, C. (1893). Notes on the Hittite Writing. *The Journal of the Royal Asiatic Society of Great Britain and Ireland*, 824.

9. Wright, W., Sayce, A., Wilson, C., Conder, C., & Rylands, W. (1884). *The Empire of the Hittites*. London: Nisbet.

10. Müller, W. M. (1893). *Asien und Europa nach altägyptischen Denkmälern*. Leipzig: W. Engelmann, 319.

11. Sayce, A. (1888). *The Hittites: The Story of a Forgotten Empire*. London: The Religious Tract Society, 124.

12. Humann, C., & Puchstein, O. (1890). *Reisen in Kleinasien und Nordsyrien: Ausgeführt im Auftrage der Königlichen Preussischen Akademie der Wissenschaften (Atlas)*. Berlin.

13. Summers, Geoffrey. 1997. "The Identification of the Iron Age City on Kerkenes Dag in Central Anatolia." *Journal of Near Eastern Studies* 56 (2): 81-94.

14. Alaura, S. (2015). Lost, Denied (Re)Constructed, 13.

15. Dr. Schliemann. (1876, November 10). *The New York Times*, p. 4, §1.

16. Traill, D. (1995). *Schliemann of Troy: Treasure and Deceit*. New York: St. Martin's Press, 243.

17. Miller, W. (1908). *The Latins in the Levant, a history of Frankish Greece (1204-1566)*. New York: E. P. Dutton and Co., 401.

18. Chantre, E. (1898). *Recherches archéologiques dans l'Asie occidentale. Mission en Cappadoce 1893-1894*. Paris: Leroux, §XIV.

19. Boissier, A. (1895). Fragments de

tablettes couvertes de caractères cunéiformes, recueillies par M. Chantre etcommuniqués par M. Menant. *Compte Rendu des séances—Académie des Inscriptions et des Belles Lettres,* 4(39), 348–360.

Chapter 4

1. EA292, as translated via Moran, W. L. 1992. *The Amarna Letters.* Baltimore: Johns Hopkins University Press, 355.
2. EA41 as translated via Moran, W.L, 114.
3. EA31 as translated via Moran, W.L, 101.
4. Winckler, H. (1888). Bericht über die Thontafeln von Tell-el-Amarna im Königlichen Museum zu Berlinund im Museum von Bulaq. *Sitzungsberichte der Königlich Preussischen Akademie der Wissenschaften zu Berlin,* 2(51), 1341–1357.
5. Winckler, H. (1888). Bericht über die Thontafeln, 1341–1357.
6. Sayce, A. (1889). The Cuneiform Tablets of Tel el-Amarna, now Preserved in the Boulaq Museum. *Proceedings of the Society of Biblical Archaeology,* 11, 327, 339.
7. Sayce, A. (1893). Transactions of the Ninth International Congress of Orientalists (held in London, 5th to 12th September 1892). London, 169–186.
8. Chantepleure, G. 1900. *Le Fiancée d'Avril.* Paris: Calmann-Lévy.
9. Beckman, G. (1986). The Hittite Language and Its Decipherment. *Bulletin of the Canadian Society for Mesopotamian Studies,* 31, 26.
10. Knudtzon, J. A. (1902). *Die Zwei Arzawa-Briefe, die Ältesten Urkunden in Indogermanischer Sprache.* Leipzig: J. C. Hinrichs'sche Buchhandlung.
11. Pedersen, H. (1903). Zu den Arzawa-Briefen. *Anzeiger Indogermanische Forschungen,* 14(1), 280–283.
12. Horn, P. (1903). Knudtzon (review). *Anzeiger fur Indogermanische Sprach- und Altertumskunde,* 14, 1.
13. Kretschmer, P. (1903). Knudtzon (Review). *Deutsche Literaturzeitung für Kritik der internationalen Wissenschaft,* 13, 779–780.
14. Messerschmidt, L. (1903). Die Zwei Arzawa-Briefe (Review). *Orientalistische Literaturzeitung,* 2, 82.
15. Bloomfield, M. (1904). On Some Alleged Indo-European Languages in Cuneiform Character. *American Journal of Philology,* 13–14.
16. Weber, O., & Ebeling, A. (1915). *Die El Amarna Tafeln.* Leipzig: J C Hinrichs, 1074.

Chapter 5

1. Alaura, S. (2006). "Nach Boghazköi!" Zur Vorgeschichte der Ausgrabungen in Bogazköy-Hattusa und zu den archäologischen Forschungen bis zum Ersten Weltkrieg. *Sendschrift der Deutschen Orient-Gesellschaft*(13), 136.
2. AN, F17 294c, Chantre dossier 8, Chantre au ministère de l'Instruction publique, 8/5/1894.
3. Thobie, J. (2000). Archéologie et diplomatie française au Moyen-Orient des années1880 au début des années 1930. *Les Politiques de l'archéologie du milieu du XIXeme siècle à l'orée du XXIeme* (pp. 79–111). Athens: Ecole Française d'Athènes, 89.
4. Sayce, A. (1923). *Reminiscences.* London: Macmillan and Co., 327.
5. Schäffer, E. (1895). Die Ruinen von Boghas-köi. *Mitteilungen des Deutschen Archäologischen Instituts, Athenische Abteilung*(20), 465.
6. Alaura, S. (2002). La prima trattativa diplomatica dei "Musei reali di Berlino" per una concessione di scavo a Boğazköy. In S. de Martino, & F. Pecchioli Daddi, *Anatolia Antica. Studi in memoria di F. Imparati* (pp. 23–46). Firenze: Eothen, 30.
7. Matthes, O. (2008). Deutsche Ausgräber im Vorderen Orient. In *Das große Spiel. Archäologie und Politik zur Zeit des Kolonialismus (1860–1940)* (pp. 226–235). Essen: DuMont, 226–228.
8. Klock-Fontanille, I. 2012. "Les débuts de l'hittitologie : le rôle de la science allemande." *Revue Germanique Internationale* 119–133.
9. Gernot, W. (1998). 100 Jahre Ausgrabungen der Deutschen Orient-Gesellschaft , Mayence. In *Zwischen Tigris und Nil. 100 Jahre Ausgrabungen der Deutschen Orient-Gesellschaft in Vorderasien und Ägypten.* Mainz: Philip von Zabern, 5.
10. Virchow, R. (1898). Die orientalische Altertumsforschung preußichen

im Landtag. *Orientalische Literatur-Zeitung*, 1(4), 120.
 11. Mangold-Will, S. (2017). Wilhelm II.—Archäologie als wissenschaftliche Herrschaftslegitimation in der Ambivalenz der Moderne. In *Wilhelm II: Archäologie und Politik um 1900* (pp. 123–126). Stuttgart: Franz Steiner, 123–126.
 12. Pears, E. (1917). *Abdülhamid II, Sultan of the Turks, 1842–1918*. London: Constable & Co., 116.
 13. Sayce, A. (1923). *Reminiscences*. London: Macmillan and Co., 327–328.
 14. A.H. Sayce to J. Garstang, november 10, 1907, Griffith Institute, Oxford, Sayce. Mss. B 32.4. Quoted in Alaura, S. 2018. "Austen Henry Layard and Archibald Henry Sayce. An Anatolian Perspective." *Rethinking Layard 1817–2017*. Venice: Istituto Veneto di Scienze, Lettere ed Arti. 25–62.
 15. Klengel, H. (1991). Das Berliner Boğazköy-Archiv: Geschichte und Textedition. *Ägypten, Vorderasien, Turfan. Probleme der Edition und Bearbeitung altorientalischer Handschriften (Schriften zur Geschichte und Kultur des Alten Orients)*. Berlin, 75.
 16. Winckler, H., & Puchstein, O. 1907. "Excavations at Boghaz-keui in the Summer of 1907." *Annual Report of the Board of Regents of the Smithsonian Institution*, 678.
 17. All quotations of Makridi Bey in this chapter are via Eldem, E. (2015). Theodor Makridi Bey ve 1907 Boğazköy Kazısı. *The Discovery of an Anatolian Empire. A Colloquium to Commemorate the 100th Anniversary of theDecipherment of the Hittite Language*. Istanbul, 170.
 18. Bittel, K. (1941). Theodor Makridi. *Archiv für Orientforschung*, 380.
 19. Picard, C. (1944). Theodoros Makridy-Bey (1941). *Revue Archeologique*, 6(21), 48–50.
 20. Winckler, H., & Puchstein, O. 1907. "Excavations at Boghaz-keui in the Summer of 1907." *Annual Report of the Board of Regents of the Smithsonian Institution*, 678.
 21. Quoted in Bittel, K. (1941). Theodor Makridi. *Archiv für Orientforschung*, 380.
 22. Wood, M. (1998). *In Search of the Trojan War*. Berkeley: University of California Press, 174.
 23. Winckler, H., & Puchstein, O. 1907. "Vorläufige Nachrichten über die Ausgrabungen in Boghaz-koi imSommer 1907." *Mitteilungen der deutschen Orient-Gesellschaft zu Berlin*, 10.
 24. Alaura, S. (2006). "Nach Boghazköi!", 136.
 25. Jansen, C., & Diebner, S. (2016). Ludwig Curtius (1874–1954). In *2016, Lebensbilder. Klassische Archäologen und der Nationalsozialismus, Bd. 2*. Berlin: Marie Leidorf GmbH, 83.
 26. Curtius, L. (1958). *Deutsche un antike Welt. Lebenserinnerungen*. Stuttgart: Deutsche Verlags-Anstalt.
 27. Miller, J. L. (2015). The Tablet Finds of Temple I from the Early Excavations at Boğazköy-Hattusa (1906–1912). *The Discovery of an Anatolian Empire. A Colloquium to Commemorate the 100th Anniversary of the Decipherment of the Hittite Language* (pp. 69–84). Istanbul, 73.
 28. Alaura, S. (2001). Archive und Bibliotheken in Hattuša. *Akten des IV. Internationalen Kongresses für Hethitologie, Würzburg, 4.-8. Oktober 1999*. Wiesbaden, 17.

Chapter 6

 1. Curry, A. (2015, September 2). Here Are the Ancient Sites ISIS Has Damaged and Destroyed. *National Geographic*, §1.
 2. Alaura, S. (2015). Bedřich Hrozný and the Imperial Ottoman Museum in Constantinople at the Outbreak of World War I. *Bedřich Hrozný and 100 Years of Hittitology*, Prague, 130.
 3. Rieken, E. (2015). Hrozný's Decipherment: Method, Success and Consequences for Indo-European Linguistics. *The Discovery of an Anatolian Empire. A Colloquium to Commemorate the 100th Anniversary of the Decipherment of the Hittite Language*. Istanbul, 96–97.
 4. Hrozný, F. (1915). Die Lösung des hethitischen Problems. *Mitteilungen der Deutschen Orient-Gesellschaft*(56), 17–50.
 5. Velhartická, Š. (2015). Rezeption der Entzifferung der hethitischen Sprache in der österreichischen und deutschen Presse. *Mitteilungen der Deutschen Orient-Gesellschaft*, 12–13.
 6. Schoepfer, A. (1915, December 11). Eine wichtige Entdeckung. *Allgemeiner Tiroler Anzeiger*.
 7. Hrozný, F. (1917). *Die Sprache der Hethiter : ihr Bau und ihre Zugehörigkeit*

zum indogermanischen Sprachstamm. Leipzig: Hinrichs.
  8. Hrozný, F. (1919). *Hethitische Keilschrifttexte aus Boghazköi. In Umschrift, mit Übersetzung und Kommentar.* Leipzig: Hinrichs.
  9. Sommer, F. 1920. *Hethitisches.* Leipzig: J. C. Hinrichs.
  10. Beckman, G. (2014). From Hattusa to Carchemish, the latest on Hittite history. In *Current Issues in the History of the Ancient Near East* (pp. 97-112). Claremont: Regina Books, 100-101.
  11. Košak, S., Müller, G., Görke, S., & Steitler, C. (2020, 01 27). *Catalogue of Hittite Texts (CTH).* Retrieved 09 04, 2021, from https://www.hethport.uni-wuerzburg.de/CTH/index_en.php
  12. Goedegebuure, P., Güterbock, H., Hoffner, H., & Van den Hout, T. (1975). *The Hittite Dictionary of the Oriental Institute of the University of Chicago (CHD).* Chicago: Oriental Institute of the University of Chicago.
  13. Van den Hout, T. (2011). *The Elements of Hittite.* Cambridge: Cambridge University Press, 2.
  14. Hoffner, H., & Melchert, C. (2008). *A Grammar of the Hittite Language.* Winona Lake: Eisenbrauns, 12-13.

Chapter 7

  1. Forrer, E. (1922). *Wissenschaftliche Veröffentlichungen der Orient-Gesellschaft 41. Die Boghazköi-Texte in Umschrift 1.* Leipzig: J.C. Hinrichs.
  2. The quotations of Forrer in this chapter are from Oberheid, R. (2007). *Emil O. Forrer und die Anfänge der Hethitologie. Eine wissenschafts historische Biografie.* Berlin and New York: Walter de Gruyter, 27-35.
  3. Ceram, C. (. (1955). *The Secret of the Hittites.* London: Phoenix Press, 92-93.
  4. Gimbutas, M. (1970). Proto-Indo-European Culture: The Kurgan Culture during the Fifth, Fourth, and Third Millennia B.C. *Indo-European and Indo-Europeans. Papers Presented at the Third Indo-European Conference at the University of Pennsylvania.* Philadelphia, 155-156.
  5. Spretnak, C. (2011). Anatomy of a Backlash: Concerning the Work of Marija Gimbutas. *The Journal of Archaeomythology, 7,* 23.
  6. Özgüç, T. (1956). "The Dagger of Anitta." *Belleten* 33-36.
  7. Van den Hout, T. (2011). *The Elements of Hittite.* Cambridge: Cambridge University Press, 2.
  8. Forrer, E. (1919). Die Acht Sprachen der Boghaz-koi Inschriften. *Sitzungsberichte der Preussischen Akademie der Wissenschaften.* Berlin.
  9. Otten, H. 1981. *Die Apologie Hattusilis III. Das Bild der Überlieferung.* Wiesbaden: Otto Harrassowitz.
  10. Collins, B.J. 2007. *The Hittites and Their World.* Atlanta: Society of Biblical Literature, 40.
  11. Sommer, F., & Falkenstein, A. (1938). *Die hethitisch-akkadische Bilingue des Hattusili I (Labarna II).* Munich: Verlag der Bayerischen Akademie der Wissenschaften.
  12. Rawlinson, H. C. (1870). *The Cuneiform Inscriptions of Western Asia, vol. III.* London: R.E. Bowler, §63.
  13. Collins, B. J. 2007. *The Hittites and Their World.* Atlanta: Society of Biblical Literature, 58.
  14. Bechtel, G., & Sturtevant, E. H. (1935). *A Hittite Chrestomathy.* Philadelphia: University of Pennsylvania Press, 194.

Chapter 8

  1. Grote, G. (1846). *A History of Greece.* London: John Murray, §15.
  2. Forrer, E. (1924). Vorhomerische Griechen in den Keilschrifttexten von Boghazköi. *Mitteilungen der Deutschen Orient-Gesellschaft zu Berlin,* 1-24.
  3. Forrer, E. (1931). Apollon, Vulcanus, und die Kyklopen in den Boghazköi-Texten. *Revue hittite et asianique,* 141-144.
  4. Bryce, T. (1985). A Reinterpretation of the Milawata Letter in the Light of the New Join Piece. *Anatolian Studies*(35), 14.
  5. Bryce, T. (1998). *The Kingdom of the Hittites.* Oxford: Oxford University Press, 395-396.
  6. Sommer, F. (1932). *Die Ahhijava-Urkunden.* Munich: Verlag der Bayerischen Akademie der Wissenschaften.
  7. Page, D.L. 1959. *History and the Homeric Iliad.* Berkeley and Los Angeles: University of California Press, §1.

8. Friedrich, J. 1927. "Werden in den hethitischen Keilschrifttexten die Griechen erwähnt?" *Kleinasiatische Forschungen* 87–107.
9. Friedrich, J. (1964). Ferdinand Sommer (1875–1962). *Zeitschrift der Deutschen Morgenländischen Gesellschaft*, *114*(1), 14.
10. Page, D.L. 1959. *History and the Homeric Iliad*. Berkeley and Los Angeles: University of California Press, 2.
11. Bryce, T. (1985). A reinterpretation of the Milawata letter, 14.
12. Muhly, D. 1974. "The Hittites and the Aegean World." *Expedition Magazine* 2–10.
13. Güterbock, H. G. 1984. "Hittites and Akhaeans: a New Look." *Proceedings of the American Philosophical Society* 114–122.
14. Ünal, A. E. & Ediz, İ. 1990–1991. "The Hittite Sword from Bogazköy-Hattusa, found in 1991, and Its Akkadian Inscription." *Müze-Museum* 46–52.
15. Carruba, O. 1977. "Beiträge zur mittelhethitischen Geschichte I—Die Tuthaliyas und die Arnuwandas." *Studi Micenei ed Egeo-Anatolici* 137–174.
16. Hansen, O. (1994). A Mycenaean sword from Bogazkoy-Hattusa found in 1991. *The Annual of the British School at Athens*, *89*, 213.
17. Cline, E. H. (1996). Assuwa and the Achaeans: the "Mycenaean" sword at Hattusas and its possible implications. *The Annual of the British School at Athens*, *91*, 150.
18. Rizza, A. (2002). Linguistic and cultural layers in the Anatolian myth of Illuijanka. In *Syggraphé* (pp. 9–24). Como: New Press, 14.

Chapter 9

1. Erimtan, C. (2008). Hittites, Ottomans and Turks: Ağaoğlu Ahmed Bey and the Kemalist Construction of Turkish Nationhood in Anatolia. *Anatolian Studies*, *58*, 142.
2. Gedikli, Y. (2002). *Pontus Meselesi. Arap alfabesinden akarilan, notlu ve tenkitli sekilde*. Istanbul: Bilge Karinca.
3. Tunçay, M. (1981). *Türkiye Cumhuriyeti'nde Tek-Parti Yönetiminin Kurulması 1923-1931*. Ankara: Miladi, 300.
4. Shaw, W. M. (2004). Whose Hittites, and Why? Language, Archaeology and the Quest for the Original Turks. In *Archaeology under Dictatorship* (pp. 131–153). New York: Springer, 150.
5. Güterbock, H. G. (1992). Kurt Bittel (5 July 1907–30 January 1991). *Proceedings of the American Philosophical Society*, *136*(4), 579.
6. Ceram, CW (pseud). 1955. *The Secret of the Hittites*. London: Phoenix Press, 202.
7. EA31, via Moran, W. L. 1992. *The Amarna Letters*. Baltimore: Johns Hopkins University Press, 101.
8. Nyland, A. (2009). *The Kikkuli Method of Horse Training*. Armidale, Australia: Maryannu Press, 1–144.
9. Güterbock, H. G. (1956). The Deeds of Suppiluliuma as Told by His Son, Mursili II. *Journal of Cuneiform Studies*, *10*(2), 41–68.
10. Bryce, T. (2003). *Letters of the Great Kings of the Ancient Near East: The Royal Correspondence of the Late Bronze Age*. London: Routledge, 35.
11. All quotations from the *Deeds of Suppiluliuma* in this chapter are translated by Güterbock, H. G. (1956). The Deeds of Suppiluliuma as Told by His Son, Mursili II. *Journal of Cuneiform Studies*, *10*(2).
12. EA4, via Moran, W. L. 1992. *The Amarna Letters*. Baltimore: Johns Hopkins University Press, 8.

Chapter 10

1. EA96, via Moran, W. L. 1992. *The Amarna Letters*. Baltimore: Johns Hopkins University Press, 170.
2. Trevisanato, S. (2007). The "Hittite Plague", an epidemic of tularemia and the first record of biological warfare. *Medical Hypotheses*, *69*, 1371.
3. Norrie, P. (2016). How diseases affected the end of the Bronze Age. In *A History of Disease in Ancient Times* (pp. 61–101). London: Palgrave Macmillan, 88–91.
4. Goldacre, B. (2009, September 12). *The Guardian*. Retrieved August 8, 2022, from https://www.theguardian.com/commentisfree/2009/sep/12/bad-science-peer-review-goldacre §1.
5. Finkelstein, J. J. (1972). Albrecht Goetze, 1897–1971. *Journal of the American Oriental Society*, *92*(2), 197.

6. All quotations from the *Annals* in this chapter are translated by Götze, A. (1933). *Die Annalen des Muršiliš.* Leipzig: Hinrichs, 161.
7. CTH394, translated by Friedrich, 1925, via Gurney, O. (1976). *Some Aspects of Hittite Religion.* Oxford: Oxford University Press, 48–49.
8. Khamsi R. 2007. *New Scientist.* 26 November. Accessed August 27, 2022. https://www.newscientist.com/article/dn12960-were-cursed-rams-the-first-biological-weapons/.
9. Sanders, P. 2006. "Argumenta ad Deum in hte Plague Prayers of Mursili II and in the Book of Psalms." *Psalms and Prayers: Papers Read at the Joint Meeting of the Society of Old Testament Study and Het Oudtestamentisch Wekgezelschap in Nederland en België, Apeldoorn, August 2006.* Leiden: Brill, 181–217.
10. Sedulius Scottus *Contra plagam*, via Waddell, Helen. 1948. *Mediaeval Latin Lyrics.* New York: Henry Holt, 125.
11. All quotations from the *Plague Prayers* in this chapter are from Götze, A. (1930). Die Pestgebete des Muršiliš. *Kleinasiatische Forschungen, 1*, 161–251.
12. Torri, G. 2019. "Strategies for Persuading a Deity in Hittite Prayers and Vows." *Die Welt des Orients* 48–60.
13. CTH 70, Mursili's Accusations against Tawananna via Singer, I. & Hoffner, H.A. 2002. *Hittite Prayers.* Atlanta: Society of Biblical Literature, 76.
14. Singer, I. 2011. *The Calm Before the Storm, Selected Writings of Itamar Singer on the Late Bronze Age in Anatolia and in the Levant.* Atlanta: Society of Biblical Literature, 609–617.
15. HDT 24A I 1–19, translated by Beckman, G., via Tugendhaft, A. (2012). How to Become a Brother in the Bronze Age: An Inquiry into the Representation of Politics in Ugaritic Myth. *Fragments, 2*, 94–95.
16. All quotations from the *Apology* in this chapter are translated by Otten, H. 1981. *Die Apologie Hattusilis III. Das Bild der Überlieferung.* Wiesbaden: Otto Harrassowitz.
17. Bryce, T. *Letters of the Great Kings of the Ancient Near East: The Royal Correspondence of the Late Bronze Age.* London: Routledge, 113.
18. KBo I 14 via Archi, A. 1966. "Trono reale e trono divinizzato nell'Anatolia ittita." *Studi Micenei ed Egeo-Anatolici*, 208.
19. KBo I 29 via Friedrich, J. 1925. *Aus dem hethitischen schrifttum.* Leipzig: J.C. Hinrichs, 23.
20. KUB 21.38 via Beckman, G., & Hoffner H. 1996. *Hittite Diplomatic Texts.* Ann Arbor, Michigan: University of Michigan Library, 132.
21. KUB XXI 38, via Singer, I. 1991. "The title "Great Princess" in the Hittite Empire." *Ugarit-Foschungen* 327–328.
22. Bo 86/299 via Otten, H. 1988. *Die Bronzetafel Aus Bogazkoy: Ein Staatsvertrag Tuthalijas IV (Studien zu den Bogazköy-Texten. Beiheft).* Wiesbaden: Harassovitz.
23. Seeher, J. (2011). *Gods Carved in Stone: The Hittite Rock Sanctuary of Yazilikaya.* Istanbul: Ege Yayinlari, 154–164.
24. Zangger, E., & Gautschy, R. (2019). Celestial Aspects of Hittite Religion: An Investigation of the Rock Sanctuary Yazılıkaya. *Journal of Skyscape Archaeology*, 5.
25. CTH105, Treaty between Tudhaliya IV of Hatti and Shaushgamuwa via Beckman G., Bryce T. & Cline E.H. 2011. *The Ahhiyawa texts (Writings from the Ancient World).* Atlanta: Society of Biblical Literature, 61.
26. CTH105, Treaty between Tudhaliya IV of Hatti and Shaushgamuwa via Beckman G., Bryce T. & Cline E.H. 2011. *The Ahhiyawa texts (Writings from the Ancient World).* Atlanta: Society of Biblical Literature, 63.
27. Cline, E. H. 2007. "Rethinking Mycenaean International Trade with Egypt and the Near East." In *Rethinking Mycenaean Palaces*, 190–200. Los Angeles: Cotsen Institute of Archaeology.
28. Pulak, C. 1998. "The Bronze Age Shipwreck at Ulu Burun, Turkey: 1985 Campaign." *American Journal of Archaeology* 1–37.
29. KUB 3.73 via Hagenbuchner, A. 1989. *Die Korrespondenz der Hethiter. Teil II.* Heidelberg: Carl Winter, 275–277.

Chapter 11

1. Barnett, R. D. (1953). Karatepe, the Key to the Hittite Hieroglyphs. *Anatolian Studies, 3*, 63.

2. Ceram, CW (pseud). 1955. *The Secret of the Hittites*. London: Phoenix Press, 108.
3. Bahadir Alkim, U. (1961). Prof. Dr. H. Th. Bossert (11.IX.1889–5.II.1961). Belleten, 25(99), 467.
4. Weidner, E. (1963). Helmuth Theodor Bossert. (11. September 1889 bis 5. February 1961). *Archiv für Orientforschung, 20*, 305.
5. Bittel, K. (1998). *Reisen und Ausgrabungen in Ägypten, Kleinasien, Bulgarien und Griechenland 1930-1934*. Stuttgart: Steiner, 380–385.
6. Alaura, S. (2020). Hittite Studies at the Crossroads: Albrecht Goetze's and Hans Gustav Güterbock's Flight from Nazi Germany. In *Perspectives on the History of Ancient Near Eastern Studies* (pp. 3–24). Philadelphia: Pennsylvania State University Press, 9.
7. Darga, M. (2001). Istanbul üniversitesi'nde Hititologji'nin ilk yillari. In *Boğazköy'den Karatepe'ye: Hititbilim ve Hitit Dünyasının Keşfi* (pp. 44–61). Istanbul: Yapı Kredi Yayınları, 45.
8. Alaura, S. (2020). Hittite Studies at the Crossroads, 9.
9. Alet, Ç. (1948). Karatepe: An Archeological Introduction to a Recently Discovered Hittite Site in Southern Anatolia. *Oriens, 1*(2), 147.
10. Ceram, CW (pseud). 1955. *The Secret of the Hittites*, 225.
11. Steinherr, F. (1949). Karatepe: the Key to the Hittite Hieroglyphs. *Archaeology, 2*(4), 177–180.
12. Glanzman, G., Rowley, H. H., Marcus, R., Speiser, E. A., & Albright, W. F. (1954). In Memoriam Roger T. O'Callaghan, S. J. *Bulletin of the American Schools of Oriental Research, 134*, 3.
13. O'Callaghan, R. T. (1949). The Phoenician Inscription on the King's Statue at Karatepe. *The Catholic Biblical Quarterly, 11*(3), 233.
14. Ünal, A. (1976). Dr. Franz Steinherr (1902–1974). *Belleten Périodique Trimestriel, Société Turque d'Histoire, 40*(158), 347.
15. Bossert, H. T. (1948). Die phönizisch-hethitischen Bilinguen vom Karatepe. *Oriens, 1*(2), 163–192.
16. Glanzman, G. et al. (1954). In Memoriam Roger T. O'Callaghan, 3
17. Bossert, H. T. (1949). Die phönizisch-hethitischen Bilinguen vom Karatepe: 1. Fortsetzung. *Oriens, 2*(1), 72.
18. Meriggi, P. 1932. "Sur le déchiffrement et la langue de hiuéroglyphes 'hittites.'" *Revue Hittite et Asianique* 1–57.
19. Collins, B. J. 2007. *The Hittites and their World*. Atlanta: Society of Biblical Literature, 31.
20. Payne, A. 2004. "Writing Systems and Identity." *Anatolian Interfaces: Hittites, Greeks and Their Neighbors, Proceedings of an International Conference on CrossCultural Interaction, September 17-19, 2004*. Atlanta: Emory University.
21. Güterbock, H. G. (1957). Toward a Definition of the Term Hittite. *Oriens, 10*(2), 233–239.

Chapter 12

1. Drews, R. (1993). *The End of the Bronze Age: Changes in Warfare and the Catastrophe, ca. 1200 B.C.* Princeton, NJ: Princeton University Press, 167.
2. Edgerton, W., & Wilson, J. (1936). *Historical Records of Ramses III, the Texts in Medinet Habu, Volumes I and II*, translated with explanatory notes. Chicago: University of Chicago Press, 53.
3. Nibbi, A. (1975). *The Sea Peoples and Egypt*. Park Ridge, New Jersey: Noyes Press, 48.
4. RS 34.129 via Lackenbacher S. & Malbran-Labat F. 2016. *Lettres akkadiennes de la «Maison d'Urtēnu». Fouilles de 1994*. Leuven-Paris-Bristol: Peeters, 38–39.
5. Drews, R. (1993). *The End of the Bronze Age*, 167.
6. Divon, S. A. (2006). The City of Emar among the Late Bronze Age Empires. *Proceedings of the Konstanz Emar Conference* (pp. 101–109). Konstanz, 103.
7. Nougayrol, J. (1960). Nouveaux textes accadiens de Ras-Shamra. *Comptes rendus des séances de l'Académie des Inscriptions et Belles-Lettres, 104*, 165.
8. Karnak Inscription in Breasted, H. J. (1906). *Ancient Records of Egypt*, vol. III. Chicago: University of Chicago Press, 572–592.
9. Sandars, N. (1978). *The Sea Peoples: Warriors of the Ancient Mediterranean. 1250-1150*. London: Thames and Hudson, 11.
10. Singer, I. (1985). The Battle of Niḫriya and the End of the Hittite Empire. *Zeitschrift für Assyriologie*

und vorderasiatische Archäologie, 75(1), 120–121.
11. Seeher, J. (1999). Die Zerstörung der Stadt Hattusa. *Akten IV. Internationalen Kongresses für Hethitologie*. Würzburg, 623.
12. Mellaart, James. 1984. "Troy VIIA in Anatolian Perspective." *The Trojan War: Its Historicity and Context : Papers of the First Greenbank Colloquium*. Liverpool: 1981, 78–79.
13. Bryce, Trevor. 1998. *The Kingdom of the Hittites*. Oxford: Oxford University Press, 382.
14. Harl, Kenneth. 2005. *Origins of Great Ancient Civilizations*. Chantilly, VA: The Great Courses / The Teaching Co.
15. Collins, Billy Jean. 2007. *The Hittites and Their World*. Atlanta: Society of Biblical Literature, 81.
16. Bryce, T. 2003. "History." In *The Luwians*, 27–127. Leiden and Boston: Brill, 98.
17. Hawkins, J.D. 2000. *Corpus of Hieroglyphic Luwian Inscriptions*. Berlin and New York: Walter de Gruyter.
18. Bryce, T. 1986. *The Lycians in Literary and Epigraphic Sources*. Copenhagen: Musem Tusculanum Press, 29–35.
19. Bryce, T. 2012. *The World of the Neo-Hittite Kingdoms: A Political and Military History*. Oxford: Oxford University Press, 29, 85.
20. Bryce, Tr. 1986. *The Lycians*, 29–35.
21. Marchetti, N., & Peker, H. 2018. "The Stele of Kubaba by Kamani and the Kings of Karkemish in the 9th Century BC" *Zeitschrift für Assyriologie* 81–99.
22. Inscription of King Adad-Nirari III from Calah via Hallo, W.W. & Younger, K.L. 1997. *Context of Scriptures*. Leiden: Brill, 1.214G:276.
23. Collins, B. J. 2007. *The Hittites and Their World*. Atlanta: Society of Biblical Literature, 88.
24. Van den Hout, T. 2006. "Institutions, Vernaculars, Publics: The Case of Second-Millennium Anatolia." In *Margins of Writing, Origins of Cultures*, 221–260. Chicago: The Oriental Institute of the University of Chicago, 237.
25. Hawkins, J.D. 2003. "Scripts and Texts." In *The Luwians*, 128–169. Leiden and Boston: Brill, 151.
26. Singer, I. 2006. "The Hittites and the Bible Revisited." In *"I will Speak the Riddles of Ancient Times": Archaeological and Historical Studies in Honor of Amihai Mazar on the Occasion of His Sixtieth Birthday*, 754. Winona Lake: Eisenbrauns.
27. Hoffner, H. A., Jr. 1973. "The Hittites and Hurrians." In *Peoples of Old Testament Times*, 197–228. Oxford: Oxford University Press, 215.
28. Wood, B. G. 2011. "Hittites and Hethites: a proposed solution to an etymological conundrum." *Journal of the Evangelical Theological Society* 239–250.
29. Vieyra, M. 1939. "Parallèle ḫurrite au nom d'Urie "le hittite." *Revue Hittite et Asiatique*, 113.
30. Clay, A.T. 1919. *The Empire of the Amorites*. New Haven: Yale University Press, 161.

Bibliography

Adkins, Lesley. 2003. *Empires of the Plain: Henry Rawlinson and the Lost Languages of Babylon*. New York: Thomas Dunne Books.
Alaura, Silvia. 2001. "Archive und Bibliotheken in Hattuša." *Akten des IV. Internationalen Kongresses für Hethitologie, Würzburg, 4.-8. Oktober 1999*. Wiesbaden.
―――. 2002. "La prima trattativa diplomatica dei "Musei reali di Berlino" per una concessione di scavo a Boğazköy." In *Anatolia Antica. Studi in memoria di F. Imparati*, by S. de Martino and F. Pecchioli Daddi, 23–46. Firenze: Eothen.
―――. 2006. ""Nach Boghazköi!" Zur Vorgeschichte der Ausgrabungen in Bogazköy-Hattusa und zu den archäologischen Forschungen bis zum Ersten Weltkrieg." *Sendschrift der Deutschen Orient-Gesellschaft* (13): 191.
―――. 2015. "Bedřich Hrozný and the Imperial Ottoman Museum in Constantinople at the Outbreak of World War I." *Bedřich Hrozný and 100 Years of Hittitology*. Prague. 126–138.
―――. 2015. ""Little by little the obscurity is being cleared away from the earlier history of Asia Minor." Searching for the Hittites, from Sayce to Winckler." *The Discovery of an Anatolian Empire. A Colloquium to Commemorate the 100th Anniversary of the Decipherment of the Hittite Language*. Istanbul. 13–27.
―――. 2015. "Lost, Denied (Re)Constructed: The Identity of the Hittites and Luwians in the Historiographical Debate of the Late 19th and Early 20th Centuries." *Transformations and Crisis in the Mediterranean. "Identity" and Interculturality in the Levant and Phoenician West during the 12th-8th Centuries BCE*. Pisa—Rome.
―――. 2017. "Setting the stage for Hittite studies in Victorian England: practices and methods of the 1870s." *Anabases* (26): 33–55.
―――. 2018. "Austen Henry Layard and Archibald Henry Sayce. An Anatolian Perspective." *Rethinking Layard 1817-2017*. Venice: Istituto Veneto di Scienze, Lettere ed Arti. 25–62.
―――. 2020. "Hittite Studies at the Crossroads: Albrecht Goetze's and Hans Gustav Güterbock's Flight from Nazi Germany." In *Perspectives on the History of Ancient Near Eastern Studies*, 3–24. Philadelphia: Pennsylvania State University Press.
Alet, Çambel. 1948. "Karatepe: An Archeological Introduction to a Recently Discovered Hittite Site in Southern Anatolia." *Oriens* 1 (2): 147–162.
Archi, Alfonso. 1966. "Trono reale e trono divinizzato nell'Anatolia ittita." *Studi Micenei ed Egeo-Anatolici* 76–120.
Bahadir Alkim, Ulug. 1961. "Prof. Dr. H. Th. BOSSERT (11.IX.1889--5.II.1961)." *Belleten* 25 (99): 467–469.
Barnett, Richard David. 1953. "Karatepe, the Key to the Hittite Hieroglyphs." *Anatolian Studies* 3: 53–95.
Bechtel, George, and Edgar H Sturtevant. 1935. *A Hittite Chrestomathy*. Philadelphia: University of Pennsylvania Press.
Beckman, Gary. 1986. "The Hittite Language and its Decipherment." *Bulletin of the Canadian Society for Mesopotamian Studies* 31: 23–30.

———. 2014. "From Hattusa to Carchemish, the latest on Hittite history." In *Current Issues in the History of the Ancient Near East*, 97–112. Claremont: Regina Books.
Beckman, Gary, and Harry Hoffner. 1996. *Hittite Diplomatic Texts*. Ann Arbor, Michigan: University of Michigan Library.
Beckman, Gary, Trevor Bryce, and Eric H. Cline. 2011. *The Ahhiyawa Texts (Writings from the Ancient World)*. Atlanta: Society of Biblical Literature.
Bittel, Kurt. 1941. "Theodor Makridi." *Archiv für Orientforschung* 380–381.
———. 1998. *Reisen und Ausgrabungen in Ägypten, Kleinasien, Bulgarien und Griechenland 1930–1934*. Stuttgart: Steiner.
Bloomfield, Maurice. 1904. "On Some Alleged Indo-European Languages in Cuneiform Character." *American Journal of Philology* 1–14.
Boissier, Alfred. 1895. "Fragments de tablettes couvertes de caractères cunéiformes, recueillies par M. Chantre et communiqués par M. Menant." *Compte Rendu des séances— Académie des Inscriptions et des Belles Lettres* 4 (39): 348–360.
Bossert, Helmuth Thomas. 1948. "Die phönizisch-hethitischen Bilinguen vom Karatepe." *Oriens* 1 (2): 163–192.
———. 1949. "Die phönizisch-hethitischen Bilinguen vom Karatepe: 1. Fortsetzung." *Oriens* 2 (1): 72–120.
Breasted, Henry James. 1906. *Ancient Records of Egypt, vol. III*. Chicago: University of Chicago Press.
Brugsch, Karl Heinrich. 1860. *Geographische Inschriften altägyptischer Denkmäler Band II*. Leipzig.
Bryce, Trevor. 1985. "A reinterpretation of the Milawata letter in the light of the new join piece." *Anatolian Studies* (35): 13–23.
———. 1986. *The Lycians in Literary and Epigraphic Sources*. Copenhagen: Museum Tusculanum Press.
———. 1998. *The Kingdom of the Hittites*. Oxford: Oxford University Press.
———. 2003. "History." In *The Luwians*, 27–127. Leiden and Boston: Brill.
———. 2003. *Letters of the Great Kings of the Ancient Near East The Royal Correspondence of the Late Bronze Age*. London: Routledge.
———. 2012. *The World of the Neo-Hittite Kingdoms: A Political and Military History*. Oxford: Oxford University Press.
Burckhardt, Johan Ludwig. 1822. *Travels in Syria and the Holy Land*. London: Association for Promoting the Discovery of the Interior Parts of Africa.
Burton, Richard F. 1873. "Notes on the Hamah Stones, with Reduced Transcripts." *The Journal of the Anthropological Institute of Great Britain and Ireland* 2: 41–52.
Carruba, Onofrio. 1977. "Beiträge zur mittelhethitischen Geschichte I—Die Tuthaliyas und die Arnuwandas." *Studi Micenei ed Egeo-Anatolici* 137–174.
Ceram, CW (pseud). 1955. *The Secret of the Hittites*. London: Phoenix Press.
Chantepleure, Guy. 1900. *Fiancée d'Avril*. Paris: Calmann-Lévy.
Chantre, Ernest. 1898. *Recherches archéologiques dans l'Asie occidentale. Mission en Cappadoce 1893–1894*. Paris: Leroux.
Clay, Albert Tobias. 1919. *The Empire of the Amorites*. New Haven: Yale University Press.
Cline, Eric H. 1996. "Assuwa and the Achaeans: The "Mycenaean" Sword at Hattusas and its Possible Implications." *The Annual of the British School at Athens* 91: 137–151.
———. 2007. "Rethinking Mycenaean International Trade with Egypt and the Near East." In *Rethinking Mycenaean Palaces*, 190–200. Los Angeles: Cotsen Institute of Archaeology.
Colebrooke, Thomas E. 1877. "Royal Asiatic Society. Proceedings of the Fifty-Third Anniversary Meeting of the Society. Held on the 29th of May, 1876." *Journal of the Royal Asiatic Society* 9 (2): 1–63.
Collins, Billy Jean. 2007. *The Hittites and Their World*. Atlanta: Society of Biblical Literature.
Curry, Andrew. 2015. "Here Are the Ancient Sites ISIS Has Damaged and Destroyed." *National Geographic*, 2 September.
Curtius, Ludwig. 1958. *Deutsche un antike Welt. Lebenserinnerungen*. Stuttgart: Deutsche Verlags-Anstalt.

Bibliography

D'Alviella, Goblet. 1894. *The Migration of Symbols*. Westminster: Archibald Constable and Co.
Darga, Muhibbe. 2001. "Istanbul üniversitesi'nde Hititologji'nin ilk yillari." In *Boğazköy'den Karatepe'ye: Hititbilim ve Hitit Dünyasının Keşfi*, 44–61. Istanbul: Yapı Kredi Yayınları.
Davis, Edwin John. 1879. *Life in Asiatic Turkey: A Journal of Travel in Cilicia (Pedias and Trachoea), Isauria, and Parts of Lycaonia and Cappadocia*. London: Stanford.
Divon, Shai Andre. 2006. "The City of Emar among the Late Bronze Age Empires." *Proceedings of the Konstanz Emar Conference*. Konstanz. 101–109.
Drews, Robert. 1993. *The End of the Bronze Age: Changes in Warfare and the Catastrophe, ca. 1200 B.C*. Princeton, NJ: Princeton University Press.
———. 2000. "Medinet Habu: Oxcarts, Ships, and Migration Theories." *Journal of Near Eastern Studies* 59 (3): 161–190.
Edgerton, Willian, and John Wilson. 1936. *Historical Records of Ramses III, the Texts in Medinet Habu, Volumes I and II, translated with explanatory notes*. Chicago: University of Chicago Press.
Eldem, Edhem. 2015. "Theodor Makridi Bey ve 1907 Boğazköy Kazısı." *The Discovery of an Anatolian Empire. A Colloquium to Commemorate the 100th Anniversary of the Decipherment of the Hittite Language*. Istanbul.
Erimtan, Can. 2008. "Hittites, Ottomans and Turks: Ağaoğlu Ahmed Bey and the Kemalist Construction of Turkish Nationhood in Anatolia." *Anatolian Studies* 58: 141–171.
Finkelstein, Jacob J. 1972. "Albrecht Goetze, 1897–1971." *Journal of the American Oriental Society* 92 (2): 197–203.
Flinders Petrie, William Matthew. 1914. "The Poem of Pentaur—Battle of Kadesh." In *The World's Story: A History of the World in Story, Song and Art*, 154–162. Boston: Houghton Mifflin.
Forrer, Emil. 1919. "Die Acht Sprachen der Boghaz-koi Inschriften." *Sitzungsberichte der Preussischen Akademie der Wissenschaften*. Berlin.
———. 1922. *Wissenschaftliche Veröffentlichungen der Orient-Gesellschaft 41. Die Boghazköi-Texte in Umschrift 1*. Leipzig: J.C. Hinrichs.
———. 1924. "Vorhomerische Griechen in den Keilschrifttexten von Boghazköi." *Mitteilungen der Deutschen Orient-Gesellschaft zu Berlin* 1–24.
———. 1931. "Apollon, Vulcanus, und die Kyklopen in den Boghazköi-Texten." *Revue hittite et asianique* 141–163.
Friedrich, Johannes. 1925. *Aus dem hethitischen schrifttum*. Leipzig: J.C. Hinrichs.
———. 1927. "Werden in den hethitischen Keilschrifttexten die Griechen erwähnt?" *Kleinasiatische Forschungen* 87–107.
———. 1964. "Ferdinand Sommer (1875–1962) ." *Zeitschrift der Deutschen Morgenländischen Gesellschaft* 114 (1): 13–15.
Gedikli, Yusuf. 2002. *Pontus Meselesi. Arap alfabesinden akarilan, notlu ve tenkitli sekilde*. Istanbul: Bilge Karinca.
Gernot, Wilhelm. 1998. "100 Jahre Ausgrabungen der Deutschen Orient-Gesellschaft, Mayence." In *Zwischen Tigris und Nil. 100 Jahre Ausgrabungen der Deutschen Orient-Gesellschaft in Vorderasien und Ägypten*, 5–13. Mainz: Philip von Zabern.
Gimbutas, Marija. 1970. "Proto-Indo-European Culture: The Kurgan Culture during the Fifth, Fourth, and Third Millennia B.C." *Indo-European and Indo-Europeans. Papers Presented at the Third Indo-European Conference at the University of Pennsylvania*. Philadelphia.
Ginsburg, Christian David. 1871. *The Moabite Stone; A Fac-Simile of the Original Inscription, with an English Translation, and a Historical and Critical Commentary*. London: Reeves and Turner.
Glanzman, George, Harold Henry Rowley, Ralph Marcus, Ephraim Avigdor Speiser, and William Foxwell Albright. 1954. "In Memoriam Roger T. O'Callaghan, S. J." *Bulletin of the American Schools of Oriental Research* 134: 3.
Goedegebuure, Petra, Hans Güterbock, Harry Hoffner, and Theo Van den Hout. 1975. *The Hittite Dictionary of the Oriental Institute of the University of Chicago (CHD)*. Chicago: Oriental Institute of the University of Chicago .

Goldacre, Ben. 2009. *the Guardian.* 12 September. Accessed August 08, 2022. https://www. theguardian.com/commentisfree/2009/sep/12/bad-science-peer-review-goldacre.
Götze, Albrecht. 1930. "Die Pestgebete des Muršiliš." *Kleinasiatische Forschungen* 1: 161–251.
———. 1933. *Die Annalen des Muršiliš.* Leipzig: Hinrichs.
Grote, George. 1846. *A History of Greece.* London: John Murray.
Grotefend, Georg Friedrich. 1805. "Über die Erklärung der Keilschriften, und besonders der Inschriften von Persepolis." In *Ideen über die Politik den Verkehr und den Handel der vornehmsten Völker der alten Welt,* 931–960. Gottingen: Vandenhoek und Ruprecht.
Gurney, OR. 1976. *Some Aspects of Hittite Religion.* Oxford: Oxford University Press.
Güterbock, Hans Gustav. 1956. "The Deeds of Suppiluliuma as Told by His Son, Mursili II." *Journal of Cuneiform Studies* 10 (2): 41–68.
———. 1957. "Toward a Definition of the Term Hittite." *Oriens* 10 (2): 233–239.
———. 1984. "Hittites and Akhaeans: a New Look." *Proceedings of the American Philosophical Society* 114–122.
———. 1992. "Kurt Bittel (5 July 1907–30 January 1991)." *Proceedings of the American Philosophical Society* 136 (4): 578–583.
Hagenbuchner, Albertine. 1989. *Die Korrespondenz der Hethiter. Teil II.* Heidelberg: Carl Winter.
Hallo, William W., and K. Lawson Younger. 1997. *Context of Scriptures.* Leiden: Brill.
Hansen, O. 1994. "A Mycenaean sword from Bogazkoy-Hattusa found in 1991." *The Annual of the British School at Athens* 89: 213–215.
Harl, Kenneth. 2005. *Origins of Great Ancient Civilizations.* Chantilly, VA: The Great Courses / The Teaching Co.
Hawkins, John David. 2000. *Corpus of Hieroglyphic Luwian Inscriptions.* Berlin and New York: Walter de Gruyter.
———. 2003. "Scripts and Texts." In *The Luwians,* 128–169. Leiden and Boston: Brill.
Hoffner, Harry, and Craig Melchert. 2008. *A Grammar of the Hittite Language.* Winona Lake: Eisenbrauns.
Hoffner, Harry A., Jr. 1973. "The Hittites and Hurrians." In *Peoples of Old Testament Times,* 197–228. Oxford: Oxford University Press.
Horn, Paul. 1903. "Knudtzon (review)." *Anzeiger fur Indogermanische Sprach- und Altertumskunde* 14 (1,2,3): 1.
Hrozný, Friedrich. 1915. "Die Lösung des hethitischen Problems." *Mitteilungen der Deutschen Orient-Gesellschaft* (56): 17–50.
———. 1917. *Die Sprache der Hethiter : ihr Bau und ihre Zugehörigkeit zum indogermanischen Sprachstamm.* Leipzig: Hinrichs.
———. 1919. *Hethitische Keilschrifttexte aus Boghazköi. In Umschrift, mit Übersetzung und Kommentar.* Leipzig: Hinrichs.
Humann, Carl, and Otto Puchstein. 1890. *Reisen in Kleinasien und Nordsyrien: Ausgeführt im Auftrage der Königlichen Preussischen Akademie der Wissenschaften (Atlas).* Berlin.
Jansen, Christian, and Sylvia Diebner. 2016. "Ludwig Curtius (1874–1954)." In *2016, Lebensbilder. Klassische Archäologen und der Nationalsozialismus, Bd. 2,* 79–111. Berlin: Marie Leidorf GmbH.
Johnson, Augustus J. 1871. *Inscriptions Discovered at Hamath in Northern Syria.* Palestine Exploration Fund Quarterly Statement, New York: Palestine Exploration Society.
Khamsi, Roxanne. 2007. *New Scientist.* 26 November. Accessed August 27, 2022. https://www. newscientist.com/article/dn12960-were-cursed-rams-the-first-biological-weapons/.
Klengel, Horst. 1991. "Das Berliner Boğazköy-Archiv: Geschichte und Textedition." *Ägypten, Vorderasien, Turfan. Probleme der Edition und Bearbeitung altorientalischer Handschriften (Schriften zur Geschichte und Kultur des Alten Orients).* Berlin.
Klock-Fontanille, Isabelle. 2012. "Les débuts de l'hittitologie : le rôle de la science allemande." *Revue Germanique Internationale* 119–133.
Knudtzon, Jörgen Alexander. 1902. *Die Zwei Arzawa-Briefe, die Ältesten Urkunden in Indogermanischer Sprache.* Leipzig: J. C. Hinrichs'sche Buchhandlung.
Košak, S., GGW Müller, S. Görke, and Ch. Steitler. 2020. "Catalogue of Hittite Texts

Bibliography

(CTH)." 27 01. Accessed 09 04, 2021. https://www.hethport.uni-wuerzburg.de/CTH/index_en.php.
Kretschmer, Paul. 1903. "Knudtzon (Review)." *Deutsche Literaturzeitung für Kritik der internationalen Wissenschaft* 13: 778–781.
Lackenbacher, Sylvie, and Florence Malbran-Labat. 2016. *Lettres akkadiennes de la «Maison d'Urtēnu». Fouilles de 1994.* Leuven-Paris-Bristol: Peeters.
Langdon, S., and A. H. Gardiner. 1920. "The Treaty of Alliance between Ḫattušili, King of the Hittites, and the Pharaoh Ramesses II of Egypt." *The Journal of Egyptian Archaeology* 6 (3): 179–205.
Luckenbill, Daniel David. 1926. *Ancient Records of Assyria and Babylonia.* Chicago, Illinois: University of Chicago Press.
Mangold-Will, Sabine. 2017. "Wilhelm II. - Archäologie als wissenschaftliche Herrschaftslegitimation in der Ambivalenz der Moderne." In *Wilhelm II: Archäologie und Politik um 1900*, 123–126. Stuttgart: Franz Steiner.
Marchetti, Nicolò, 2014. *Karkemish: An Ancient Capital on the Euphrates (OrientLab 2).* Bologna: AnteQuem.
Marchetti, Nicolò, and Hasan Peker. 2018. "The Stele of Kubaba by Kamani and the Kings of Karkemish in the 9th Century BC." *Zeitschrift für Assyriologie* 81–99.
Matthes, Olaf. 2008. "Deutsche Ausgräber im Vorderen Orient." In *Das große Spiel. Archäologie und Politik zur Zeit des Kolonialismus (1860–1940)*, 226–235. Essen: DuMont.
Mellaart, James. 1984. "Troy VIIA in Anatolian Perspective." *The Trojan War: Its Historicity and Context : Papers of the First Greenbank Colloquium.* Liverpool: 1981. 63–82.
Meriggi, Piero. 1932. "Sur le déchiffrement et la langue de hiéroglyphes "hittites."" *Revue Hittite et Asianique* 1–57.
Messerschmidt, Leopold. 1903. "Die Zwei Arzawa-Briefe (Review)." *Orientalistische Literaturzeitung* 2: 80–86.
Miller, Jared L. 2015. "The Tablet Finds of Temple I from the Early Excavations at Boğazköy-Hattusa (1906–1912)." *The Discovery of an Anatolian Empire. A Colloquium to Commemorate the 100th Anniversary of the Decipherment of the Hittite Language.* Istanbul. 69–84.
Miller, William. 1908. *The Latins in the Levant: A History of Frankish Greece (1204–1566).* New York: E. P. Dutton and Co.
Moran, William L. 1992. *The Amarna Letters.* Baltimore: Johns Hopkins University Press.
Muhly, D. 1974. "The Hittites and the Aegean World." *Expedition Magazine* 2–10.
Müller, Willhelm Max. 1893. *Asien und Europa nach altägyptischen Denkmälern.* Leipzig: W. Engelmann.
The New York Times. 1876. "Dr Schliemann." 10 November: 4.
Nibbi, Alessandra. 1975. *The Sea Peoples and Egypt.* Park Ridge, New Jersey: Noyes Press.
Norrie, Philip. 2016. "How diseases affected the end of the Bronze Age." In *A History of Disease in Ancient Times*, 61–101. London: Palgrave Macmillan.
Nougayrol, Jean. 1960. "Nouveaux textes accadiens de Ras-Shamra." *Comptes rendus des séances de l'Académie des Inscriptions et Belles-Lettres* 104: 163–171.
Nyland, Ann. 2009. *The Kikkuli Method of Horse Training.* Armidale, Australia: Maryannu Press.
Oberheid, R. 2007. *Emil O. Forrer und die Anfänge der Hethitologie. Eine wissenschaftshistorische Biografie.* Berlin—New York: Walter de Gruyter.
O'Callaghan, Roger Timothy. 1949. "The Phoenician Inscription on the King's Statue at Karatepe." *The Catholic Biblical Quarterly* 11 (3): 233–248.
Otten, Heinrich. 1958. "Vorläufiger Bericht über die Ausgrabungen in Boğazköy im Jahre 1957. Keilschrifttexte." *Metteilungen der Deustchen Orient Gesellschaft* 91: 73–84.
———. 1981. *Die Apologie Hattusilis III. Das Bild der Überlieferung.* Wiesbaden: Otto Harrassowitz.
———. 1988. *Die Bronzetafel Aus Bogazkoy: Ein Staatsvertrag Tuthalijas IV (Studien zu den Bogazköy-Texten. Beiheft).* Wiesbaden: Harassovitz.
Özgüç, Tahsin. 1956. "The Dagger of Anitta." *Belleten* 33–36.

Page, Denys L. 1959. *History and the Homeric Iliad*. Berkeley and Los Angeles: University of California Press.
Panayotov, Strahil. 2014. "George Smith's Identification of Karkemish: From the Account of his Assistant Mathewson." In *Karkemish: An Ancient Capital on the Euphrates*, 44–51. Bologna: Ante Quem.
Payne, Annick. 2004. "Writing Systems and Identity." *Anatolian Interfaces: Hittites, Greeks and Their Neighbors, Proceedings of an International Conference on CrossCultural Interaction, September 17–19, 2004*. Atlanta: Emory University.
Pears, Edwin. 1917. *Abdülhamid II, Sultan of the Turks, 1842–1918*. London: Constable & Co.
Pedersen, Holger. 1903. "Zu den Arzawa-Briefen." *Anzeiger Indogermanische Forschungen* 14 (1): 280–283.
Perrot, George. 1872. *Exploration archéologique de la Galatie et de la Bithynie d'une partie de la Mysie de la Cappadoce et du Pont exécutée en 1861, avec Edmond Guillaume et Jules Delbet*. Paris: Firmin Didot.
Picard, Charles. 1944. "Theodoros Makridy-Bey (1941)." *Revue Archeologique* 6 (21): 48–50.
Pulak, Cemal. 1998. "The Bronze Age Shipwreck at Ulu Burun, Turkey: 1985 Campaign." *American Journal of Archaeology* 1–37.
Rawlinson, Henry Creswicke. 1848. "The Persian Cuneiform Inscription at Behistun, Decyphered and Translated; With a Memoir on Persian Cuneiform Inscriptions in General, and on That of Behistun in Particular." *Journal of the Royal Asiatic Society of Great Britain and Ireland* 10 (i): 349.
———. 1870. *The Cuneiform Inscriptions of Western Asia, vol. III*. London: R.E. Bowler.
Rieken, Elisabeth. 2015. "Hrozný's Decipherment: Method, Success and Consequences for Indo-European Linguistics." *The Discovery of an Anatolian Empire. A Colloquium to Commemorate the 100th Anniversary of the Decipherment of the Hittite Language*. Istanbul.
Rizza, Alfredo. 2002. "Linguistic and cultural layers in the Anatolian myth of Illuijanka." In *Syggraphé*, 9–24. Como: New Press.
Robinson, Andrew. 2012. *Cracking the Egyptian Code: The Revolutionary Life of Jean-François Champollion*. Oxford: Oxford University Press.
Ronder, C. 1893. "Notes on the Hittite Writing." *The Journal of the Royal Asiatic Society of Great Britain and Ireland* 823–853.
Saint-Martin, Antoine-Jean. 1823. "Extrait d'un mémoire relatif aux antiques inscriptions de Persépolis lu à l'Académie des Inscriptions et Belles Lettres." *Journal Asiatique* 65–90.
Sandars, Nancy. 1978. *The Sea Peoples: Warriors of the Ancient Mediterranean. 1250–1150*. London: Thames and Hudson.
Sanders, Paul. 2006. "Argumenta ad Deum in the Plague Prayers of Mursili II and in the Book of Psalms." *Psalms and Prayers: Papers Read at the Joint Meeting of the Society of Old Testament Study and Het Oudtestamentisch Wekgezelschap in Nederland en België, Apeldoorn, August 2006*. Leiden: Brill. 181–217.
Sayce, Archibald. 1876. "George Smith." *Nature* 14: 421–422.
———. 1880. "A Forgotten Empire in Asia Minor." *Fraser's Magazine*, NS 22: 223–233.
———. 1888. *The Hittites: The Story of a Forgotten Empire*. London: The Religious Tract Society.
———. 1889. "The Cuneiform Tablets of Tel el-Amarna, now Preserved in the Boulaq Museum." *Proceedings of the Society of Biblical Archaeology* 11: 326–414.
———. 1890. *The Hittites: The Story of a Forgotten Empire*. Oxford: The Religious Tract Society.
———. 1893. "Transactions of the Ninth International Congress of Orientalists (held in London, 5th to 12th September 1892)." London.
———. 1907. *The Archaeology of the Cuneiform Inscriptions*. London: Society for Promoting Christian Knowledge.
———. 1923. *Reminiscences*. London: Macmillan and Co.
Schäffer, E. 1895. "Die Ruinen von Boghas-köi." *Mitteilungen des Deutschen Archäologischen Instituts, Athenische Abteilung* (20): 451–465.
Schoepfer, A. 1915. "Eine wichtige Entdeckung." *Allgemeiner Tiroler Anzeiger*, 11 December.

Seeher, Jurgen. 1999. "Die Zerstörung der Stadt Hattusa." *Akten IV. Internationalen Kongresses für Hethitologie.* Würzburg.

———. 2011. *Gods Carved in Stone: The Hittite Rock Sanctuary of Yazilikaya.* Istanbul: Ege Yayinlari.

Shaw, Wendy M. K. 2004. "Whose Hittites, and Why? Language, Archaeology and the Quest for the Original Turks." In *Archaeology under Dictatorship,* 131–153. New York: Springer.

Singer, Itamar. 1985. "The Battle of Niḫriya and the End of the Hittite Empire." *Zeitschrift für Assyriologie und vorderasiatische Archäologie* 75 (1): 100–123.

———. 1991. "The title "Great Princess" in the Hittite Empire." *Ugarit-Foschungen* 327–328.

———. 2006. "The Hittites and the Bible Revisited." In *"I Will Speak the Riddles of Ancient Times": Archaeological and Historical Studies in Honor of Amihai Mazar on the Occasion of His Sixtieth Birthday,* 754. Winona Lake: Eisenbrauns.

———. 2011. *The Calm Before the Storm, Selected Writings of Itamar Singer on the Late Bronze Age in Anatolia and in the Levant.* Atlanta: Society of Biblical Literature.

Singer, Itamar, and Harry A Hoffner. 2002. *Hittite Prayers.* Atlanta: Society of Biblical Literature.

Smith, George. 1876. "Letter from George Smith to Samuel Birch, Department of Oriental Antiquities at British Museum, Aleppo April 5th." London: British Museum Original Papers 51 May-July 1876, c5 Aug. 76 Stamp: BM 14 Jun 1876 No. 3024.

Sommer, Ferdinand. 1920. *Hethitisches.* Leipzig: J. C. Hinrichs.

———. 1932. *Die Ahhijava-Urkunden.* Munich: Verlag der Bayerischen Akademie der Wissenschaften.

Sommer, Ferdinand, and Adam Falkenstein. 1938. *Die hethitisch-akkadische Bilingue des Hattusili I (Labarna II).* Munich: Verlag der Bayerischen Akademie der Wissenschaften.

Spretnak, Charlene. 2011. "Anatomy of a backlash: concerning the work of Marija Gimbutas." *The Journal of Archaeomythology* 7: 1–27.

Steinherr, Franz. 1949. "Karatepe: The Key to the Hittite Hieroglyphs." *Archaeology* 2 (4): 177–180.

Summers, Geoffrey. 1997. "The Identification of the Iron Age City on Kerkenes Dag in Central Anatolia." *Journal of Near Eastern Studies* 56 (2): 81–94.

Texier, Charles. 1839. *Description de l'Aise Mineure: faite par ordre du gouvernement francais de 1833 á 1837.* Paris: Didot Frères.

———. 1862. *Asie Mineure, Description Géographique, Historique et Archéologique.* Paris: Didot Frères.

Thobie, Jacques. 2000. "Archéologie et diplomatie française au Moyen-Orient des années1880 au début des années 1930." *Les Politiques de l'archéologie du milieu du XIXeme siècle à l'orée du XXIeme.* Athens: Ecole Française d'Athènes. 79–111.

Torri, Giulia. 2019. "Strategies for Persuading a Deity in Hittite Prayers and Vows." *Die Welt des Orients* 48–60.

Traill, David. 1995. *Schliemann of Troy: Treasure and Deceit.* New York: St. Martin's Press.

Trevisanato, Siro. 2007. "The "Hittite Plague," an epidemic of tularemia and the first record of biological warfare." *Medical Hypotheses* 69: 1371–1374.

Tugendhaft, Aaron. 2012. "How to Become a Brother in the Bronze Age: An Inquiry into the Representation of Politics in Ugaritic Myth." *Fragments* 2: 89–104.

Tunçay, Mete. 1981. *Türkiye Cumhuriyeti'nde Tek-Parti Yönetiminin Kurulması 1923–1931.* Ankara: Miladi.

Ünal, Ahmet. 1976. "Dr. Franz Steinherr (1902–1974)." *Belleten Périodique Trimestriel, Société Turque d'Histoire* 40 (158): 347–349.

Ünal, Ahmet, and İsmet Ediz. 1990–1991. "The Hittite Sword from Bogazköy-Hattusa, found in 1991, and Its Akkadian Inscription." *Müze-Museum* 46–52.

———. 2011. *The Elements of Hittite.* Cambridge: Cambridge University Press.

Van den Hout, Theo. 2006. "Institutions, Vernaculars, Publics: The Case of Second-Millennium Anatolia." In *Margins of Writing, Origins of Cultures,* 221–260. Chicago: The Oriental Institute of the University of Chicago.

Velhartická, Šárka. 2015. "Rezeption der Entzifferung der hethitischen Sprache in der

österreichischen und deutschen Presse." *Mitteilungen der Deutschen Orient-Gesellschaft* 9–23.
Vieyra, Maurice. 1939. "Parallèle ḫurrite au nom d'Urie "le hittite."" *Revue Hittite et Asiatique* 113–116.
Virchow, Rudolf. 1898. "Die orientalische Altertumsforschung preußichen im Landtag." *Orientalische Literatur-Zeitung* 1 (4): 120–124.
Waddell, Helen. 1948. *Mediaeval Latin Lyrics*. New York: Henry Holt.
Ward, Thomas. 1926. *History of the Athenæum 1824–1925*. London: Athenæum Club.
Weber, O., and A. Ebeling. 1915. *Die El Amarna Tafeln. Anmerkungen und Register*. Leipzig: J C Hinrichs.
Weidner, Ernst. 1963. "Helmuth Theodor Bossert. (11. September 1889 bis 5. February 1961)." *Archiv für Orientforschung* 20: 305–306.
Winckler, H., and O. Puchstein. 1907. "Vorläufige Nachrichten über die Ausgrabungen in Boghaz-koi im Sommer 1907." *Mitteilungen der deutschen Orient-Gesellschaft zu Berlin* 1–71.
———. 1909. "Excavations at Boghaz-keui in the Summer of 1907." *Annual Report of the Board of Regents of the Smithsonian Institution* 677–696.
Winckler, Hugo. 1888. "Bericht über die Thontafeln von Tell-el-Amarna im Königlichen Museum zu Berlin und im Museum von Bulaq." *Sitzungsberichte der Königlich Preussischen Akademie der Wissenschaften zu Berlin* 2 (51): 1341–1357.
Wood, Bryant G. 2011. "Hittites and Hethites: a proposed solution to an etymological conundrum." *Journal of the Evangelical Theological Society* 239–250.
Wood, Michael. 1998. *In search of the Trojan War*. Berkeley: University of California Press.
Wright, W., Sayce, A.H, Wilson, C.W., Conder, C.R., and Rylands, W.H. 1884. *The Empire of the Hittites*. London: Nisbet.
Wright, William. 1874. "The Hamah Inscriptions: Hittite Remains." *British and Foreign Evangelical Review* 23: 90–99.
Zangger, Eberhard, and Rita Gautschy. 2019. "Celestial Aspects of Hittite Religion: An Investigation of the Rock Sanctuary Yazılıkaya." *Journal of Skyscape Archaeology* 5–38.

Index

Abdulhamid II, Sultan 57–58, 70
Académie des Inscriptions et Belles Lettres (Academy of Inscriptions and Literature) 41
Adad-nirari I, King of Assyria 127, 130
Adad-nirari III, King of Assyria 160
Adda-danu 45
Ağaoğlu Bey, Ahmet 109
Ahhiyawa question 97–106
Akhenaten 45
Akhetaten 45
Akkadian 42, 46–47, 79–84; decipherment of 11–15
Alashiya *see* Cyprus
Aleppo 21–23, 32
Amarna Letters 44–50, 92, 110, 112–113, 116, 120
Amazons 34
Amenhotep III, Pharaoh 47
Amman, Mount 116
Ammisaduqa tablet 94
Ammurapi, King of Ugarit 155
Amurru 32, 45, 135
Anatolian hieroglyphs *see* Luwian hieroglyphs
Ancient Near East chronology 94–95, 125
Anitta 90–91; dagger 91; *Proclamation* 91
Ankara silver bowl 103
Antiochus, King of Commagene 56
Anu and Adad, Temple 15
Arinna 124, 133–134, 158
Armenian revolt 58–59
Arnold, Matthew 3
Arnuwanda I 121
Arnuwanda III 136
Artatama II, King of Mitanni 115
Aryan race 108–110
Arzawa 47–48, 93, 152
Arzawa Letters 46–48, 50–53, 112–113
Ashtata 115
Assur 15
Assurbanipal's library 29
Assur-uballit, King of Assyria 128n1
Assuwa 103
Atatürk *see* Kemal, Mustafa

Athenaeum 3–4, 28
Atreya 99
Ay 117
Azitawanda 147

Babylon, Hittite sack of 93–94
Balkan, Kemal 91
Baltimore Museum 37
Barnett, Richard 144
Behistun inscription 12–13
Belck, Waldemar 59
Bellerophon 104–105
bilingual 7, 12, 36, 138, 145–148
Birch, Samuel 35
Bittel, Kurt 62, 71, 111–112, 137–141, 154
Bloomfield, Maurice 53
Blosse Linch, Henry 4
Boğazköy 25–27, 33–34, 37–42, 53, 56, 59, 62–65, 139; *see also* Hattusa
Boissier, Alfred 41
Bosse, Julius Robert 57
Bossert, Helmuth Theodor 138–148
Boustrophedon 20
British and Foreign Bible Society 18
British Museum 22, 39, 144
Broca, Paul 40
Broteas 30
Brugsch, Karl Heinrich 9–10
Bryce, Trevor 115, 157
Bugge, Sophus 52
Burckhardt, Ludwig 16–17
Burton, Sir Richard 18
Byblos 45, 115, 120

Cairo 17
Çambel Alet 142
Cambon, Paul 55
Canaan, Canaanite 4, 28, 21
Canning, Sir Stratford 29
Caylus Vase 12
Çelebi, Kâtip 24–25
Chabas, François Joseph 35
Champollion, Jean François 7–12, 66, 130
Chantepleure, Guy *see* Violet, Jeanne-Caroline

185

Index

Chantre, Ernest 40–41, 55, 59
Chenery, Thomas 4
Children of Heth 4, 9
clay tablets 64
Cline, Eric 135
Collins, Billie Jean 148
Constantinople 28–29, 37
Conze, Alexander 68
cuneiform, decipherment of 9–15
Curtius, Ludwig 60, 67–69
Cyprus 134, 136, 152

Dakhamunzu 115n1
Danuhepa 128
Darius the Great, King of Persia 12
Darling Buck, Carl 77
Darwin, Charles 3, 23, 45n1
Davis, Edwin John 24
de Mortillet, Gabriel 40
de Rouge, Emmanuel 152
Deutsche Orient-Gesellschaft (German Orient Society) 57, 66–67
Dickens, Charles 3
Dupont-Sommer, André 144

EA 31 46–48; see also Arzawa letters
EA 32 47–48; see also Arzawa letters
EA 96 120
Edgerton, William Franklin 152
Edhem, Halil Eldem 59, 85
Egyptian hieroglyphs, deciphrement of 7–8
Egyptomania 8
Elamite 12
embargo 135–136
Encyclopaedia Britannica 15, 35
Eteokles 99
Eufrates, River 21–22

famine 155
Ferguson, James 3
Fischer, Major 25
Flinders Petrie, William 44–45
Forrer, Emil 85–88, 91–92, 97–101, 106
Fourier, Joseph 7
Fox Talbot, Henry 14–15
Francisella tularensis 120
Fraser's Magazine 31
Friedrich, Johannes 100, 144

Galton, Francis 45n1
Garstang, John 60
Gasga see Kaska
Gassulawiya 125
Gezer 45
Gilgamesh, Epic of 21, 94
Gimbutas, Marija 89–90
Gladstone, William 21, 29
Götze, Albrecht 121–122
Great War see World War I
Grote, Arthur 3
Grotefend, Georg Friedrich 11–12

Gurney, Oliver Robert 123
Güterbock, Gustav 114, 140–141, 149

Hajji Khalifa see Çelebi, Kâtip
Hakpis 127–129
Hamah Stones 17–20
Hamidiye 58
Hani 117
Hansen, Ove 103–104
Hantili 95
Harar 18
Harl, Kenneth 157
Hartapu, King of Tarhuntassa 159
Hattians 90–92
Hattusa 43, 48, 91–93, 102–103, 112–113, 126–129, 156–157; excavation of 63–72, 111–114, 138, 154; see also Boğazköy
Hattusa-ziti 116
Hattusili I 92–93; *Annals* 93; *Testament* 93
Hattusili II 96
Hattusili III 33, 99, 127–133, 159; *Apology* 129–130
Hawkins, John David 158
Hayes Ward, William 20
Henderson, Patrick 23
Herodotus 25, 26, 31; *Historiae* 25–26
Herriot, Éduard 140
Hierapolis see Mabog
Hincks, Edward 14
Hittite hieroglyphs see Luwian hieroglyphs
Hittite-Egyptian peace treaty 10, 65–66
Hittite language 78–80; decipherment 74–78; Indo-European origins 50, 76–78; writing system 80–84, 137
Hittitomania 108
Hogarth, George David 23
Horn, Paul 52
Houwink ten Cate, Hendrik Jan 101
Hrozný Bedřich 74–79; *Die Lösung des hethitischem Problems* 76, 77
Humann, Carl 37–39, 56
Hurrians 110, 113–114
Hüyük 33, 41

The Iliad 34, 97–106
Ir-Tesub 159
İvriz 24, 158; relief 24–25
İzmir 30, 55–56

Jessup, Henry Harris 17
Johnson, Augustus J 17
Jovanov, Aleksander 33

Kadashman-enlil I, King of Babylon 116
Kadashman-enlil II, King of Babylon 132
Kadesh, battle of 31–33, 127–130
Kadirli 142
Kamani, King of Karkemish 159
Kammergruber, Lieutenant 75–77
Kanesh see Nesa
Karabel relief 24–26, 30

Index

Karahöyük 159
Karatepe 143–147
Karkemish 15, 22–23, 34, 115, 152, 159
Karnak 8
Kārum 90
Kaska 96, 112, 124, 128, 157
Kassites 127, 154
Kemal, Mustafa 107–110
Kheta 9–10, 15
Kikkuli text 113
Kili-Tesub, General 115
Kizzuwatna 130, 152
Klengel, Horst 60
Knudtzon, Jørgen Alexander 50–53
Kohl, Heinrich 68
Krencker, Daniel 67–68
Kretschmer, Paul 52–53
Kudur-enlil, King of Babylon 132
Kültepe *see* Nesa
Kunzi-Tesub 159
Kurgan hypothesis 89–90
Kurunta, King of Tarhuntassa 132–133, 159
Kuscu, Ekrem 143–144

Labarna 92
Late Bronze Age collapse 153–157
Lawazantiya 131
Lawrence, Thomas Edward (Lawrence of Arabia) 23, 73
Layard, Austen Henry 4, 28–30, 60
Lenormant, François 37, 47
Lower Lands 126
Lucian of Samosata 34
Lukka 153–158
Luwian hieroglyphs 17–27, 36–39, 48–49, 137–138, 145–149, 158–159
Luwian language 148–149, 160
Lycaonia 24
Lycia 158

Mabog (Mabij) 34
Makridi Bey, Theodor 61–72
Manapa-Tarhunta letter 101
Mar'asch Lion 38–39
Massanauzzi 130
Masturi, King of Mira 130
Matthewson, Peter (Mateev, Peter) 21–22
Medinet Habu, Egypt 151–152
Meissner, Bruno 87
Menant, Joachim 41–42
Meriggi, Piero 148
Merneptah, Pharaoh 153
Messerschmidt, Leopold 52–53, 138
Meyer, Eduard 39, 85–88
Milawata letter 99
Mira 130
Mitanni (Hanigalbat) 45, 92, 110, 113–117, 127–128
Mordtmann, Andreas David 36
Mosul 29

Muhly, James David 101–102
Müller, Wilhelm Max 35–36
Mursili I 93, 95
Mursili II 114, 121–126; *Accusation Against Tawananna* 126; *Annals* 121–122; *Plague Prayers* 123–126
Mursili III 127–129, 132, 159
Mushki 157
Muwatalli II 33, 126–127

Nature 23
Nazism 108, 110, 121–122, 138, 140–141
Nefertari 131
Nemrut Dağ 56
Neo-Hittites 157–163
Nerik 128
Nesa 90–91
Nihriya (Nairi) 136
Nineveh 13
Niobe 30
Nyland, Ann 113

O'Callaghan, Roger 144
Old Persian 11–12
Old Testament 4–5, 20, 160–163
Oppert, Julius 14
Oriental Archaeology Group at the Athenaeum 3–4
Orientalische Literatur Zeitung 57
Origins of the Hittites 88–89
Orontes, River 17–31
Osman Hamdi Bey 54–56, 61
Otten, Heinrich 93
Otter, Jean 25
Ottoman Empire 58–59, 73, 107
Ozguc, Tahsin 91

Page, Sir Denys Lionel 100
Palestine 4, 25, 55, 161–163
Palestine Exploration Fund 19–20
Pausania 30–31
Pax Hethitica 130
Pedersen, Holger 52
Peleset 153
Pentaur 31–32
Pentisarri 131
Pergamon 38
Perrot, George 26–27, 33, 40
Petra 17
Phoenicians 143
Picard, Charles 61
Pithana 90
Piyama-Radu 99, 101
Piyassili 115
plague 120–125
Pontus Meselesi (The Pontus Question) 108
Pteria 26, 39
Puchstein, Otto 38–39, 56, 68
Puduhepa 130–133
Punch 29

Index

Ramesses II, Pharaoh 8–9, 31–33, 128–132
Ramesses III, Pharaoh 151–153
Ramesseum 8–9
Rawlinson, Sir Henry 4, 13–14, 21–23, 159
Reşit Galip Bey 139
Rib-Addi, King of Byblos 120
Ritual of Askhella 123
Rosetta Stone 7–8
Royal Asiatic Society 22

Sain-Martine, Antoine-Jean 12
Samuha 128
Sandars, Nancy 155–156
Sargon II, King of Assyria 158
Sarre, Friedrich 56
Sausgamuwa, King of Amurru 135
Sayce, Archibald 3–4, 23–31, 33–37, 39–40, 48–49, 53, 59–60, 152
scapegoat ritual *see* Ritual of Askhella
Schaeffer, Claude 155
Schäffer, Lieutenant 56
Schede, Martin 111
Schliemann, Henrich 39–40, 98, 101, 104
Schroeder, Otto 77
Schythians 9
Scientific Racism 35
Sea People 152–156
Sedulius Scottus 124
Seha, River 101
Sesostris 25
Shattuara 127
Shekelesh 153
Sherden 153
Simon, Henri James 65, 111
Simyra 120
Singer, Itamar 125, 156
Sinuhe the Egyptian 114
Skene, James Henry 21
Smenkhkhare, Pharaoh 45
Smith, George 20–23
Smyrna *see* İzmir
Society of Biblical Archaeology 21, 31, 48
Sommer, Ferdinand 78, 86–88, 100–101
Speke, John Hanning 18
Steinherr, Franz 145–148
Storm-God 126, 133–134
Subhi Pasha 19
Sumerian 13, 21, 47, 75, 80–84
Sumerogram 47, 80–83
Suppiluliuma I 46, 113–119; *Deeds* 114–115
Suppiluliuma II 136, 153–157
Susgamuwa 135
Sylipos, Mount 30, 34
Syncretism 133

Tabal 157–158
Tantalus 30
Tarhundaradu, King of Arzawa 47
Tarhuntassa 127, 159

Tarkondemos seal 36–37
Tawagalawa letter 99
Tawananna 125–126
Telipinu 95–96, 112; *Edict* 95–96
Tell el Amarna 44–45, 67; *see also* Akhetaten
Tell el Jerablus 21
Texier, Charles 25
Tiglath-Pileser I 14–15, 159
Tiglath-Pileser III 158
Torp, Alf 52
Troy 40, 97–104
Truwisa 97–103
Tudhaliya I/II 97; sword 102–104
Tudhaliya III 112–113
Tudhaliya IV 99, 133–136
Tukulti-Nimurta, King of Assyria 136
Turk Tarih Texi (Turkish History Thesis) 108
Tushratta, King of Mitanni 114–115
Tutankhamun, Pharaoh 45, 115n1

Ugarit 155
Uluburun wreck 135
Upper Lands 127
Urhi-Tesub *see* Mursili III

Van den Hout, Theo 80
Vaux, William Sandys Wright 3
Venus (planet) 42, 94
Violet, Jeanne-Caroline 49
von Landau, Wilhelm Freiherr 61
Vorderasiatische Gesellschaft (Near Eastern Society) 57, 63

Walters, Henry 37
Warpalawa, King of Tuwana 158
Washukanni 127
Weber, Otto 85
Weidner, Ernst 77
Westenholz, Aage 64
Wilhelm II, Kaiser 57–58, 111
Willoughby Cole, William 4
Wilson, John Albert 152
Wilusa 97–103
Winckler, Hugo 46–48, 53, 60–72, 112
Wirchow, Rudolph 57
World War II 141
Wright, William (I) 18n1
Wright, William (II) 18–20, 24

Yazilikaya 26–27, 33–34, 133–134
Yersinia pestis 121
Young Turks movement 70
Yuruks 30, 142

Zangger, Eberhard 134
Zannanza affair 115–119
Zia Bey 63, 69, 112